W9-BIE-994

Advance Praise for *Centered*

"*Centered* is a captivating and uplifting story about pursuing dreams, pushing through difficult times, and reaching one's full potential. Anthony Ianni's story shows what can happen when young people and their families hold themselves to the highest standard of accountability."
—Nick Saban, Head Football Coach, University of Alabama

"Anthony Ianni is such an inspirational success story, and his new book provides tremendous motivation and practical experience in how to adapt, overcome, and achieve, despite the obstacles. Anthony's story provides a thoughtful and influential guide to doing your best and being your best self, no matter what."
—Jay Bilas, ESPN College Basketball Analyst

"Anthony loved sports ever since he was a little kid and he did not let autism hold him back. He was bullied and classes were really difficult for him. He succeeded in earning his degree and playing college basketball. When he talks to students at schools, he tells them to chase every dream and to work hard."
—Temple Grandin, author of *Thinking in Pictures*

"Everyone will benefit from reading Anthony's firsthand account of living life on the autism spectrum. They say you can never judge a book by its cover, and he is the perfect example of that. You look from the outside and he is a tall, athletic, accomplished athlete, husband and father. You assume his struggles have been minimal, which in fact could not be more inaccurate. He has, with the tireless efforts from his family and friends, overcome daily struggles to live a 'normal' life, and he continues to do so with great resiliency. His willingness to be the face of autism is brave, and this book shows you what that *really* means."
—Allie LaForce, sports reporter, TNT

"Anthony Ianni's story reminds me of my journey growing up. It was very inspirational and encouraging to know that I am not the only one. With all of the hard work and great support of family, kids like us can accomplish anything we want to do in life. Anthony's story is a great example of how to navigate difficult issues in life of being impacted by autism."
—Armani Williams, first NASCAR driver with autism

# CENTERED

RED ⚡ LIGHTNING BOOKS

# CENTERED

## Autism, Basketball, and One Athlete's Dreams

### ANTHONY IANNI
#### and Rob Keast

*This book is a publication of*

Red Lightning Books
1320 East 10th Street
Bloomington, Indiana 47405 USA

redlightningbooks.com

This book is printed on acid-free paper.

Manufactured in Canada

Cataloging information is available from the
Library of Congress.

ISBN 978-1-68435-154-1 (hardback)
ISBN 978-1-68435-153-4 (paperback)
ISBN 978-1-68435-152-7 (ebook)

First printing 2021

# CONTENTS

# FOREWORD

THE FIRST TIME I MET Anthony Ianni, he was nine years old, and he told me he was going to play basketball at Michigan State for me.

Little did I know that bold statements like that from A.I. should not have surprised me.

For as long as I've known him, Anthony has been defying the odds and doing things that people have said he wouldn't be able to do.

The fact that he is now a motivational speaker and someone who will stand in front of large crowds, both young and old, not only shows how much confidence he has but, to me, is just another demonstration of Anthony showing everyone that he can do anything he puts his mind to.

When I was approached by Anthony to write the foreword to his book, I readily accepted. I don't hesitate to speak about him and his family because I have great admiration and respect for his parents, Greg and Jamie, his sister, Allison, and, of course, for A.I., who confidently shook my hand that night more than twenty years ago and did in fact end up playing for me at Michigan State.

From the moment his father, Greg, returned to Michigan State in 1993, Anthony was always a part of the Michigan State basketball program. He attended games with his parents, worked as a ball boy for us at practice and games, and bled Green and White as much as any kid I had ever met. He even traveled with us a few times and once took my seat on the bus!

I knew he faced challenges growing up, challenges that other kids his age wouldn't have to face, because he was autistic.

He was bullied. Doctors told his parents that he probably wouldn't finish high school. And the chances of him going to college and getting a "regular job" and living on his own were marginal. Becoming a Division I athlete wouldn't even be in the realm of possibility.

But he found his passion in basketball, and that drove him to show anyone who doubted him that he would survive and succeed.

When Anthony was fifteen years old, Greg told me that he wanted to play for an AAU team to help him make that next step in his basketball career.

I suggested he try the Michigan Mustangs, a team based out of Kalamazoo, because I knew their coach and thought he'd be a good mentor for Anthony. Not only did he make the team, but it was there that his nickname, A.I., first came about.

When it came time for him to go to college, I knew he wanted to come to Michigan State, and he wanted to try and play here. And I understood that. He grew up here and he loved it here.

But I also knew that he had to be realistic. He had a scholarship offer at Grand Valley State, and I knew their coach, their program, and their school. I didn't have a scholarship to give and couldn't promise him anything.

He ended up taking the opportunity to go to Grand Valley and stayed there for two years. After his second year, he was back in my office, asking me about walking on to our team again.

When we played Grand Valley in an exhibition game—a game they won—I told A.I. afterward that I would always be there for him.

I knew his heart was in East Lansing and that he wanted to be at Michigan State. But I also told him—autism or not—that I was going to treat him like any other player on our roster. It was a pretty frank discussion, and not once did he back down.

I knew what autism was, but I had never dealt with anyone who had it. You have those preconceived notions of, "He can't do this," or "He can't do that," but what I learned was that he could do anything.

It took a little while for our coaches to learn what the best way was to communicate with him, but he worked harder and harder to show that he belonged and that he could handle playing with our team.

By the same token, he wanted to be treated like everyone else. During summer workouts, at practice, in the weight room, and in the locker room, he bonded with those guys, and that just made him part of the group.

Once we started workouts and practices, Draymond Green took him under his wing after learning about his background.

A.I. had a tremendous work ethic, and that's what made him stand out. He eventually became the captain of our scout team and made guys like Draymond and our starters better simply because of how hard he played.

A testament to that was A.I. winning the Tim Bograkos Walk-On award as a junior. It was not a fun job for him or anyone else in those roles, but to A.I., winning the award was like winning the Big Ten Player of the Year.

Like all walk-ons, Anthony had to do a lot of dirty work, but he loved it, and that's one of the things I admire about him.

It was that belief in himself, the belief that if he truly put his mind to it, he could accomplish anything, including being the first player with autism to play Division I basketball.

I really can't say enough about A.I. Like all of my former players, he is family to me, to my wife, Lupe, and to my kids, Raquel and Steven.

Since he graduated from Michigan State and began working for the Autism Alliance of Michigan, telling his story has become his passion. This book shows how he faced his challenges and was able to overcome and achieve. It is a tremendously inspirational success story that I think could benefit anyone.

Telling his story is his passion; it is his life. Just like coaching is for me. The ability to tell his story and show people with autism that they can do anything they put their mind to is what Anthony Ianni wants to do with his life.

I once said that his passion comes through when he speaks. Just as easily, his passion comes through when you read his story.

*Tom Izzo*
*Head Basketball Coach, Michigan State University*

# ACKNOWLEDGMENTS

A.I. AND R.K.

Thanks to the following: Susan Hall, for introducing us and anticipating how well we would work together—we can't wait to give your signed copy to you; Chris Solari, for your early contributions to this story—you were the first to see that this story wouldn't fit in a newspaper article; Joe Perry, for representing us and believing in this project from the start; Dave Hulsey, Anna Francis, and everyone at Indiana University Press for your collaboration and support; Tom Bissell, for your help with the title and for your advice and encouragement; Warren Baker, for your work on several of the photos that appear in this book; and Dan Helton, for your legal assistance.

A.I.

There are so many people I want to thank as I write this. First off to my family that I love so much. To my wife, Kelly, words can't describe how lucky I am to have you in my life. Thank you for your endless support, for always believing in me and sticking by my side through everything. To my sons, Knox and Nash, Daddy loves you to the moon and back, and I'm so proud to be your father. When you're old enough to read this, always know that no dream is too big to accomplish in life. Follow your dreams, boys, because you can achieve and accomplish anything you want in life as long as you work hard, use your support system, and always believe in yourself, even when those around may not. To Mom and Dad, you guys are the reason I am the man and person that I am today. Your belief and support for me was the biggest reason I was able to achieve and do so much in my life despite having autism. I'm so lucky to have such great parents, and thank you both for giving me your love and guidance and for lighting the way for me on my life's journey. To my sister, Allison, thank you for protecting me and helping me when others around us didn't understand why I said and did the things I did when I was a kid or just didn't understand me in general.

To all of the teachers and administrators in Okemos Public Schools, especially the ones I had at Wardcliff Elementary, Chippewa Middle School, and Okemos High School: words can't describe how thankful I am to every single one of you. You all went the extra mile to help me become the best student I could possibly be, and you all adapted to my learning style to help me succeed in the classroom and beyond. I also want to give a huge thank-you to the late Sandy McDonald, who was the assistant director of special education during my time in Okemos Schools. Sandy helped give us a path at a time when there were few resources for those on the autism spectrum. Because of Sandy's guidance, we were able to succeed and find the strategies that benefited me in Okemos Public Schools.

To my high school coaches, Dan Stolz and Carter Briggs, thank you both for helping me become a better player and for adjusting some of your coaching style to help me learn the game better. Your guidance and lessons on the court helped me become a better person off the court, and I will never forget the incredible seasons and memories we had during my three years on the Okemos varsity basketball team. To my AAU coach,

Anthony Stuckey, thank you for believing in me, encouraging and supporting me, and giving me the nickname "A.I." I will never forget those summer practices and tournaments with the Michigan Mustangs out of Kalamazoo.

To GVSU Coach Ric Wesley and Coach Burt Paddock, thank you both for giving me my start in college athletics. You saw something in me that other schools didn't when you recruited me, and I can't thank you both enough for giving me the honor of wearing the Laker uniform and being a part of the GVSU program. Coach Paddock, thank you for being by my side during my freshman year and allowing me to lean on you whenever I needed to ask questions or was confused on things such as drills, plays, and games. Coach Wesley, it was an honor to play under you, even if it was only for two years. Although we had our differences, I'm always proud to say that I played for one of the greatest coaches in GV history and one of the best D2 programs in the country. I will always be grateful for the time I had with you and your staff. Dr. Damon Arnold, thank you for being my go-to guy at GV. During all the ups and downs, thank you for keeping me positive and giving me guidance when I felt like I didn't have any.

To MSU coaches Tom Izzo, Dwayne Stephens, Mike Garland, Dane Fife, Mike "Vork" Vorkapich, and Jordan Ott: words can't describe how much you all mean to me and how thankful I am for each of you. Thank you all for not only making a kid's dreams come true but also for adapting your coaching and teachings to help me be successful in our program. You all didn't just help me become a better player; you also helped me become a better person off the court. To Elliot Daniels, SASS (Student Athlete Support Services), Gretchen Paige, and RCPD (Resource Center for Persons with Disabilities), thank you all for giving me the encouragement, path, resources, and guidance to be the best student I could be during my time at Michigan State. Without you all, I wouldn't have gotten my degree. I am forever proud to be a Spartan for Life!

To all my teammates at Okemos, Grand Valley State, and Michigan State: you all are my brothers for life, and it was an honor to step onto the court with you. We had some incredible moments together, and we all made history. The banners in the gym at Okemos, the Fieldhouse at GV, and the Bres all prove that. To my friends, especially to Geoff Hall and Mike Przydzial, thank you both for being not only my best friends but also the brothers that I never had. I will always cherish my friendships with you both as well as all my friendships with those in Okemos, Grand Valley State, and Michigan State. Thank you for your continued support and sticking by my side. I love you all.

To Brian Calley, thank you for giving me my start in the field of public speaking and autism advocacy. Your support doesn't go unnoticed, and I promise you, as well as the entire autism community, that I will continue to be that hero and role model for those with autism and their families.

Last, but not least, I'd like to thank my coauthor Rob Keast. It's been a fun ride working on this manuscript with you. I can't thank you enough for your hard work, time, dedication, and effort to make this project a reality. More than that, thank you for believing in my story and helping me share my life journey with the world. I will forever value our friendship!

R.K.

Thank you to the Keast family, both extended and immediate, and especially to my parents—my work on this book began decades ago, when you first took me to the Lapeer library; my friends and colleagues in the Wyandotte Public Schools, especially Warren Baker (for your photo work as well as your friendship) and Janet Haddad (for your advice on automated interview notes—I can't imagine the manuscript without them!); John Freeman and Michael Lauchlin for being good readers and good friends over the years; Craig Pajak, because you nudged me back to books in high school after I had drifted away from them; Landon Thorpe—sometimes I forget that we're not related, as you feel like family to me—I'm grateful for our closeness, not to mention all of your great book and TV suggestions (dating back to Narita Airport 1999); Marty, for more than two decades of honesty about each other's writing; and Mary, for your love, patience, and enthusiasm—reading an entire manuscript once is truly a generous act, and you read this twice (and some parts more than that).

Thank you, A.I. This has been one of the most satisfying endeavors of my career. If our readers get half of the optimism and energy from your story that I have, they will be changed forever.

I dedicate my share of this book to Nora—I love you, and I hope you find some inspiration in this story, though you are already doing fine in the inspiration department. Your creativity and your commitment to your own art continue to impress me.

# CENTERED

# PROLOGUE: THE BRES

I ATTENDED MY FIRST MICHIGAN STATE basketball game when I was four years old. It was December of 1993, and we'd moved to East Lansing that summer. I'd gone to basketball games before at Ohio University—my dad's previous job—but Mom warned me that this game would be different.

"It's a bigger arena than what you're used to," she said, "so it's going to be more crowded. When people cheer, it will be louder."

"I know, Mom."

"And the lights won't be like before. The lights might seem brighter."

"OK."

"But we want to see Daddy, right?"

"Right."

"I'm not sure what the horn is going to sound like. Is it OK if the horn is different from what you're used to?"

"Yeah," I said.

But it wasn't OK. None of it was OK.

Even with Mom's preparations, the Breslin Center overwhelmed me. It was everything she said and a lot more. The music pounded and the lights blazed. The scoreboard flared chaotically. We sat twenty rows from the floor, close enough that it felt like every sight and sound was aimed right at me. I did my best to endure the surges of stimulation. I lasted through the player introductions, the opening tip-off, and the first home-court points of the season. But something triggered the crowd—was it a dunk? a ferocious blocked shot?—and they roared. And I wigged out.

I buried my head in my mom's lap, squeezed my eyes shut, and struggled to cover my ears with the palms of my hands. "It's too loud!" I wailed. "It's too loud!"

Mom put her hands over mine, trying to block out the sound, but it didn't work. "It's still too loud!" I said, again and again. My body writhed.

Mom suggested popcorn. She guided me up the stairs to the concourse, and my older sister, Allison, followed. She wasn't annoyed or disappointed. Allison was used to my outbursts.

The concourse was no better. The lines and the crowds were nothing like what I'd known at the Convocation Center in Athens, Ohio. Michigan State's fans swarmed, and their shouts echoed. I didn't want popcorn; I wanted to go home.

"It's too much!" I cried, still pressing my palms to my ears. Tears ran down my face, unwiped.

People shot judgmental looks at Mom. I was *very* tall for my age, so they assumed I was a bratty, immature, spoiled third grader.

Not a four-year-old on the autism spectrum.

Somehow we made it to the front of the concession line, and Mom bought our popcorn. The game hit a lull—the Spartans held a comfortable lead against East Tennessee State—and we returned to our seats. I munched my popcorn and tried to follow the game. I was conflicted. I wanted to be there, supporting Michigan State and spending a few minutes with Dad, who stopped by our seats when he had a free moment, but I also was desperate to escape the stimulation.

The Spartans made another big play, and the crowd roared again.

"Too loud! Too loud!"

Mom showed me her Mickey Mouse watch; his big white gloves were the watch's hands. "See this hand? When it makes it to the nine, we can go."

Every few minutes I grabbed her wrist and checked the watch. I didn't want to bail on the Spartans, but I had to escape the throbbing music, the thousands of people, and the glaring court. It all slammed into my brain. I needed to escape, to retreat to my bedroom. My room at our new house was quiet, and it had a carpet that I loved: soft and white with red, green, and blue dots. I wanted to sit on my floor, alone, and surround myself with my familiar toys.

\* \* \*

We returned to our same seats in the Breslin Center, game after game and season after season. By the time I was eight, I'd adjusted to the lights and the roaring fans. I didn't shield my eyes, and whenever fans erupted, I could cover my own ears, ride out the barrage of noise, and enjoy the big play. Dad, who was MSU's associate athletic director, started taking me down to the floor and introducing me to people at the scorer's table. He led me to the locker room, and I met Coach Tom Izzo and some of his players. On off days, Dad let me shoot baskets in the empty arena. By then I knew the Bres as well as I knew my elementary school. The problem was, I'd learned to follow the game. I'd learned to care, deeply, about the outcome. Crowds and buzzers were no big deal, but I couldn't stand losing.

The Spartans had to win every contest. They *had* to. Every loss devastated me, even if it was not a rivalry game, or an NCAA tournament game, or even a Big Ten game. Back then I didn't distinguish a conference game from a non-conference game. To me, every game was the most important game in the history of MSU basketball.

Michigan State hosted the Detroit Mercy Titans in December 1997, a few weeks before the Big Ten season started. Though MSU and Detroit Mercy are both Michigan schools, they are not rivals. No disrespect to Detroit Mercy—it has had many strong teams over the years, and the Titans actually put together a three-game winning streak against the Spartans in the 1990s—but it does not have the program that Michigan State has. Still, upsets happen, and Detroit Mercy came to the Breslin Center ready to play that Saturday evening. Michigan State fell behind by twelve points early in the second half, and I balled my fists and pounded my legs.

"Why can't we catch up?" I cried to my mom. "We're losing!"

"Never give up on your team, Anthony. You have to believe in them, even when they're down."

"But we're losing!"

Finally, some shots started falling for us, and we grabbed a few rebounds. We got closer. Mom was right: never give up on the Spartans. With twelve minutes left in the game, Mateen Cleaves made a basket off the glass and tied the game. Back and forth it went for the next eleven minutes. Up by a few, then down by a few. Most of the Breslin Center seemed to be loving the drama, but not me. It was pure torture. I wanted to win every game by a hundred points.

The game was tied with under a minute to go, and the Titans had the ball. Their guard drove the basket. There was chaos in the lane. What was happening?

The guard's shot went up and in, and the ref blew a foul on MSU.

"No!" I screamed. "It doesn't count! The basket shouldn't count!"

"What did I say, Anthony," Mom reminded me, "about never giving up?"

After the free throw, Michigan State trailed by three and just thirty seconds remained.

Mateen Cleaves attempted a three-pointer as the clock ticked down, but it clanked off the front of the rim.

Watching Cleaves's shot fall short tortured me as much as horns and buzzers once did. I'd met some of those players, and they were my heroes. They couldn't lose—they just couldn't. Coach Izzo couldn't lose, either. They had to win.

But they didn't win. I cried my eyes out. My Spartans had lost, right there in front of me.

By now I was as tall as a middle-school kid, but I still bawled like a preschooler. Not that I noticed, but the critical looks again must have poured down on Mom from the seats around us.

"Remember, Anthony," she said, "that nobody wins and nobody loses. OK? Nobody wins and nobody loses."

I didn't know what it meant, but somehow it comforted me. *Nobody loses.* OK. The Spartans didn't lose. It was just a score.

"Nobody wins and nobody loses," I said. All the way up the stairs, I repeated Mom's words. "Nobody wins and nobody loses," I said as we passed the shuttered concessions and veered toward the exit. *Nobody loses,* I assured myself. *Especially not Michigan State.*

\* \* \*

A few years after witnessing the loss to Detroit Mercy, I stood on the court at the Breslin Center, practicing jump shots on a side basket. I was between seventh and eighth grades, taking part in a summer basketball camp. Those were good years for Spartan fans. We'd gone to the Final Four three straight years, and Mateen Cleaves and his fellow Flintstones had won the national championship in 2000. I'd played enough basketball by then to know that I wanted to wear the green and white someday.

We'd finished lunch, and this was shootaround time before the afternoon clinics and scrimmages. I recognized many of my fellow campers from seventh-grade basketball. I played for Okemos, a middle-class suburb whose residents worked in the state capital or for Michigan State University. Many of the other boys played for our two biggest rivals, Holt and Mason. They drifted over to my basket and started jabbering.

"Okemos is a joke," they told me. "You guys are weak."

"You're wrong," I answered, unnerved, my voice shaking. "Okemos is good." I didn't know how to ignore them. Empty trash talk is a part of basketball, but I was incapable of brushing it off. *Nothing they said was true. Okemos was the greatest!* I loved Okemos.

I walked away from them, down the sideline to the next empty hoop, but they followed. Trying to ignore them, I lined up for a free throw.

"Your free throw is the worst. I'll bet a million dollars you miss it."

I growled, which cracked them up.

"You need to stop!"

"Go ahead and shoot."

I heaved a free throw toward the basket. It glanced off the rim and rolled away.

"That was the ugliest shot I've ever seen."

"Stop!"

I growled again. I balled my hands into fists and shoved them against my skull, all but punching myself. It was like I was trying to shove the explosion back down before it could come out. These guys couldn't see me cry. I was beyond talking. All I could do was growl and moan. Why would they do this to me? Why was I their target?

Some of the boys stood only as high as my shoulders, and others came up to my chin. If I'd been a fighter, I could have flattened them. But they knew I wouldn't fight back. They knew I would fall apart. By the time the camp coaches took the floor and sent us off to our afternoon clinics, I was a visible and audible mess, clutching my head and all but howling.

Not a soul at that camp would have guessed that a few years later I'd be standing on that same floor, starting at center for Okemos in the high school state championship game. Or that I'd return to the Breslin Center in college as a redshirt junior and trot onto the court wearing number 44. I had done it. I was a Michigan State Spartan, and this time every light and every cheer truly were aimed at me. I loved every decibel of it.

*   *   *

Is it all right that the Bres holds a few tough memories for me? Of course. A home is still a home, even though you endure some hard times there. And that's what the Bres is for me: home. I grew up there and had family time there. I learned to love basketball, and I became devoted to Michigan State. I settled on my first favorite player at the Breslin Center: a power forward named Antonio Smith. He was one of the Flintstones, but he was a year ahead of the trio that won the national championship. On the court Big Tone was ferocious. He grabbed every rebound that came his way, played tough defense, and never backed down from a challenge from anyone on the court. Off the court, though, he was friendly with me from the start, treating me like his little brother. Whenever I was around the team, Big Tone said hello and asked how I was doing in school. Antonio's senior year, the Spartans made it to the Final Four in St. Petersburg, Florida. I was ten. My family had good seats for the semifinal, and I was decked out in my green and white gear—which was what I wore every day of the week, anyway.

My Spartans were facing the overall number-one seed, Duke. I cried when Duke won, 68–62, not just because the season was over, one game short of a chance to play for the championship, but because Big Tone lost his last game. I knew his career as a Spartan was over. My favorite player would never wear an MSU jersey again. Sometimes after a loss, tears really are appropriate.

*  *  *

All Spartan careers come to an end, even my own. To be honest, I wasn't overwhelmed with sadness as I took the court for the last time, because I was so damned proud that my career had happened at all.

The Michigan State basketball team has a Breslin Center tradition. Every year at our last practice before the team leaves for the NCAA tournament, the team's seniors climb to the arena's very top row and take it all in. Coach Izzo, the other coaches, and the underclassmen stay back on the floor far below. There is a column up there that the seniors have signed for years—it may be a tradition almost as old as the Bres itself. In 2012, I signed that column.

To finish the ritual, each senior then heaves a basketball toward the court, hoping to sink the longest three-pointer in the building's history. By my senior year, nobody had ever made it. One of my teammates, junior Derrick Nix, told me his money was on me to be the first. Coach Izzo also said he had a feeling. From the rafters I could see my teammates and coaches—some stood around midcourt, and the rest lounged in the first row. They all looked up, waiting for a basketball to come hurtling down from the upper atmosphere. I was up. I gave the ball a bounce on the concrete floor, almost like I was taking a fifteen-foot free throw. I decided not to aim straight for the basket. Instead I picked out a spot on the floor well behind the three-point arc, not far from the sideline. My plan was to sink it on the bounce.

My throw hit the floor near my target. The ball rocketed skyward and toward the hoop.

"Come on! Get there!"

The shot curved downward . . . and sailed past, missing both the rim and the backboard.

If I'd taken the shot from the court, it would have been an ugly airball. But, given that I chucked it from the rafters, I'd say it was a pretty good attempt.

I've defied the odds so many times in my life, but not on that shot.

But here is what I *have* done at the Breslin Center: In 2010 I wore a Michigan State jersey for the first time, becoming the first person known to be on the autism spectrum to play Division I basketball. Also in 2010, I scored my first Division I points, on a pass from future NBA great Draymond Green. In 2012, as part of a Senior Day tradition, I kissed the Spartan logo at center court. And, a few months after kissing the floor, I crossed the stage in my green cap and gown to receive my diploma.

The Breslin Center is my home. It is where I first dreamed my dreams. Few people who knew me when I was young would have believed my dreams had any chance of becoming realities. But they did. At the Bres.

# 1

## "WE ARE OKEMOS"

LIKE THE BRESLIN CENTER, THE Okemos High School gym has popped up in my life again and again. It was my family's version of childcare, it is the place where my basketball career took off, and it is where my current life as a public speaker connected with my past.

On September 5, 2017, ten years after I graduated from Okemos, I went back to the gym. My gym.

I speak in a lot of school gyms and auditoriums. I give public talks all the time to raise awareness about autism and to stress how painful bullying can be. But this speech was different.

First, my wardrobe was different. Normally I wear an MSU polo shirt and jeans, but for this event, the principal, Christine Sermak, gave me a "We Are Okemos" T-shirt. It wasn't a tough switch to make. I bleed maroon and white, and I will be part of the Chiefs family forever.

Second, a few months before my appearance, Principal Sermak asked if I could emphasize my personal connections.

"Can you tailor your message around family," she asked, "and say what Okemos meant to you? We want to bring back the family atmosphere to the building that was here when you went to school here."

"That's perfect," I said. "I talk about family all the time. It's always in my presentations."

I first started hanging out in the Okemos gym when I was in elementary school, when my mom became the varsity volleyball coach (a job she still has today, more than twenty years later). Mom took me to practices with her, and to pass the time I went off to the side hoops. I shot baskets the whole time. Usually the boys' varsity basketball team would wrap up practice just before the volleyball team took the floor. One of the seniors, a guy named Mark Kissling, often headed over to my basket. He'd play one-on-one with me, or he would rebound while I shot. I always thought that was pretty cool of Mark, and I became a big Okemos hoops guy from then on.

In this gym, I developed as a center who attracted interest from college coaches.

In this gym, the student section—the crazy O-Zone—had a chant for me: "A.I.! A.I.!" My rowdy classmates even synched their arm movements: tenting their arms for "A," just like in the song "Y.M.C.A.," then straight above their heads for the "I."

"A.I.! A.I.!"

They hollered for me every game in here, giving me love and support—giving me community.

This gym . . . this gym comes with a lot of emotions.

It was a coping mechanism when I needed it most. Because of my autism, I was prone to frustration in class—and tantrums anywhere. In class all I could do was fidget and tap and pound the floor and hyperventilate. Math assignments swamped me. Multiple-choice questions rattled my sense of logic. Some days it felt like my classes were walls that closed in around me and squashed me. I felt suffocated.

Until I was in the gym.

The Okemos gym was my happy place. I could shoot for two hours straight, honing my post moves and jump shots. My mind cleared, and my breathing settled. I forgot that I even had autism.

So in 2017 when I returned, I wanted the students to appreciate the special place they had.

Unlike at other schools where I speak, no one had to steer me toward the gym. I could have found it with my eyes closed. On my way through the halls, I stopped by Danielle Tandoc's room. Mrs. Tandoc was one of my science teachers. When I broke my humerus bone my junior year, she displayed the X-ray in her classroom. Mrs. Tandoc had been one of the teachers to suggest me as a speaker.

"Thank you," I told her. "This is the chance of a lifetime."

"It was a no-brainer! You're pretty good at what you do, and your message is something our kiddos need."

The students entered the gym and filled one side. (This is my preference. When students sit on both sides of the gym, I end up with my back to half the kids.)

"I don't care what city, state, or town you are originally from," I told them. "I want you all to remember this. The rest of the time you are here at Okemos High, you should respect everyone here at this school. And here's the funny part: I don't care if you *like* each other or not. I don't care if you *know* each other or not, you should *respect* everyone at Okemos. When I drove home this morning, I was crazy excited to be back. I was excited because I'm coming back to my community, but not just a community—a community that made me and helped me become who I am today."

As someone on the autism spectrum, I told them, I knew how much it could hurt when respect was missing from a school. And I knew how great it felt when respect was there.

I paced before the bleachers, making a lot of eye contact. I wanted them with me and not looking at their phones.

"You should respect everyone in this school," I urged them, "because guess what? You're part of the same group. You're on the same team. You're part of the Okemos Chiefs family for life!"

To finish my speech, I did something I've never done anywhere else: I trotted to center court, dropped to a push-up position, and kissed the Chiefs logo that blazed across the floor.

The honors didn't stop there. Afterward, a senior crossed the floor to me and said he was the head of the homecoming parade committee. "Would you like to be our grand marshal?" he asked.

I didn't even hesitate.

A month later, on a beautiful fall Friday evening, with the sun low in the sky and Michigan's leaves turning colors, I took my seat of honor in a silver convertible.

Near me in the church parking lot, the middle school football team assembled in their jerseys. Fifteen years earlier, I'd been one of them. I had marched in this parade before, as a tall, awkward, twelve-year-old football player.

As my convertible's driver started our car, a big Hercules float rolled past—the homecoming theme that year was "Greek and Roman gods."

The parade started, with my car in front and the marching band behind me. I heard the Okemos fight song a lot that day, and it made me a very proud alum.

The route went south from the church toward the high school. The entire way, people stood and cheered. There wasn't an empty spot on the street. I tossed candy and my "Relentless Tour" wristbands to kids, and I waved to former teachers and classmates when they shouted "Anthony!" or "A.I.!"

One of my friends from the class of 2007 was there with her kids. She jumped up and down, and I waved to her and her family. (I saw her again a month later at our ten-year reunion. She told me how surprised her son was that his mom had known me in high school. "That's pretty cool!" he'd told her.)

Even though I was wearing Okemos gear, people knew I'd played basketball for Michigan State. "Go Green!" they shouted, and I responded with all my heart: "Go White!"

The best moment of the parade came near the end, when my mom and my wife brought my son Knox out to me. He sat on my lap and helped me wave. I've seen a lot of pro athletes take their kids onto the court or the field after a championship game. Some bring their sons and daughters into pressers, and the world gets to see that they are more than just athletes. They are fathers and mothers. I won't ever get a post-NBA championship presser that my kids can attend, but this was better. I got to show my son to my hometown, and I got to show my hometown to my boy.

# 2

## THE DIAGNOSIS

BOTH OF MY PARENTS ARE from Michigan, but that's not where they met. Mom grew up in Morenci, a small town just north of the Ohio border. She played four sports at Morenci High School: volleyball, basketball, softball, and track. After high school she attended Adrian College, a Division III school thirty minutes to the northeast. Mom continued to play volleyball, basketball, and softball at Adrian. She was an AIAW (Association for Intercollegiate Athletics for Women) all-state athlete in all three sports. Mom also earned Division III All-American honors for basketball, and she was an academic All-American, too.

After college, Mom went to Athens, Ohio, to coach the high school's volleyball, basketball, and track teams. It wasn't long before the University of Rio Grande (which is in southeastern Ohio, not Texas) hired her to coach volleyball and women's basketball. Mom's next coaching move was back to Athens. She coached Ohio University's women's volleyball team, and she was an assistant coach for the women's basketball team. Mom has always loved working with young people; she gets so much satisfaction from seeing them grow. She even owned her own dance studio for a time, where she taught tap, jazz, ballet, and tumbling. Because she loves teaching, and because she had so much success as an athlete, coaching was a natural fit.

Dad is from southeastern Michigan and grew up in towns within an hour of Detroit. His father, my Grandpa Nick, was a school administrator, and new opportunities came along from time to time that required the family to move. When my dad was a boy, they lived in the Detroit suburb of Livonia. From there they moved to Byron, a rural district not far from Flint. Grandpa Nick was the high school principal in Byron and was then promoted to district superintendent. Next, Grandpa Nick became the superintendent of schools in Dexter, near Ann Arbor, and Dad's family moved again.

Grandpa Nick eventually left his job as the Dexter superintendent to become the superintendent of the Washtenaw Intermediate School District. The Washtenaw ISD has a strong special education department, providing everything from speech and occupational therapy to early childhood education and job training for students with special needs. My grandpa was always an advocate for special education students, and he even gave input on legislation that strengthened protections and increased opportunities for special education students. I wasn't even born yet, but I later benefited from the accommodations he fought for.

Dad was a three-sport athlete at Dexter High School: football, basketball, and baseball. Dad is one of six kids, and most of his siblings also played sports. His brother Mark played basketball at Michigan Tech, and his brother Rob played basketball for Northwood University.

Grandpa Nick, too, had been an athlete and coach. He grew up in New Kensington, Pennsylvania, and played football at Pitt. After college he taught high school social studies, and he coached football and baseball before switching to administration.

Dad attended Michigan State in the early 1970s, where he pitched on the baseball team. When Dad graduated from MSU, he initially intended to have a career in radio and television. (MSU's broadcasting program is a great one, and that attracted my dad as much as the chance to play baseball did.) His first job out of college was selling ads for a radio station in Saginaw. When that career didn't pan out, Dad went to Ohio University to get a master's degree in sports administration. He stayed on at Ohio University as the ticket manager and assistant business manager.

When my parents met in Athens, they had instant connections: they were both from Michigan, and they were both athletes who had stayed in the world of sports. They got married at the chapel on Adrian College's campus in 1982 but continued to live in Ohio for another decade. My older sister, Allison, was born in 1985, and they had me four years later. Both of my parents traveled a lot for Ohio University (Mom as a coach and Dad as an athletics administrator), so after I came along, Mom retired from coaching at the college level. It had been nearly impossible with one child, let alone two!

My parents always assumed Allison and I would be involved in sports. As athletes themselves, they know what great values sports instill in kids: teamwork, discipline, effort, commitment, and loyalty. They also know that teams can be like families. Early on, some signs indicated that I would be another Ianni athlete. I could hit a baseball well and strike a golf ball cleanly when I was only three.

My toddler years in Ohio looked like any other kid's toddler years. I played on swing sets and watched *Sesame Street* and *Mister Rogers' Neighborhood*. I pushed my Thomas the Tank Engine toys across the floor while watching *Thomas & Friends*. (The TV must have stayed on when my shows ended, because I also remember watching *The Joy of Painting*.) We had a black lab named Nipper, and I chased him around the house and let him jump up on the couch with me. Sometimes Nipper knocked over the kitchen trash can or got rambunctious, but I loved him and knew he had a big heart.

Some afternoons a couple we knew, Floyd and Ermyl Ballinger, watched me at their house. Floyd and Ermyl maintained an old-fashioned way of living; they were throwbacks to simpler times. They spent every minute they could in their giant garden, and Allison and I learned to pick green beans, shuck corn, and pop peas from their pods. Ermyl canned or froze everything they grew and maintained stores of tomatoes, peppers, cucumbers, and just about anything else that a gardener could raise in an Ohio backyard. Ermyl cooked everything from scratch, and their TV and its rabbit-ears antenna sat tucked away in a corner of a back room, rarely used. Every time I visited, Ermyl whipped up homemade peanut butter crackers using Peter Pan peanut butter and saltines. Floyd was my sparring partner. Whenever I heard him come home and open the back door, I bolted through the kitchen, yelling, "Aaaaaarrrrggghhh!" I started throwing punches, determined to take him down.

"Not today," he'd taunt. "You're not going to get me today!"

Floyd pretended to fight back, but I ended up winning every one of our scuffles. "Ha ha!" I bragged. "I won, you lost!" Then I ran away before he could recover. Floyd and Ermyl were two of the kindest people I've ever known, and they'll have a place in my heart for the rest of my life.

Dad's office was in the Convocation Center, where Ohio University's basketball and volleyball teams played. If the arena was dark, I sprinted around the concourse, loving the echoes I generated. But if the lights were on and the hardwood court was down, I shot baskets in front of 13,000 empty seats. Every visit, I insisted we see the large, stuffed bobcat near the arena's main entrance. "We have to see the big bobcat before we leave," I told Mom. "We have to."

We *had* to. If we skipped the bobcat, I went berserk. That's how it was with me. The bobcat was just one of the rituals I insisted on. Bedtime was another. First, I lined up every Thomas the Tank Engine train I had on a shirt-sleeves ironing board. I arranged them in a precise order: first Thomas, followed by Percy, Gordon, Toby, Mavis, James, and finally Edward the Blue Engine. Once the trains were in place, I flipped on my Thomas the Tank Engine nightlight that sang a tinny little song, hit the switch on my ceiling fan, and pressed play on my lullaby tape.

At first my parents thought the orderly row of toys was endearing: their three-year-old was so organized! They'd never have to worry about me misplacing homework or losing junk under my bed. But my tidiness came with a dark side: if something wasn't the way I wanted or *expected* it to be, I exploded.

Other things about my development also didn't seem quite right.

"Anthony, go put this in your toy box," Mom said to me one afternoon, handing me an action figure. I trotted off . . . and came back with a second action figure.

"Anthony, you're going to wear your red shirt today," Mom said to me while I finished my breakfast. "Go to your closet and get your red shirt." I hustled to my room, went to my dresser instead of the closet, yanked open a drawer, and returned with a shirt that didn't have a stitch of red in it.

It wasn't defiance, but my parents didn't know what it was. They decided to have my ears checked. My cousin Sara is hearing impaired, and she needed a cochlear implant at an early age, so my parents wondered if I had a similar problem. The hearing tests came back fine.

Often, I jumbled language. I liked to ask "Why" questions. *Why do cows eat grass? Why is the store closed? Why is Allison going to school?* Except I got so used to hearing my parents' answers start with the word "because" that I started anticipating it. So my questions sounded like this:

"Why because do cows eat grass?"

"Why because is Allison going to school?"

They took me for a second hearing test and then a third. The results stayed the same. My ears weren't the problem.

I watched a lot of Disney back then: *Aladdin, Beauty and the Beast, One Hundred and One Dalmatians*, and *The Little Mermaid*. Whatever I heard, I repeated: "Darling it's better, down where it's wetter, take it from me!" I could say a line hundreds of times. "Darling it's better, down where it's wetter, take it from me!"

Clinicians call this "perseverative speech."

"Tale as old as time," I'd sing. "Tale as old as time. Tale as old as time. Tale as old as time. . . ."

My parents enrolled me in a preschool—briefly. What I remember is walking down a ramp into a room swarming with kids. There were lots of areas to play in and stations to explore. The teachers encouraged us to roam and do what interested us. To me, it was chaos. I craved an assigned seat and appointed toys and tasks, not a free-range approach. I wigged out almost daily, and the intensity of my flailing and screaming was off the charts. My outbursts provoked judgmental looks from other parents. I didn't notice, but my mom did.

The preschool staff speculated that I had an extreme case of attention deficit disorder. I don't remember damaging anything, but I screamed angrily and cried. Even in preschool I was tall, so at the age of three, I looked like a five-year-old who was acting like a one-year-old. Before long, my parents pulled me from the preschool, probably to everyone's relief: the teachers', the other parents', and definitely mine.

The preschool teachers weren't the only people telling my parents that I had attention deficit disorder. My pediatrician in

Athens seconded the diagnosis. But that didn't make any sense to my parents. Mom coached players with ADD and taught dancers with ADD, and she knew what to look for. When Mom and I stayed home, just the two of us, I didn't break down nearly as much. Besides, I didn't seem to lack focus. If anything, I had too much concentration. I noticed the world around me and mimicked the words and songs I heard, over and over and over: "Darling it's better, down where it's wetter! Darling it's better, down where it's wetter!"

ADD wasn't the issue, and Ritalin sure wasn't going to be the solution.

\* \* \*

I butted heads with my big sister the way all siblings do. Sometimes I took her toys, and she wanted them back. We fought over the TV. She kicked me out of her bedroom whenever I wandered in. Allison could stride into the living room giving orders, ponytail swinging, wearing an Ohio University sweatshirt and already looking like the confident athlete she would become. Allison had a little toy keyboard that I liked to play with. It ran on batteries, so I could easily take it from her room to mine. I banged out random notes while silly drumbeats pulsed on and on.

Allison heard me plunking away and charged into my room. "Give that back now! It's not yours."

"Yes it is!"

"No it's not!"

She grabbed her keyboard and stomped back to her own bedroom. As always, I threw a fit. Not a normal three-year-old fit, but a nuclear bomb–level fit, leaving my parents to wonder, yet again, what was wrong with their son.

My parents made an appointment at Children's Hospital in Columbus, a little over an hour away. The hospital mailed an eighty-page questionnaire to my parents ahead of time, and Mom sat at the kitchen table and worked her way through it.

A few weeks before my appointment at Children's Hospital, Dad received a call from Michigan State University, his alma mater. MSU offered him a job as associate athletics director. The problem was, MSU needed him in East Lansing right away. Dad accepted the position. My parents agreed that Allison should see out the school year in Athens, so my mom, my sister, and I stayed on in Ohio.

Mom and I made the drive from Athens to the hospital in Columbus on a winter morning shortly before my fourth birthday. It was a typical car ride for us. I drove my Thomas trains along the windowsill, and Mom told me to search for letters on passing billboards. "Find an 'A,' Anthony," she said. "Just like the 'A' in your name." When I found one, she said "B" was next.

We sang songs, just like we always did: "Skidamarink a dink a dink, Skidamarink a doo, I love you."

Mom belted out the lyrics cheerfully, but she must have been stewing in uncertainty. Would somebody finally figure out what was happening with her son? Could somebody give her the prescription or the therapy that would turn me into an average boy with average-size outbursts?

As we rolled toward the hospital, I asked my questions:

"Why because does it snow?"

"Why because is that truck stopped?"

At Children's Hospital we met with one therapist after another. I remember lots of elevator rides. The hospital had a kind of gymnasium, and the physical therapist told me what to do: run, skip, hop, trot. She put me on a bike with training wheels and told me to go for a spin. I swung on the swing and slid down the slide.

No surprise—I performed just fine in the gym.

But when I met with the psychologist, things went less well. She pulled out flash cards, which was a good start. I knew flash cards from home. She showed me a drawing of a pond. Some cartoon ducks swam in the middle, while others rested on the shore. "How many ducks do you see, Anthony?"

"Six."

"How many do you see *on* the pond?"

"Six."

"Just count the ducks that are on the pond."

I was confused. There were six ducks. What was she asking? She tried another picture.

"Tell me, Anthony: Is the ball on the table or under the table?"

I pointed. "There's the ball."

There was a ball, and there was a table. What else did she want?

* * *

They scheduled another appointment, just under a month later, when Mom could go back for the results. A few days before the follow-up, Mom told our neighbor, Lynne, that she had an appointment at Children's Hospital.

"I think you need me to go with you," Lynne insisted. Lynne was a nurse and knew how to talk with other medical professionals. "I'll take notes, ask questions."

I stayed with the Ballingers when Mom and Lynne went to the hospital. I couldn't have guessed or even understood that they were about to receive a diagnosis that would set a course for the rest of my life.

This time, Mom spent most of her time with the developmental pediatrician. That's who broke the news to her.

"Your son has something called Pervasive Developmental Disorder, Not Otherwise Specified," he said. "PDD-NOS, for short. It's a form of autism."

Mom was stunned.

"It's a milder form," the pediatrician continued. He handed Mom a heavy book of medical diagnoses and pointed at the PDD-NOS entry.

She read the description: a delay in social development; a lag in abstract language development; mimicking, repetitive behaviors.

It was all there. That was me. Mom knew they had it right.

"Our pediatrician suggested Ritalin," she told the doctor. "Would that do anything for Anthony?"

He shook his head. "I prescribe more Ritalin than any other doctor in this county. For some kids it certainly has benefits. But not Anthony. Believe me, if I thought it would help him, I'd prescribe it."

Mom didn't understand. "So, if you can't prescribe him anything, what are we supposed to do?"

"What your son needs is very strict behavioral management. Consistency. It's going to be all about how you manage life for him and for your family. To function, Anthony needs routine. You need to make schedules and stick to them. He wants a world that is extremely ordered. Very black and white."

And that was it. There was no plan past that. "Give him structure." Everything beyond that was up to my parents.

Walking out of the hospital, Mom started crying. All she had was six letters, PDD-NOS, and a brief entry in some medical book.

"What are we supposed to do next?" she asked Lynne. "Why can't they tell me what to do?"

Lynne stayed optimistic. "We know what we're dealing with, so it's going to be OK. We'll make a plan," she assured my mom. "We don't have a plan yet, but we'll make one, and there is no one better to handle this than you."

That evening Mom called Dad in East Lansing.

"Anthony has a form of autism," she told him. Mom knew it was the right diagnosis. She had no idea what to do next, but she at least knew what to call it.

Dad wasn't quite ready to buy it.

"He's going to be OK. Boys are always behind," he said. "So what if Allison was ahead of him when she turned four? That's normal."

They could try a new doctor in East Lansing in a few months, he said.

But Mom knew. I was autistic.

The pediatrician had prescribed consistency, but my dad was living in another state, and we were packing up everything we owned—the clothes I wore, the toys I played with, the plates I ate off of, everything. We were leaving the only town and neighbors I'd ever known, I was saying goodbye to the bobcat, and we were about to live in a small apartment for several months while our new house was being built.

Life with an autistic child was not off to a good start.

# 3

## THAT ANTHONY KID

> Ball skills—Anthony uses a right side preference with a mature pattern for throwing . . . With a regulation basketball, Anthony will steal the ball, dribble, shoot and make baskets or catch the ball after it bounces off the backboard. He participates in jumping when a "jump ball" is called.
>
> From my kindergarten physical therapy report

MOM AND I SAT ON my bedroom floor with some empty boxes between us.

"The new house isn't all the way built yet, Anthony," she said, "so we're going to live in an apartment by Daddy's work for a few months."

Allison and I would be sharing a small bedroom, Mom explained, so most of our toys would stay in storage until our house was ready.

"Let's pick out a few things to not pack," she instructed. "Those will be the toys you'll have all summer. And we're going to put the rest in these boxes."

That was easy: every Thomas the Tank Engine toy stayed out, and Mom and I began to load the rest into the boxes. We packed gradually, over many days, so I could adjust to the disappearances.

We said goodbye to Athens on Memorial Day weekend and headed north. Instead of driving straight to the apartment, we swung by Mom's parents' house to drop off Nipper. Michigan State's married housing complex didn't allow dogs.

Mom grew up on a sixty-acre farm. When she was a kid her parents grew wheat, corn, and soybeans, and they raised chickens and pigs. They had steers, too, and at one point owned a completely untamable horse that snorted and stomped and didn't let anyone come near it. The animals were gone before I was born, though, and my grandparents rented their cropland to another farmer. The two-story farmhouse was yellow, with a small front porch. The cellar door seemed like a hatch to a dungeon. My grandparents had a long driveway and a large yard—perfect for football, baseball, Red Rover, and other games I could play with my cousins at holidays and other family gatherings.

Mom had explained the Children's Hospital visits to her parents, but my grandpa was skeptical. "What he needs is some good spankings," Grandpa told my mom. "He's spoiled is what he is."

My autism wasn't like my cousin Sara's hearing impairment. With Sara, you could see her hearing aids. My grandpa needed a similar visual cue for me—but autism doesn't have one. He did his best, though. Before we left, Grandpa sat on the riding mower and lifted me onto his lap. "Let's go for a ride, Anthony." He took me to the end of the driveway and back.

It was time to say goodbye to Nipper and continue the trip to East Lansing.

\*   \*   \*

Lynne was right about Mom: if anybody could figure out how to give me structure, she could. As soon as we arrived at the apartment, Mom hung the dark blue window shades from my old room in the bedroom I would share with Allison. She and Dad pushed the bunkbeds near the window—exactly where my bed had been in Ohio. Then she plugged in the Thomas nightlight and the cassette player. The lullabies tape was still loaded. Allison watched quietly as they made all of the accommodations for me and none for her.

I don't recall spending much time inside the apartment that summer. Mom got us out as much as she could. Married housing apartments at Michigan State attracted families from all over the world, and our complex's playground was full of children. On hot days, while Dad worked, Mom took us to MSU's aquatic center to swim. Most days we drove out to the building site to check on the progress of our new house. Then we'd stop at Tasty Twist for an ice cream before heading back to the apartment. Once Tasty Twist became part of the routine, my mom had to stop every time. My need for consistency could have surprising benefits!

Whenever we ran errands, Mom laid out the agenda for me, stop by stop.

"First, we're going to get gas. The next stop is the post office. OK?"

"OK. That's all the stops?"

"No. The third stop is Target."

"Can I get a toy?"

"Today you can look, but we're not going to buy one today."

The errands went fine until we hit the toy aisle. I spotted a Batman action figure that I didn't have.

"I want that one!"

"Remember what we said? Today we're not going to buy any toys."

"I want that one!"

I stomped and growled. My face trembled.

"Anthony . . ."

"Aaaagggghhh!"

When our errands didn't match the agenda, my rage was even worse. If Mom prepped me for stops at the building site and Target but forgot to mention that we were dropping off paperwork at Allison's new elementary school, I howled and cried.

At night the apartment complex could be noisy. I played my Thomas nightlight and turned up the lullaby tape even louder than usual. Allison, sleeping in the upper bunk, somehow tolerated this cacophony.

*　*　*

We made a lot of trips to my grandparents' farm in Morenci that summer. I missed Nipper, and I couldn't wait to jump out of the car, rush inside, and roll around on the living room floor with him.

"Take him outside," my grandpa ordered.

So Nipper and I bolted outside with a tennis ball. I was proud of how far I could throw it. Nipper shot across the yard, chasing the bouncing ball.

We had two cousins who lived nearby, Angie and Sara. Sara was close to Allison's age, and Angie was a few years older. They came by whenever we were at the farm, mainly to play with my sister. My grandparents' bedroom was on the farmhouse's first floor, so the two upstairs bedrooms served mainly as a play area for us grandkids. The three girls ran upstairs to play school or to act out Dorothy's journey through Oz with all of the *Wizard of Oz* dolls. Uninvited, I followed them up.

The girls looked at me apprehensively.

"I'm playing, too!" I seized the Cowardly Lion.

Whenever I opened my mouth, Sara took three steps back. Because of her hearing impairment, she relied heavily on reading gestures, and everything about the way I moved was loud and aggressive. I crashed right through the personal space Sara needed. I didn't mean to be that way, but that's how I was.

The girls retreated to the other bedroom, but I pursued them.

"I'm playing, too!" I said again.

To give the girls a break, Grandpa offered to take me for a ride in his pickup down the road a quarter mile to visit his neighbor, Steve. Steve had cows, so I was game.

When we stood near the fence, I waved at each cow I saw.

"Hi, Steve the Cow."

Grandpa laughed; I didn't know why.

"Steve the Cow," I repeated, pointing at a different cow.

Lots of cows named Steve grazed in that pasture.

\* \* \*

Our subdivision was largely unfinished when we arrived—our house was only the third to be completed. My "neighborhood" was mostly dirt hills that I could run up and down. In Ohio we had lived in a ranch-style home, but now we had a two-story house. The stairs were like a playground: I'd dash to the top, then slide down to the bottom, bouncing on my butt the whole way.

One by one, builders completed the houses around ours, and families moved in. Just about everyone had children. Many of the kids were Allison's age, while others were a few years younger than I was. I landed in the gap between.

When I began kindergarten, I had no idea that I was autistic. It would be years before my parents shared my diagnosis with me. I'm glad they waited. Trying to explain autism to me when I was five or six would have been, at the very least, confusing. It may have even discouraged me. I may have set low expectations for myself. Instead, when I heard it for the first time as a teenager, it lit a fire in me. The six-year-old me wasn't ready to go out there and prove people wrong.

From the first time I entered Wardcliff Elementary as a kindergartener, trailing behind Allison, I could tell that my sister was a leader in that school. She was starting her fourth-grade year. Teachers seemed excited to see her, and kids were eager to say hello.

My kindergarten teacher's name was Mrs. Woodruff. What I loved about her class were the things that most kindergarteners like about their first year of school: going outside for recess, playing with paint in art class, and listening to my teacher read stories. Some days our counselor, Mrs. LaVine, stopped by and performed with a puppet—a dolphin named Duso. Whenever Mrs. LaVine pulled out Duso, I knew we were in for a good show.

It didn't take much, though, for a great day to become a nightmare. Another kid could be playing with a toy I wanted. A certain color of crayon wasn't in the box. A fire drill rang.

And then I'd unravel. I cried and screamed. I thrashed my arms and clutched at my head.

One day I stomped out into the hall and saw a parent I didn't recognize.

"Do you have a car?"

The parent stared, too stunned to speak.

"Will you drive me home? I got to get out of here. I got to get out of here."

Another time I went AWOL. I wandered toward the main office and took a seat on the picnic table in the school's common area. One of the secretaries peeked through a window and noticed me. I smacked the table repeatedly and breathed heavily. It was the middle of the school day, and everyone else was in their classrooms. The secretary came out of the office and approached me.

"Anthony, aren't you supposed to be in class?" she asked.

"Yes."

"Well, what are you doing out here?"

"Call me a cab," I told her. "I'm outta here."

One morning Mom walked me in, said hello to the parents and teachers she knew, and sent me on my way. Heading back to her car, Mom passed another mother and son stepping out of their car. "Now remember," the mother said, "I do not want you to play with that Anthony kid today." That broke my mom's heart. She knew I loved people. I didn't intend to threaten anyone. But, in a moment of overstimulation, I could wig out. I never hurt anybody during a tantrum, but I was very big for a kindergartener. Mom retreated to her car. "That Anthony kid" was her son. The other families were judging me without attempting to understand me or consider what I was going through. It made Mom so sad. Not that Mom was blind—she knew my behavior could be inappropriate. But she also knew the good intentions behind my behavior. I *wanted* to bond with people—I just didn't know how.

*   *   *

Mom became a volunteer parent aide in my building. Volunteering let Mom work with young people again, something she loves to do. It's in her blood. But being in my school also allowed her to be nearby to deal with my outbursts. Sometimes she could calm me with soothing words and a big hug. Other times there was no getting me back, and we left for the day.

Something needed to change. The school knew it, and so did my parents. So, I went through another battery of tests. I don't remember being singled out for all of these evaluations, but apparently I met with all sorts of specialists: speech and language therapists, a social worker, a physical therapist, and an occupational therapist all conducted assessments.

The end product was my individualized education plan—or IEP, for short.

They needed a large conference table for the IEP meeting to fit all of the specialists. I wasn't there; not until high school did I even hear about this meeting.

"Based on our tests with Anthony," one of the evaluators began, "we do believe he'll be able to graduate from high school. We think that can happen. And then, there are group homes he will be able to live in and live a relatively normal life."

A group home.

Next was a physical therapist who had done a wheelbarrow test with me, with me walking on my hands. The physical therapist said to my parents, "I know you're both athletic people, but he will never be an athlete."

It was like a punch to the face.

Around the table, the specialists kept going. More negativity. More dire predictions. My mom began crying. It had been two years since Children's Hospital had told my mom that I was autistic, but this was the first time anyone had declared what her son's sad future would look like. It was one of the worst moments of my parents' lives. To this day, they can't think about that first IEP meeting without either tearing up or becoming flushed with anger.

My dad finally interrupted.

"First of all, I respect each and every one of you as a professional, and I appreciate the time you've taken to test our son," he said. "But let me tell you what our expectations are for Anthony. He *will* graduate from high school. He *will* go to college, and he *will* graduate from college."

The evaluators looked at my dad like he had three heads. A college degree? The specialists around the table must have thought Dad was delusional. They must have been dreading the next twelve years of my education—working with this father who couldn't accept reality.

"Here's what we're going to do," my dad continued. "We're going to figure out a way to make that happen. I don't know how we're going to do it, but we're going to figure it out."

The specialists filed out one by one. Sandy McDonald, who was the assistant director of special education in Okemos Schools, had been in charge of the meeting. Now, she and my parents were the only three left in the room. My parents were flummoxed. *Maybe they're right*, my mom thought. How many times had she yanked me from school, just in the previous three months? How often did I rage at my classmates and at the world? Maybe the therapists had a point. I was only in kindergarten, and already I was so far behind: socially, emotionally, and, in some ways, linguistically.

McDonald, in that moment, became our angel.

"You're right," she told my dad. "We *are* going to figure out what to do. We can't solve it all in one day, but we're not going to give up."

That may seem too vague to call an actual plan—*let's try anything and everything*—but it was the perfect answer. It was the first step on our journey.

To be fair to my more pessimistic evaluators, my behavior in kindergarten did stand out. To shape my initial IEP, the Okemos Schools had its district psychologist observe me. This is what the psychologist reported, right around my sixth birthday:

Anthony began nursery school in September of 1992 and attended until January 1993. His parents took him out of nursery school as the classroom tended to over-stimulate Anthony. He is overly sensitive to loud and unexpected noises. Anthony had difficulty playing with the other children cooperatively. He did not have any interest in writing, coloring or learning the alphabet. Mrs. Ianni reports that Anthony has a keen sense of hearing and vision. He is also a very tactile young man who likes the feel of silky materials, especially ladies' hosiery.

Anthony exhibited many behaviors which made him look different from the other children including making loud noises, throwing tantrums, moving around a lot, talking to inanimate objects and touching and smelling things. Socially, Anthony tends to take things away from other children and often pretends to punch them. Because of his large physical size, Anthony often intimidates other children. His mother reports that Anthony has always had great difficulty changing activities and reacts strongly to changes in his routine. Anthony often repeats phrases from television or movies in a perseverative manner. He injects the utterances into conversations in an inappropriate manner. Mrs. Ianni is concerned about Anthony's gross and fine motor skills at this time. He is unable to button without assistance and cannot tie his shoes. . . . He is a very restless sleeper. Anthony typically awakens between 1 and 3 a.m. and goes to get his mother who then lies down with him in his bed. Anthony often screams in his sleep.

Was this really me? Pretending to punch my classmates? I never meant to intimidate other kids, ever.

The detail I am most embarrassed to read, and most embarrassed to share, is my interest in women's stockings. I don't like to talk about it. When people ask me now what I was like as a child, I'll say, "I used to have an obsession with certain fabrics," but I don't get more specific than that. What I remind myself, though, is that admitting this will help other autistic kids with their own fixations and their own shame. They're not alone. They're not weird. They're just at a place on the spectrum that includes some obsessions they need to address, and that's OK. I worked through it, and they can, too.

The psychologist's report continues:

Mr. and Mrs. Ianni have been reluctant to pursue medication. Instead, the Iannis try very hard to structure Anthony's time to minimize temper tantrums and behavioral difficulties. Anthony becomes over stimulated easily in public places, particularly with large amounts of people. Socially, Mrs. Ianni continues to worry because Anthony does not have any peers that call him to make play dates. He has one female friend in the neighborhood whom he plays with in a mostly parallel fashion. Children tend to think that Anthony is mean because of his loud voice, large size and his difficulty sharing. Anthony is very competitive and has difficulty taking turns in games. He hates to lose. Anthony's sister often gives in to him in an effort to keep peace. Mrs. Ianni reports that her daughter and her friends are very good to Anthony and tolerant of his behavior.

Well, "very competitive" is right. If anything, it's an understatement! I hated to lose back then, and I hate to lose now. I'm competitive as a speaker now, wanting not just to be *good* and *helpful*, but somehow *better*—better than my last time in front of an audience, and better than other speakers. I serve as an assistant coach for a girls' high school basketball team now, and a loss pisses me off as much now as it did when I was five. Sometimes after a loss—whether it's the high school team or an MSU game on TV—I have to find a room where I can be alone and calm myself down.

It's strange, though, to read that my classmates were afraid of me. In my heart I was a teddy bear. I wanted connections. I wanted friendships. The last thing I wanted was to come off as mean. But that's autism for you. How I perceived my social interactions did not jive with how everyone else in the room—kids, teachers, and district psychologists—perceived those same interactions.

Was the one neighbor girl really the only person who even came close to being a friend? That's not how I remember it. Devin McGee was next door, and there were other boys in the neighborhood. They were my buddies. I'm sure of it. But I do admit that my sense of those friendships is traveling through two layers of autistic perceptions: the five-year-old Anthony who wanted those bonds and also the adult Anthony who is still autistic and still misperceives social cues.

It's completely true that I was "over stimulated easily in public places." I have vivid memories of that. It took me a long time to get used to places like Spartan Stadium and the Breslin Center. To think: two of the venues I used to hate have become some my favorite places in the world!

There was more in the IEP:

Anthony's kindergarten teacher reports that Anthony's behavior is much improved from the beginning of the school year. At this time there is an extra classroom aide working in Anthony's class. The kindergarten teacher and the aide continue to use a behavior plan that is aimed at helping Anthony transition out of the classroom quietly, follow the classroom rules and rejoin the class activity when he has to leave. This program includes having the classroom aide sit down with Anthony every morning to review the day's schedule, which seems to reduce his anxiety and behavioral outbursts with changes in routine. There is a designated place for Anthony to take himself to when his behavior becomes disruptive and he needs to calm down. The physical education teacher reports that Anthony has difficulty with body awareness. He often has difficulty stopping a movement once he has started and consequently bumps into people accidentally. Anthony also attends the kindergarten half-day child care program two days per week. His teacher there reports that behavior problems tend to escalate near the end of the day. Anthony's play in that setting is also typically parallel. By the end of the afternoon, Anthony seems more anxious and tends to frustrate easily. He will often make grunting or growling noises as he becomes more frustrated. Anthony moves from one activity to another, barely spending a minute at each activity center.

I know exactly when the grunting and growling started. I picked it up from *The Lion King*. The animals in the movie grunt and growl to express frustration and anger, and the sounds made sense to me. They were true and honest. I started using them myself, not aware that, even though they are perfectly appropriate in the context of the movie, they stood out in a kindergarten classroom. It took me at least another year to cut the grunts and growls from my vocabulary.

The psychologist came to my kindergarten classroom on a few occasions. This is what she noticed:

During free time, Anthony often played near other students and typically chose make believe activities such as playing store or restaurant. Anthony was observed sniffing pieces of items he found on the floor. Anthony became very angry when another student picked up a car that he had left unattended. He had difficulty controlling his anger and the classroom aide had to intervene. On the first day of observation, Anthony had two time-out periods during a half-hour observation time. When the aide sat him down to discuss the problem, Anthony continued to try to swing at her and act out. On the second day of observation, Anthony's behavior was more appropriate although he continued to move from one center to another and sometimes took items away from other students. At one point another student stood up to him and informed Anthony that she was not finished playing with the item. Anthony then walked away from that confrontation. Anthony then placed a puppet on his hand and walked around the room scaring others and making loud noises. When the teacher gave the direction that it was time to clean up, Anthony continued to build and play with the blocks. With an extra reminder from his teacher, Anthony did join in and help to clean up. At the end of the observation period, Anthony approached this examiner and asked if he could touch her leg and feel her stockings.

There it is again: my fixation with nylons. I remember that fixation, and part of me wishes that I could erase it from my past. But putting it out there for autistic kids and their families to see—I hope sharing this will help them.

When I was in high school and in college, my mom told me about some of this behavior: taking toys, scaring other kids, always on the verge of an outburst. I used to think she was kidding. I was sure she was exaggerating, just to tease me. Reading this twenty-five-year-old document, though, I realize that Mom didn't exaggerate. That's how I was. That's not how I saw myself, or how I remember myself, but that's how I was.

Reading my IEP now stirs such a mix of emotions in me. I'm sad about how I stood out, and I'm sad that few people saw the big heart and teddy bear personality I was sure were my main features. And I'm angry at my younger self for some of my behavior. I didn't treat my peers well. Even though such behavior was directly related to my autism, I still feel anger. I can't help it. I'm also surprisingly happy—happy to know that my admissions could inspire others to keep working through the obstacles that autism has thrown at them.

Another emotion in the blend is gratitude. My teachers, aides, and parents were so patient. They rode out the bad days in the classroom and the sleepless nights at home. They made things as consistent as they could, and they braced me for changes as thoroughly as possible. They kept their expectations high, even though it must have been tempting to lower them. It takes effort for teachers and aides to stick to an IEP. Shortcuts can be alluring, given all the tasks educators must juggle in a day. Mine never took shortcuts, and they never gave up. I hope every autistic student out there can have what I've had: parents who kept their expectations high and educators who were diligent when it came to my accommodations.

I may not remember some of this, and I may question a few spots, but there is one part of my IEP I absolutely agree with. One page had a list of behaviors and asked an evaluator to identify them as either strengths or weaknesses for me. A "+" indicated a strength, and an "o" meant weakness. "Class discussions" had a "+," while "hands-on tasks" had an "o," to give two examples.

And the mark next to "parent involvement/support"?

++.

Extra strong.

# 4

## TALKING TO NOBODY

Anthony's relative strength is in the area of language arts. He said that he enjoys reading and has learned many words from sight. When he came upon a word he did not know, he usually "passed" on the word instead of using any phonetic approaches to sound out the word. When more complicated abstract questions were required in the reading comprehension section, he was unable to understand the concept and would pick out one or two non-meaningful words in the sentence.

From an evaluation done during second grade

DURING RECESS IN THE FIRST few months of kindergarten, I scampered around the playground and scaled the equipment with my classmates, riding down the slides and crossing the bridges. For a while I thought I was just another kid, doing what everyone else was doing. But I wasn't just another kid. For one thing, I talked to myself all through recess.

"Ow! What was that for?"

I'd say that out loud—to nobody. And I wasn't even hurt. It was a line from *The Lion King*. I'd blurt, "Don't turn your back on me!" Then I'd growl, the way Mufasa does. Next I'd jump to *Aladdin*: "Let's make some magic!" Over and over I'd say that, roaming the playground: "Let's make some magic! Let's make some magic!"

Kids began to notice.

One recess I was watching a few older kids play four square. As they bumped the kickball back and forth, I rattled off a play-by-play:

"The ball comes back this way. He hits it across. Good shot. Bounce. Another hit. Bounce. Too far. The ball's out. The ball went out. It's outta here!"

The four square players ignored me, but a wandering fourth grader didn't.

"Who are you talking to?"

My mouth hung open—I didn't know how to answer him.

"Are you talking to nobody?"

I trembled. I was on the verge of screaming.

"That's how dumb you are. You're so dumb you talk to nobody."

"I haven't done anything," I finally stammered. "I'm not doing anything to you."

"Are you just gonna keep talking to the air? You don't make any sense."

"You need to stop, or I'm gonna tell. I'll tell the teacher, and the principal."

I was a tall kindergartener, but I was still a kindergartener, and I was as far as you can get from being a fighter.

"Do whatever you want," the fourth grader said. "You're the weirdo—talking to nobody. I'll say anything I want to you. Go ahead and tell the principal. That won't stop me."

I said, "Are you challenging me?" It was an absurd response, mainly because it was another line from *The Lion King*, and that's what started the mocking in the first place. "Are you challenging me?" I repeated, somehow with a little conviction. I definitely didn't feel like a fighter, but, thanks to my height, maybe he thought I could throw a punch.

He waved over his older brother, a fifth grader. As he turned to me, the first thought that came into my mind was "Andre the

Giant." My bully's older brother walked toward me. He stared down at me, looming, the way Andre did Hulk Hogan at WrestleMania III. Both boys wore navy blue sweatpants and tennis shoes that made them seem athletic, and tough.

I started to run. Side by side, they chased me. I hustled toward the large playscape in the middle of the playground. I've always been an awkward runner, and the more I hurried, the more I waddled. I ducked under the slide and turned toward a ladder. The brothers split up, and somehow the younger brother ended up at the top of the ladder—he'd cut me off. I froze. Andre the Giant got in my face and smirked. Then he shoved me down as hard as he could.

"Don't ever try and talk back to my brother again," he threatened, "or you'll get it worse."

The cruelty extended beyond these two brothers—and beyond the playground. When I re-entered the school after recess, so did my bullies.

I worked with a speech therapist who pulled me out of class sometimes, which sparked fresh insults from my classmates. "Why do you have to leave the class?" they'd ask. "Only the dumb kids get taken out of class. You must be too dumb for the regular class."

"You don't know what you're talking about," I said. "That's not it. That's not it."

But what *was* it?

My therapist didn't focus so much on pronunciation—I spoke clearly enough. The problem was language itself. I didn't know how sentences worked. What made "apple" a noun and "chew" a verb? Somehow "chair" was a noun, but "sit" was a verb. How could that make sense? The speech therapist showed me a picture of a computer.

"Noun or verb?"

I shook my head.

I was even worse at idioms. Take, for example, this expression: "It's raining cats and dogs outside." Say that to the average six-year-old who hasn't heard the phrase before, and they would at least *sense* that the phrase wasn't meant literally. Their intuition would tell them it was an expression, even if they weren't certain it meant a downpour. Now, if you had told the six-year-old Anthony that it was raining cats and dogs out, I would have dashed to the nearest door, hustled outside, and extended my arms—hoping a new pet would fall into my arms.

Once, in first grade, my class had been good all week. We'd behaved well, we'd worked diligently on our math assignments, and we'd earned high scores on a reading test. "Boys and girls," my teacher announced, "it's been such a great week for *all* of us. I feel like I'm living on Cloud Nine!"

Only one kid—me—didn't understand the compliment. I stood and walked straight to the window.

"Where is Cloud Nine?" I asked. "How do we get there?"

The class burst into laughter.

Why were they laughing? Somewhere out there, a stairway led up to Cloud Nine. I was sure of it. I imagined Cloud Nine to be walkable—I knew what an airplane was, and I figured you didn't need an airplane to get up there. If my teacher felt like we were there already, it had to be close. Even after she guided me back to my seat and explained that it was just an expression, I gazed out the window, looking for a ladder to a cloud.

For a long time afterward, my classmates remembered. "Hey, Cloud Nine," kids would call to me in the hallway. "How's it going, Cloud Nine?"

"My name is Anthony."

"No, it's Cloud Nine."

"It's Anthony!" I'd bellow. What was wrong with them? They knew my name was Anthony. Why would they call me something that wasn't my name?

Finally, late in the fall of first grade, I found a defender.

I was on the playground one noon recess, talking to myself and watching some fifth graders play basketball. I narrated the game: "He shoots from the baseline. Nothing but net!" I loved that expression and started repeating it: "Nothing but net. Nothing but net."

"Hey, shut up! Nobody asked you."

One of the basketball players was stepping toward me when another boy intervened.

"Leave my little brother alone," he said. "He's done nothing to you, so back off. Let him say what he wants. Got it?"

That became his new name for me: "Little Brother."

I went home feeling good. *Things will be okay*, I told myself as I got ready for school each morning. *My big brother's got my back. He's there to protect me.*

He let me tag along with his friends when they circled the playground. They gave me a turn to shoot sometimes when they played basketball. Every day my big brother called out, "Hey, Anthony." He didn't call me a dummy. He didn't refer to me as "Cloud Nine." It was the safest I had ever felt at school.

Winter arrived in Okemos. Temperatures dropped below freezing, we had our first snowfall, and teachers made sure our boots were on and jackets zipped for recess. One cold morning, my big brother and his buddies waved me over to a jungle gym that had a set of old-school metal monkey bars. "Come on over here, Anthony," they summoned. "We want to show you something."

I rushed over.

"A couple of us were sticking our tongues on the pole just now, and it feels really cool. You should try it."

I didn't give it a second thought. I opened my mouth wide and planted my tongue right on the frozen pole. I left it there for a few seconds, waiting for the good feeling to hit. Instead, my tongue began to sting. I pulled away—gently at first, and then harder. My tongue broke free, but not without leaving a bit behind. My tongue began to bleed. I grabbed a handful of snow and shoved it in my mouth, hoping to numb the pain and stop the bleeding.

They laughed and laughed. "Are you done already?" they asked. "Why don't you try it again?"

I thought they were my friends. Why would they do this to me?

For months afterward, they told me to stick my tongue to any surface they saw: the wall of the school, the plastic slide, the bark of a tree trunk. The more ridiculous the suggestion, the harder they laughed. Even well into spring, they continued the joke.

"Hey, Anthony, why don't you go stick your tongue on the monkey bars again?"

There is a well-known scene in *A Christmas Story* when, after a "triple dog dare," a boy named Flick sticks his tongue to a flagpole. I know it's supposed to be a funny scene, but I still cringe a little bit whenever it's on. I'm guessing I'll have that reaction for the rest of my life. I try to follow my cringe with positive thoughts. I focus on how that bullying—preying on my naivete, taking advantage of my deep trust in others' words—has made me a stronger person. My "big brother's" trick has become one more way for me, as an adult, to relate to the victims out there.

\* \* \*

Our school assigned classroom aides, or paraprofessionals, to special education students who required extra help. Okemos wasn't unique in this regard. Schools all over the country employ parapros to provide one-on-one attention to students with special needs. I qualified. So did a boy named Josh. Often our parapro, Mrs. Maki, invited us to the back table to work with her. The table was shaped like a thick letter "C," and Mrs. Maki sat in the indent and guided Josh and me through assignments. Sometimes they were math worksheets. Other times they were art projects that required fine motor skills. Frequently she helped us with stories that the rest of the class could read independently.

"Can you say that word?" she asked as she pointed first at Josh's sheet and then at mine.

I didn't like it when Mrs. Maki gave Josh more of the attention. I wanted her focus on me, so I could keep going with the story and finish my assignment.

"What does this word mean?" I'd interrupt, even if Mrs. Maki was right in the middle of talking with Josh. "I don't know this word. Help me. You don't need to help Josh. He's fine. He's smarter than me. Help me."

If there was a stigma to working at the back table, I didn't notice. The extra attention more than made up for it. I knew I couldn't have finished my work without Mrs. Maki. Besides, as Josh and I worked at the C-shaped table together, our friendship developed. It wasn't a friendship built on novelty or deception, the way it had been with my "big brother." Josh was a true friend. We both loved Batman, *Star Wars*, the Power Rangers, and Michigan State. We also collected trading cards, and we started bringing them to school. We both owned hodge-podge collections that mixed football with *Toy Story*, NBA players with *Goosebumps*. We saw nothing wrong with Michael Jordan and Luke Skywalker stacked next to each other in the same deck. Trades might last for just a day or a week rather than forever. I'd offer Woody from *Toy Story* in exchange for Steve Young of the San Francisco 49ers. We operated more generously than the general managers who were our counterparts in the NBA and NFL. I put Woody on the table because I knew Josh liked *Toy Story* and would appreciate taking the card home for a few days. Josh, in turn, knew I liked Atlanta's Steve Smith because he'd played for Michigan State, and he accepted a Yoda card for him.

Our willingness to share had its limits, though. "You should trade your Barry Sanders," Josh insisted one day, referring to the greatest Detroit Lions running back of all time.

"Not happening, buddy."

And that's what he was: my buddy.

Collecting cards and watching *Star Wars* and wanting friends—all those things were normal. Just about every kid I knew did those things. But not everything I did was age-appropriate. One afternoon our class was watching *Iron Will*, the Disney movie about a boy who overcomes long odds and harsh obstacles to win a dog-sled race. I'd seen the movie before at my grandparents' farmhouse, and I loved it. In the middle of the movie, I noticed the speech therapist enter the classroom. I knew why she was there: she was about to pull me out, right in the middle of *Iron Will*. Nope. Not today.

I rushed to the back of the room and crouched under the table where Josh and I worked with Mrs. Maki. It was a ridiculous hiding place and an immature response, but that's who I was. My classmates may have had the social awareness to know how babyish I looked, but I didn't. I wasn't missing *Iron Will*, end of story.

My teacher found an excuse to stop the movie while I was off with the speech therapist, and she didn't restart it until I returned. It was just one of a million acts of kindness and flexibility from my Okemos teachers and parapros over the years.

While hiding under the parapro table clearly wasn't age-appropriate, watching educational cartoons and other PBS fare was more of a gray area. Child development experts probably permit such tastes well past kindergarten, but those experts didn't roam the halls of my elementary school or sit near me at lunch. At Wardcliff Elementary there were TV shows that you just weren't supposed to watch: *Sesame Street*, *Teletubbies*, *Arthur*, and *Shining Time Station* (the Thomas the Tank Engine show) to name four. In my school, you avoided *anything* on PBS.

Me? I watched PBS all the time, especially in the morning after I'd finished my breakfast. Given the way I talked to myself and sang to myself, it was only a matter of time before I was found out.

I was on my way to the drinking fountain, unaware that I was singing: "Ask for help. Ask for help. Don't hesitay-ay-ate! Just ask for help."

A boy rushed over to me. "Are you kidding me? Are you actually singing that song? Do you watch PBS?"

"No."

"You do, too! You watch PBS. What are you, a baby?"

"No! No! That song is from FOX."

"You watch the baby channel! Why don't you go home and watch *Arthur*?"

"You're wrong—I said it's from FOX!"

It's likely that other kids still watched *Arthur* and *The Magic School Bus*. How else would he even recognize "Ask for Help" as a PBS song? But everyone else knew to keep their viewing habits to themselves. We believed we were maturing, and we wanted our tastes to reflect our newfound sophistication. My classmates had figured out how to pull off this charade. Meanwhile, I paraded down the hall singing, "Ask for help."

Though I did "ask for help" all the time from Mrs. Maki, and though I did roll through work faster at the C-shaped back table, I savored my own desk's personal touches. I'd thoroughly decorated the surface with Michigan State stickers and Power Rangers stickers. Anyone who saw me in those elementary years— talking to myself on the playground, hiding under a table when the speech therapist entered the room, looking out the window for Cloud Nine, and crying and wigging out when things didn't go my way—would have said I had a better chance of being a Power Ranger than a Michigan State basketball player. Those MSU stickers suggested something unrealistic. They were emblems of pure fantasy.

# 5

## PUSHING MY BUTTONS

KIDS PUSH EACH OTHER'S BUTTONS. That's a fact of childhood. Sometimes they mean to and other times they don't. Either way, this posed a real problem for me. First, I had so many buttons. There were a million ways to upset me: Have a toy I wanted. Say something I disagreed with. Refuse to play with me. Second, once the button was pushed, I wigged out. My thrashings and wailings could shake walls.

My grandparents hosted Easter every year at the farmhouse in Morenci. One tradition we had was an Easter egg hunt. My grandma wrote a specific grandchild's name on each egg—about fifteen or so for each of us. The plastic eggs contained candy, chocolates, little bouncy balls, quarters, or folded-up dollar bills. Every year, my dad and my uncles took the eggs outside and hid them around the farm. Eggs went in bushes and behind trees, on my grandpa's truck's bumper, on the hood of the tractor, in the seat of the riding mower, and in the barn behind the door or on the tool shelf.

Once Dad and my uncles said the eggs were ready, we dashed out of the house with our buckets. I wanted to be the first one to finish, but I was the youngest, so I was a little slower than my cousins and less familiar with the hiding spots. Soon my cousins David and Kyle filled their buckets, and they trotted over to where I was, frantically poking around the barn.

"Ha ha! We finished and you didn't," they said, waving their buckets in my face. "We won, we won."

I began to protest and whimper, revving up for a wig-out. Tears formed. My grandpa must have flashed me a critical look that said, *Why the hell are you crying?*

It was just normal teasing. Kyle and David weren't trying to trigger a massive explosion, but they were about to get one. That's when my cousin Angie rescued me.

"Come on, Anthony. I'll help you find the last few." Angie was seven years older than me, and I admired her. Everyone in the family talked about what an incredible softball player she was, and sometimes we drove across the Ohio border to watch her games.

Allison must have been relieved to have someone else play the role of big sister. Keeping me from erupting probably felt like a full-time job to her. I know my IEP says that Allison allowed me to win games in order to keep things peaceful, but that's not how I recall it. I remember her winning often at Monopoly, and whenever she did, I would slap her and scream.

"Sit next to me, Anthony," Angie said, after we'd found the last of the eggs with my name on it. "We can open our eggs together."

When I was finally calm, Kyle and David tried a different button.

"Michigan is way better than Michigan State," David said, as if it were an incontrovertible fact. "Michigan State is terrible."

"No way! Michigan State is better!"

The previous football season was months ago, and the next one was a long way away. Who cared about college football?

We did.

"Then how come Michigan won last year?" David persisted.

"MSU is better than Michigan! MSU is better!"

"In your dreams."

*  *  *

One day at recess I sought out a classmate who had the same name as my sister. "Play with me, Allison," I insisted. It didn't matter that Allison already was playing with other girls.

She tried to be nice about it. "I can't play with you today, Anthony, but I'll play with you tomorrow."

The next day, I found her on the playground. "Play with me," I demanded.

"Not today."

"But you promised."

"Sorry, Anthony. I'm already playing."

Crying, I fled. I found my mom and began to wail. "She said she would play today! She said she would play today!"

Mom held me close. "Sometimes people have to change their plans," she said gently. "Things don't always happen the way people say."

"She said she would play today!"

"It's going to be OK, Anthony." She hugged me tightly.

Always the coach, Mom actually started training me to handle disruptions. There were mornings when she announced the day's schedule, *knowing* that later she would break it.

"After school today we'll go to the park," she promised one morning at breakfast.

"Yes!" I shouted. All day in school I anticipated the trip to the park. That afternoon I reminded Mom, "It's time to go to the park now."

"I'm sorry, Anthony, but the car doesn't have enough gas. We'll have to go another day."

"But you said!"

"I know, but the car doesn't have enough gas. Things happen. Sometimes you can plan to do something, but then there's a problem."

"We're going to the park."

Mom had me take long, slow breaths. She told me to count to ten, and she bear hugged me.

Mom ran this drill again and again—not that I knew what she was up to at the time, of course. Sticking with the sports metaphor, Mom thought of these schedule changes as "curve balls." My autism made me one of the world's worst curve ball hitters.

Champions are made in practice—that's a classic sports aphorism. Coach Mom was running practices in our kitchen, and she endured tantrum after tantrum from me. Would her drills ever pay off? Would I ever improve?

*  *  *

Mom may have been throwing curve balls intentionally, but Wardcliff Elementary did its best to avoid them. A few weeks before I started first grade, my teacher invited my parents and me in for a private tour of the classroom. Mrs. Knox wanted me to acclimate.

"Follow me, Anthony," she said. "Let me show you where we are going to keep our supplies this year. Regular paper is here, and the colored paper is right here next to it."

I followed her as she went from shelf to shelf. Mrs. Knox then guided me to the classroom library and promised that we were going to read so many good stories.

"Would you like to see where you are going to sit?"

"Yes."

She led me to my seat near the front of the room.

"Go ahead and try it," she encouraged. "Do you like that one?"

"It's good."

I loved the personal tour, and it became a ritual for my family. Every August we went in a few weeks early so I could meet my teacher and test-drive my desk.

At my initial IEP meeting, Sandy McDonald had promised my parents that they would figure out how to help me succeed. Not all at once, and with some trial and error, but they would find what worked. And that's what they were doing. Okemos Schools did a lot of things right. However, many autistic kids aren't so fortunate. I'd like to see my teachers' ideas spread to other districts, so the next generation of autistic students can benefit.

*   *   *

I was either in second or third grade when I entered my classroom one morning and saw a guest teacher—a substitute— standing near the front. Normally the office called Mom and warned her about substitutes so that Mom could prep me. But no one had said anything! Desperately, I scanned the room for my parapro. There was Mrs. Maki, at our usual table.

*Mrs. Maki is still here*, I told myself. *You can still have a good day.*

This, for me, was a victory.

I'd hit a curve ball.

# 6

## SPORTS

EVEN AS A LITTLE KID, I was intensely competitive. This can be a bad combination with autism. Whenever I lost a game—whether it was a rec league T-ball game, two-hand touch football at recess, or a board game against my language therapist—I would bawl my eyes out, and the bawling threatened to escalate into a full-on outburst. Most kids possess the social awareness to keep it together after a loss, but not me.

The first team sport I tried was T-ball. I was seven years old, and it was the summer before second grade. Putting me in T-ball was not really a daring experiment for my family: I'd always loved hitting and catching the ball at home. Dad and I tossed the ball in the front yard all the time, and we always had the Detroit Tigers on the TV. Whether they were good or bad, I watched them. I loved the big power hitters of the 1990s—Barry Bonds, Sammy Sosa, and Ken Griffey Jr.—so I also followed the Giants, the Cubs, and the Mariners.

Baseball was in my genes. Dad had pitched at Michigan State, and Mom had pitched and played first base on Adrian's softball team. They never coached my teams, but they gave me lots of pointers at home: adjusting my batting stance, correcting my throwing motion, and so on.

When I moved up to machine-pitch baseball, my coach had me play catcher just about every game. I was the tallest kid on my team, and conventional baseball strategy says the big kid should play catcher so he can block more pitches and handle the collisions at home plate. I didn't mind catching, but I didn't want to get stuck there. I also liked playing outfield and first base, and sometimes I wonder if pitching was my true athletic calling. Dad tells me I could have been a great pitcher. Feeling trapped behind home plate, I quit baseball after a few years.

A few months after my first season of T-ball ended, I signed up for basketball through the same city recreation league. Like with baseball, I had a head start in more ways than one. I'd been shooting a lot of hoops in the driveway with my dad, my sister, and just by myself. Basketball, like baseball, was also an inheritance. Mom had played power forward at Adrian, and Dad had been a pretty good guard for Dexter High School. I rarely missed a Michigan State basketball game. I saw many of them live at the Breslin Center (once I could handle the stimulation), and the rest I watched on TV.

I was like every other kid in the 1980s and 1990s who could dribble a basketball: Michael Jordan was my favorite NBA player. I had Jordan's Chicago Bulls jersey—number 23—and that's what I wore every day on my driveway. Unlike Jordan, though, I wasn't a quick-footed guard. Instead, I was a slow-footed center. If I thought the tall kid always got stuck in the same position in *baseball* . . . well, basketball is even more rigid about what to do with taller players and where to put the shorter players, and I was the tallest player in the whole league!

Fortunately, I liked center. I've never played anything but center, and I'm fine with that. From an early age, my height gave me an advantage. I grabbed rebounds, blocked shots, and went above the other boys to score points. The only problem was that I'd often go up and reach over an opponent for a rebound and get called for a foul—even when I made no contact with the kid and the rebound was clean.

By fourth grade, I was playing with and against other boys in the community recreation league who would end up being my high school teammates. There we were in the mostly empty gym, botching layups, dribbling clumsily, and playing bad defense, having no clue we were seven years away from traveling to the state finals together, playing in the sold-out Breslin Center, battling together in a dramatic game that would go to double overtime.

Some health care providers steer autistic children away from team sports. They encourage parents with kids on the spectrum to sign up for swimming or track, since these require fewer social interactions. I see their point, but I'm grateful my parents let me try baseball, basketball, and football. Kids on the spectrum want relationships, too. Autistic children want to be part of a team as much as any other child. More parents are giving team sports a try, and I'm happy to see it. Not every kid on the spectrum will be comfortable on a team, but you'll never know until you try it.

\* \* \*

As I entered the ranks of the upper elementary kids, playground sports became more important. It was a way to prove myself. We played touch football all three recesses, and whenever I took the field, I told myself that if I scored enough touchdowns, intercepted enough passes, and sacked the quarterback enough times, I would earn my classmates' respect. I could silence my critics forever.

Often the other team was more stacked with the quick guys, the athletes. I couldn't outrun them, but I towered over them in the end zone, so I played wide receiver.

"Just throw it to me," I told my quarterback. "I'll go up and get it." I think I had pretty good hands for my age, and I caught my share of touchdown passes. But we still were outmatched.

By then, I couldn't stand losing. I hated when Michigan State lost, I hated when the Detroit Lions lost, and I couldn't stand losing anything I was playing, whether it was touch football or Candyland, driveway basketball or Chutes and Ladders. I hated losing enough that I cried when it happened.

One recess following a defeat, I tried a new technique: "We won," I sang to myself, ignoring the score. "We won, we won, we won—"

Immediately the other team was in my face.

"Are you that dumb? Do you really think you won?"

"We won, we won . . ."

"*We* won, you dummy. Don't you know the score?"

I stopped my song . . . and started crying. That didn't help at all.

"What a crybaby! I can't believe you're crying."

My cheeks were smeared with tears when we filed back inside. I can't even count how many times the teachers must have watched me re-enter the school like that: my face smudged and emotionally drained. Yet somehow, two hours later, I returned to my place on the field, ready to win for real this time, eager to prove them wrong about me. I was no crybaby—I was a champion.

It is no fun to relive these incidents. I can still hear those insults: "dummy" and "crybaby" and all the rest. For every insult that hit me, though, I suspect I missed about ten. Autism is a funny disorder. In the same instant, it can invite bullying *and* shield autistic children from bullying. Our lack of social cues is a vulnerability but also a form of protection. After a touchdown I might do a ridiculous and awkward dance that was supposed to look like the Atlanta Falcons' "Dirty Bird" celebration. If the other boys stared or rolled their eyes or mimicked me, I didn't notice. Maybe they laughed, and I don't even remember, since at the time, I figured they were laughing *with* me. That's autism for you. My behavior provoked laughter, which should have hurt, except that it didn't sting at all when I didn't perceive what was behind the laughter: meanness. Autism prevented me from recognizing cruelty. Is that a disability, or a gift?

*  *  *

Football never felt like a good fit for me the way basketball did. I've had plenty of football players in my family, including my dad and my Grandpa Nick, but genetics weren't enough. I did love the Detroit Lions, and I sometimes wore a Barry Sanders jersey to school and did my best to run like him during two-hand touch games at recess. Not that I came close, but there is nothing wrong with attempting to be like one of the all-time great running backs.

Like with baseball, my position was an issue. Throughout middle school, coaches put me on the offensive line, either as a tackle or as a guard. I was much more interested in tight end. That and defensive end. But the coaches took one look at my size and made up their minds. It didn't matter that my hands were good enough for tight end—I made some pretty nifty catches in practice, on the occasions when a ball was thrown my way—and I could run with the ball and stiff-arm any would-be tacklers. In the coaches' view, I was built like an offensive lineman, and the matter was settled.

In sixth grade, my coach was an energetic young guy not long out of college. He was always clapping his hands and shouting encouragement: "Shoulder down, shoulder down! That's the way to do it!" Between twenty and twenty-five boys signed up for sixth-grade football, and the coach involved every one of us. We all got whacks on the shoulders: "Good hustle, good hustle!"

One practice early in the season, he lined us up on the end line.

"You're going to the fifty-yard line," he said. "And I want to see you go hard."

I took my place between two other boys and made sure to put my toe right on the line.

"We're gonna go on two," the coach yelled.

Through my helmet's cage I stared hard at the ground, concentrating. I didn't want to miss it when he said "two."

"Hut hut."

I didn't know what that was, so I stayed focused, eyes on the ground. Then, I sensed I was alone. I looked up. Everyone else was sprinting away, already twenty yards ahead. I started running, trying to catch up but not coming close.

"What happened, Anthony?" the coach asked.

"You said to go on two."

He laughed and gave me a knock on the helmet. "Two of anything, Anthony. Two of anything. Hut hut. That's two."

Mom had witnessed it, and after practice she asked what happened.

"He said to go on two," I said.

"In football, they might say 'blue-blue' or 'green-green,'" Mom explained. "If you go on two, you go on the second sound."

"OK."

And then there were the plays.

I can't tell you why, but basketball play names made more sense to me than football play names. In basketball we had numbered plays, like "14" and "2." And we had plays named after places, like "Miami" and "Texas." But our football plays had names like "50 Gladiator" and "Pro 23 Blast." I had improved a lot from the days when I couldn't distinguish between ducks *on* the pond and ducks *next to* the pond, or when I searched for the ladder to Cloud Nine, but I still couldn't match "Pro 23 Blast" with the various intricate movements of eleven boys on a football field. What did "Pro 23 Blast" have to do with a run, or a pass, or a blocking assignment? In my mind: nothing.

# 7

## GRANDPA NICK

Anthony was referred for re-evaluation purposes in accordance with the provisions of the Individuals with Disabilities Education Act. He is currently receiving special education support services in the middle school resource room, one period each day. He also receives the services of the teacher of the speech and language impaired and a case coordinator. Those services are provided to him under state guidelines for Autistic Impairment.

From my sixth grade Individualized Education Plan

MY GRANDPA NICK WAS MANY things in his lifetime: an athlete; a coach; a teacher; a school administrator; a leader; an advocate for special-needs children; and a devoted husband, father, and grandfather. One thing he was definitely *not*, though: a Spartan fan.

It made no difference that two of his sons—my dad and my Uncle Nick—had attended Michigan State, or that my dad had pitched there, or that my dad worked in MSU's athletic department. If Grandpa Nick had lived long enough to see my sister play volleyball at Michigan State and me play basketball, it still wouldn't have mattered!

Grandpa Nick was born in western Pennsylvania in 1927. His parents had immigrated from Italy. My great-grandmother had come to the United States from Milan in 1910 and my great-grandfather had come six years later from southern Italy.

Grandpa Nick's dad operated a shoe repair shop, and his mom ran a grocery store in Pittsburgh for a time. Grandpa Nick was a star athlete in high school, both in football and in baseball. He graduated during World War II, and after high school he entered the Coast Guard and was stationed in Greenland. After his stint in the Coast Guard, he played football at the University of Pittsburgh and then went into teaching and coaching after earning his bachelor's degree. A job offer in the post–World War II booming Detroit suburbs brought him to Michigan. On a trip back home to Pennsylvania to visit family, he met my Grandma Ger. The two married and raised six children. Once he shifted into school administration, he gave up coaching.

He continued to root for the professional teams of his youth, the Pittsburgh Pirates and the Pittsburgh Steelers, but he also adopted the Detroit teams, especially the Tigers and Lions. At the college level he became devoted to Michigan State's archnemesis: the University of Michigan. (He earned a master's degree from the University of Michigan, and he lived and worked near Ann Arbor, so I guess it's forgivable that he became a Wolverine.) Despite his love of sports, student athletes weren't his highest priority or his focus. No, it was students who had special needs.

Grandpa Nick served as head of the Washtenaw Intermediate School District for twenty-one years. In those two decades, not only did he meet with lawmakers and push for more services and protections for special education students, but in the 1970s he also oversaw the construction of the High Point School in Ann Arbor. The school was designed to meet the needs of students with disabilities in a wide age-range, and it quickly became renowned. If you lived anywhere in Washtenaw County and had a child with special needs or developmental disabilities, you wanted your child in High Point. It continues to operate to this day.

Grandpa Nick retired in 1986, three years before I was born, unaware that his own grandson would one day benefit from his work.

I don't have any memories of throwing a football or baseball with Grandpa Nick. By the time I was old enough to do those things with him, his health was declining. But he still loved being outside, watching us shoot baskets and toss a baseball.

Sometimes I spent the night at Grandpa Nick and Grandma Ger's house in Dexter. On those nights, we watched the Tigers or whatever football or basketball game happened to be on. Watching those games, the coach came back out in Grandpa Nick. He snapped instructions at the players on TV, he got fired up when his teams made mistakes, and he pointed out smart plays to me.

Grandpa Nick told me stories about some of the glory days in Detroit sports. The Lions have been playing on turf in indoor stadiums for decades, but back in the 1950s my grandpa took my dad to games at the old Tiger Stadium, in Detroit's Corktown neighborhood. They watched those games in the elements—hot or cold, sunshine or rain or sleet. Grandpa Nick also loved the 1984 Detroit Tigers: Jack Morris, Alan Trammell, Lance Parrish (who was born near Pittsburgh, like Grandpa Nick), and Kirk Gibson (who played both football and baseball at Michigan State, though Grandpa Nick didn't give Gibby any points for that). Those were the last Tigers to win the World Series—a little more than four years before I was born. Grandpa Nick told me stories about Gibson's homers and Alan Trammell and Lou Whitaker's double plays, Chet Lemon's catches in center field, and great saves by the closer, Willie Hernandez.

At family gatherings, conversation often revolved around sports. My dad, my uncles, and Grandpa Nick would debate the strengths and weaknesses of that year's Lions, Tigers, or

Wolverines. Whenever Grandpa Nick weighed in, my ears perked up. He was so wise, so insightful. Sometimes he raised his voice and fixed his eyes on me. He was about to make a point, and he didn't want me to miss it.

My dad admired Grandpa Nick as much as I did. Dad admired the way his father did everything the right way, with integrity and decency. Grandpa Nick was a natural leader and motivator, and he brought out the best in the people around him. There was one issue, though, where Grandpa Nick never swayed us: Bo Schembechler. The longtime Michigan coach could do no wrong in Grandpa Nick's eyes. Bo was a great coach and an even better man, Grandpa Nick said. My grandpa told me about Bo's battles against Woody Hayes's Ohio State teams in the 1970s—the Ten-Year War, Grandpa Nick said it was called. As much as I loved my grandfather, he never convinced me of the greatness of the University of Michigan.

Grandpa Nick died in 1996, when I was seven. It was my first experience with death. The loss didn't hit me right away—I thought he would be gone for a little while and then come back. I didn't appreciate how permanent his absence would be. My lack of understanding probably had more to do with my age than it did with my autism. Eventually, it sank in that Grandpa Nick was never coming back, and I was very sad.

My parents dressed me in a shirt and tie for the viewing at the funeral home in Dexter. The room was crowded all day with family, friends, and lots of people from the world of education. Many there didn't call him "Nick"; they called him "Big Ace." That, I learned, was his nickname. He was a big man and a clear leader. "Big Ace" fit him perfectly.

During the vigil that evening, several people stood and spoke about my grandfather. They talked of his leadership at the Washtenaw ISD and in other school districts, and they listed his contributions to special education—a category that already applied to me, though I didn't know it at the time.

I leaned over to my mom, who was sitting next to me during the speeches.

"I'd like to say something about Nick," I told her.

"You mean Grandpa?"

"Yeah."

Mom worried. What would come out of my mouth? Disney lyrics? Something nonsensical?

"What do you want to say?'

I only had one thing to say, and I told Mom what it was.

My mom told me that would be acceptable, so I raised my hand, the priest called on me, and I stood up, just like I would in school during show-and-tell.

"Hi, my name is Anthony James Ianni," I announced to the congregation. "I live at 384 Lampen Drive, East Lansing, and I want to say Grandpa Nick was the best grandpa in the whole wide world."

It is not uncommon for autistic people to feel just fine speaking in front of a group. After all, the thing that triggers fear in most people is a sense of social awareness, an appreciation that all eyes are on them. They get very self-conscious. But a typical feature of autism is a lack of social awareness. So when I announced to the large assembly of people honoring my grandfather that he was the greatest grandpa in the whole world, I felt no fear.

\* \* \*

Grandpa Nick was an advocate, and now I am an advocate. Every time I prepare to go on stage—at a school, an autism awareness fundraiser, or another event—I sense a torch being passed to me from Grandpa Nick in heaven. He also was an athlete and a coach, and my sister and I both have followed in those footsteps, too. He died before he could watch my sister play high school or college volleyball, and long before he could watch me play for Tom Izzo. Still, every game of my career, I know that Grandpa Nick had a front-row seat. He still has a front-row seat. Whenever I go in front of an audience and advocate for students with special needs, he is there.

# 8

## HATING TO LOSE

Anthony Ianni is an extremely engaging, verbal young man. Anthony does not have any difficulties in initiating conversation, having direct eye contact or seeking companionship from either adults or peers. Anthony, by and large, is a very cheerful young man, who at times, has difficulty with handling disappointment and can become easily overwhelmed with the responsibilities and obligations of his schoolwork. At those times, Anthony is quick to cry and/or become angry. This worker has observed that Anthony has a very difficult time understanding his peers' tone and has a difficult time with figurative language and the meaning of his peers' language. Because of this, at times, Anthony is socially confused and/or either under- or over-reacts to certain social situations.

From an evaluation conducted during 6th grade

I LOVED SPORTS, AND I *hated* to lose. As I approached middle school, that was me in a nutshell. It's not a great combination in a child, to be deeply competitive and short on emotional control.

Some of my teachers, though, figured out how to use my competitiveness to push me academically. My elementary speech instructor, Mrs. Steinbart, played board games like Sorry! and Chutes and Ladders with me. The catch was, she didn't allow me to move until after I'd answered a language question. Every time I rolled, she'd show me a card with a word or phrase on it.

"Noun, verb, or idiom?" Mrs. Steinbart asked.

If I got it wrong, I couldn't move, and if I wasted a good "5" or "6," so be it. Sometimes when I screwed up and lost, I threw fits. I was almost as tall as my teachers by then, but that didn't matter. A temper tantrum welled up in me, and I had no choice but to let it out. I couldn't suppress it any more than another person can prevent a flinch or a wince of pain. It just blasted out of me, and it didn't matter that I was as tall as a high school sophomore.

"I don't ever want to go to this speech class again!" I'd declare.

But two or three days later, I was back at the Chutes and Ladders board. I was like an emotionally raw athlete who had just needed to vent, and Mrs. Steinbart was the patient coach who saw my potential. She gave me worksheets, and I circled the verbs. She gave me more sheets, and I drew arrows to the nouns.

In my mind, the stakes were just as high in a game of Chutes and Ladders as they were for an elite wide receiver playing in the Super Bowl, so I let Mrs. Steinbart push me to be better. No more would I gaze out the window in search of Cloud Nine. No more would I assume an actual hammer was involved if someone hit the nail on the head.

My fourth-grade teacher, Mrs. Kott, was another educator who employed my love of sports to help me. She knew I was prone to outbursts, and whenever I felt one coming on, I'd ask her if I could leave the room.

"Can I go in the hallway?" I'd ask. She must have seen the gathering storm in my face.

"OK, Anthony," Mrs. Kott would say. "Do you think you want to use a thirty-second timeout or a full timeout?"

"Full timeout."

Mrs. Kott then would lead me to the hallway for a chat. I was already winding down. The sports terminology had put me at ease before I'd even exited the room.

*  *  *

Once I entered middle school, the world became even more about sports. I turned *everything* into a competition. And not just a competition—I turned everything into Game 7 of the NBA Finals.

Like the rest of my family, I play to win. The difference is, I didn't know when to ease up emotionally. Not every game has a world championship at stake, but you couldn't tell me that in sixth grade.

Our physical education class included a volleyball unit. The PE teachers had set up six volleyball courts in the gym, and we faced a few different teams over the course of the period. Each day's games were part of a week-long tournament—a tournament some of my less competitive classmates couldn't have cared less about. I treated it like March Madness.

Most of the kids had never played volleyball before. They weren't good, and they didn't care to improve. They shanked hits all over the gym, into other courts, and off the wall—that is, when they made contact with the volleyball at all. Some kids did their best to avoid the ball, even when it flew straight to them.

But me? I was up near the net, stretching for every ball.

"Let's go!" I yelled, every time we got a point. "Keep it going! Keep it going!"

The other kids on my team milled around with almost no sense of position. Where was their focus? Where was their hunger?

One of my teammates served, and the ball didn't even make it to the bottom of the net, let alone the top. The server seemed indifferent to the error, and so did the rest of my team.

"Come on, guys!" I hollered. "Come on!" My fists clenched.

Not that I noticed, but the kids in my class must have been looking at each other and rolling their eyes. They were probably thinking, *What is with the tall oddball who cares so much about a stupid gym class volleyball game?*

Those kids probably didn't even know the score. Well, *I* knew the score. I knew exactly what the score was. I knew we were losing, and time was running out. Only a minute or two remained, and whoever was ahead at the whistle won the game.

"Come on, guys!" I yelled again, and tears started to form in my eyes.

A young substitute teacher stepped onto our court.

"Walk with me to the drinking fountain," he said. "You're working hard. Let's get you some water."

I followed him away from the court, but my intensity didn't drop a notch.

"What's wrong with them?" I bellowed. "Why aren't they trying harder?"

"I get your frustration," the substitute said. "I really do."

"We're still in the game! We can still win, if they just cared about the game! Can't they see the other team wants it more?"

The tears came. "They need to try harder!" I sobbed. "They're just talking to each other. They're not paying attention!"

The substitute, Mr. Hopper, looked up at me. (In sixth grade I was six feet tall, which made me one of the tallest people in the building, teachers included.) "Look, you've got intensity, but not everybody does. If I were out there, I'd play like you, but that's us. That's not everyone. You can't let other kids get to you like that. It doesn't matter whether they're on the other side or on your own team." He sent me back to rejoin the game. We still lost, and I still fumed at my teammates as we left the gym, but Mr. Hopper's gesture was huge, especially for a substitute.

That trip to the drinking fountain was the beginning of a bond. The district hired Mr. Hopper to teach social studies the next year, and I was in the first group of students he taught. Mr. Hopper loaded his desk with quirky trinkets: little toys, stuffed animals, and silly coffee mugs like *The Munsters*. The stuffed doll I remember most was a burglar. He had dark pants, a striped shirt, black gloves, a bandit mask, and a five o'clock shadow. This was our class's stress ball—we even took our class picture with the burglar. As often as not, the burglar was with me. Whenever Mr. Hopper saw frustration surfacing on my face, he strode past me and dropped the burglar on my desk. Somehow, squeezing that burglar settled me, and I went back to learning geography.

Mr. Hopper put a couch in his room, and when the other students and I needed a change of scenery, we could move to the couch. "As long as you stay on task, and as long as you keep listening to me," he said, "you can work on the couch."

Mr. Hopper must have heard the insults—my height, my tears—that I endured in the hallway, because one day he kept me after class.

"Middle school is full of people saying things they shouldn't," he said. "Don't let those other people get to you, even if you hear them say something mean."

"OK."

"Just try your hardest. You're a leader, and that's what you have to do."

Me, a leader?

"One day," he continued, "they're going to start following you. It'll happen. Work your hardest at everything, Anthony, and they're going to start following you. You're a leader; they just don't know it yet."

That's when Mr. Hopper became more than just my social studies teacher. I saw him as my very own Mr. Feeny, from *Boy Meets World*: full of wisdom and warmth.

I wasn't convinced other students would ever follow me, but I trusted Mr. Hopper enough to believe that things would get better.

Life would improve—on the football field, on the basketball court, in the classroom—and, somehow, the teasing would end.

However, in one report from my file, written when I was in sixth grade, I apparently told my examiner that I was thinking about giving up sports. The report reads:

> Anthony indicated that he had "blown up and embarrassed himself" in front of his mother and his classmates. Anthony asked for help in handling the "anger and pain" he felt when losing at a game. During the second evaluation session, Anthony spoke of the sadness he feels when teased by his peers. He complained that "nobody" likes him. . . .
>
> He explained that in the past, he enjoyed participating in sports. However, he claims that he does not wish to participate in sports at this time because of his hatred of losing and his difficulty in handling that possibility.

Honestly, I don't remember the idea of dropping sports *ever* crossing my mind. I have clear memories of crying and pouting after a loss, and I can recall chastising myself when I didn't play well or when I let someone else be the best player on the court. But did I ever get mad at myself for getting mad? Did I ever think that walking away from sports was the answer? If I did, those moments have been completely erased from my memory. Either way, I'm grateful that sports continued to be a part of my life. Without sports, I couldn't have met and played alongside so many of my heroes. Without sports, I don't know if I would have had a dream to chase.

You know what was my most competitive period of the day? Lunch.

The boys I ate lunch with were like me: all sports, all the time. We scarfed down our food so we could rush to play Ping-Pong at the table set up in the cafeteria. Other boys bolted for the foosball table, but I loved Ping-Pong. Day after day I battled the other boys. I reveled in every winning shot, and I became frustrated with each hit into the net or beyond the table. Our principal, Dr. Tweedy, sometimes got in on the action. Supposedly Dr. Tweedy had never lost a match with a student. Early in sixth grade, I took him on for the first time.

Dr. Tweedy wore a full suit to school every day, and he didn't so much as remove his jacket or loosen his tie for Ping-Pong. I expected him to slam the ball at me, or put a vicious spin on his hits, but he never did. Instead, shot after shot, he sent it where I least expected. He'd catch me leaning left, and he'd send it to my right. He'd get me comfortable on my backhand and then snap it at my forehand. And he didn't miss. Suit and all, he destroyed me that first match. The score was something like 21 to 8.

"Good game," he said, and shook my hand. Dr. Tweedy was always classy and a model of sportsmanship. He had attended Purdue, so whenever MSU played Purdue in football, we made a lunch bet. My first year he bought me lunch (MSU won at home, 30 to 10). The next two seasons, though, Purdue won, and I paid for Doc's lunch.

Doc was a quiet player. I only remember a little chatter. "Good shot," he might acknowledge to any kid who zipped one past him. "Coming at you," he'd announce before a serve. When his score reached 20, he sang serenely, "Game point, game point."

The first time he sang that, it unnerved me, but I soon noticed that he chanted "Game point, game point" to everyone. As trash talk goes, it was gentle.

I grabbed a spot at the table as often as I could and played my classmates every day. I quickened my shots and improved my instincts. I learned to read my opponent's paddle better and predict where the next shot would land. I also played more patiently. I stopped trying to kill every single shot, which led to fewer unforced errors.

Again and again I cajoled Dr. Tweedy into playing me, and again and again, I lost. I'd get upset, but he was so calm in victory that I relaxed a little, even in defeat.

"I'll get you next time," I said.

"Bring it," Doc always answered.

I learned to play like Doc: not fancy, but smart. I had no trick shots or vicious slams, but two school years of Ping-Pong made me consistent. I returned every shot that came at me, and I picked the corners. The games between Dr. Tweedy and me grew closer: 21–15 . . . 21–18. Near the end of seventh grade, I pestered him into yet another match. From the outset, my game felt right. Nothing went into the net, and every ball caught the last few inches of table. Each shot was my best shot. I reached 20, and now I was the one who announced "Game point." Doc, down 20–15, had service. He sent it firmly to my backhand, and I fought it off. Doc smacked a line drive deep in my forehand corner. I reached back and managed a return. His next shot wasn't as hard, and I composed myself and aimed for a corner. I struck it just right, the ball clipped the edge, and it shot straight sideways, skittering across the cafeteria floor. I threw my hands in the air. "Yes!" I hollered. "Yes!" I pumped my fist, Tiger Woods style.

Doc laughed and set his paddle on the table. "Congrats, big guy," he said, extending his hand.

It was, at the time, one of the great sports victories of my life.

I strove for victory in less official sports, too. Sports like lunch box baseball.

In seventh grade, we took a break from Ping-Pong. Michigan had a long, beautiful fall that year, and we were allowed to go into the courtyard and gardens outside the cafeteria during lunch. We couldn't take a bat outside, but tennis balls weren't banned, and neither were lunch boxes, so we quickly came up with rules for lunch box baseball, including ghost runners and home run boundaries.

Only six of us played lunch box baseball. They were boys I'd known from rec league baseball and basketball. Every one of them had grown to accept my quirks—they were all true friends who had my back.

One lunch I hit a line drive over my friend J.P.'s head. He jumped and grabbed it, robbing me of a big hit. His next time at bat, he hit a deep fly ball across the courtyard that I caught on the run.

"My catch was better," J.P. said.

What was he talking about? I had to run, and I caught his midstride on the warning track! All he did was jump a little.

"No way," I sputtered. "Mine was better. I was running. It was a running catch! Running catches are harder."

"Says you."

I stormed back inside, incredulous—and completely unaware that he was just needling me for fun. It took me years to realize that J.P. didn't really care whose catch was more astounding.

Did I take this argument too seriously? Absolutely. But was J.P. still my friend? I don't doubt it for a second.

I was lucky. When kids are bullied, a common response is to attempt invisibility. They stop putting themselves out there: they stay away from the Ping-Pong table, from the athletic fields, anywhere they might draw attention to themselves. But, thanks to my autism, I didn't have the social sense to try to disappear. Over and over I threw myself into the mix. The bullies kept finding me, since I was right out there in the middle of the action, talking to everybody and playing with everybody, but eventually some friends emerged, too. My autism did it again: it simultaneously opened me to attack and cut me a break.

\* \* \*

Not that the bullies vanished.

From what I can remember, the cruel kids targeted me more for my height than for my autism. (I still didn't know that I was autistic, and I'm not sure what my classmates sensed about me.) The advantage to my height was that I could help my teachers put things away when nobody else in the classroom could. I could stretch and touch the ceiling, a feat not one of my classmates could do. I pulled scissors and markers and other supplies down from the top shelves; I liked feeling helpful.

The downside to my height was the teasing.

"Freak."

"Jolly Green Giant."

They weren't impressed by my height or even intimidated. They were repulsed.

When kids called me the Jolly Green Giant, they said it with no warmth, and in no way did the label make me jolly. I hated that name, which made some kids say it all the more. I wore green Michigan State gear every day, and I tried to be kind around the school, so the nickname made sense to my classmates. But that wasn't me—my name was Anthony!

One boy in particular swung by my locker almost every hour, even when he had no business being in that part of the school.

"Here comes the Jolly Green Giant," he'd announce. "Ho ho ho!"

He encouraged others to call me the Green Giant, too, and before long it felt like half the school was calling me that. I couldn't make them stop.

His taunting continued, day after day. I started thinking that only a fight would stop him. I imagined taking a big swing, right at his face. One good punch would drop him. I wouldn't say a word to him; I'd just knock him out cold.

One night, though, I paced in my bedroom, looking in my mirror and thinking about my tormentor. *You're not going to fight him*, I said to myself. *You're not going to do anything, for two reasons. Number one, this isn't who you are. Your family didn't raise you to resort to violence. Number two, it's what he wants you to do. He wants you to stoop to his level and throw a punch. Don't give him the satisfaction. I'll find a way to knock him down, but it will be my way, on my terms.*

Sure enough, I found another way to handle him. This kid and I were in the same basketball league, and before long my team was scheduled to play his. I saw my opportunity.

He guarded me, and even when he wasn't guarding me, he would switch off to try and steal the ball from me. Every time my team went on offense, there he was.

*This is your chance,* I told myself. *Beat him this way, on the court.*

And I did. Basket after basket. Rebound after rebound. Jump shots. Post moves. I used everything in my arsenal against him. We crushed his team, and I'd lit him up for twenty points.

When I saw him in school on Monday, I extended my hand. I wanted to be gracious in victory, like Dr. Tweedy at the Ping-Pong table. It was time to put the past behind us.

"I know what you're gonna say to me," he snarled, ignoring my hand.

He walked away without another word. No cordiality. No mutual respect. Just his back.

The rejection didn't sting the way it often did. I knew I'd embarrassed him on the court. I had my retribution. Let him walk down the hall thinking he'd one-upped me by refusing the truce.

We never made peace, and he tossed half-hearted insults my way on occasion, but he knew not to push it, because if he continued with the "Jolly Green Giant" stuff, I'd remind him and everyone around him what had happened the Saturday he tried to guard me.

And did I continue to wear my Spartan green to school?

Every single day.

With Dad and Allison, Christmas 1989. Allison was four years old, and I was almost one. Ianni family.

In my Michael Jordan jersey on my driveway, spring 1998. Ianni family.

With my dog Nipper. I was probably nine years old. Ianni family.

*From left*: Me, Coach Izzo, and Allison at the team hotel during the 1999 Final Four in Tampa, Florida. Ianni family.

With Coach Anthony Stuckey at Kalamazoo College after
an AAU state tournament in May 2004. Ianni family.

With Coach Dan Stolz during a playoff game against rival Holt
High School, March 2006. Courtesy *Lansing State Journal*.

With my parents in the Okemos High School gym on
Senior Night, February 2007. Ianni family.

Playing for Grand Valley State University against Wayne State,
January 2009. Courtesy GVSU Sports Information.

The lowering of the flag, midgame, on the USS *Carl Vinson*, November 2011. *From left*: Dan Chapman, Austin Thornton, Keenan Wetzel, me, Adreian Payne. Courtesy Hondo S. Carpenter Sr.

The 2011–2012 MSU men's basketball team, with President and
First Lady Obama, on the USS *Carl Vinson* aircraft carrier.
November 11, 2011. Draymond Green and I are standing directly
behind the president. Courtesy Michigan State University.

With Coach Tom Izzo during a preseason game my senior
year, October 2011. Courtesy Michigan State University.

Cutting down the net in Indianapolis after winning the Big Ten tournament, March 2012. Courtesy Michigan State University.

With my parents and my sister Allison outside the Breslin Center after I graduated from Michigan State University, May 2012. Ianni family.

Speaking to middle school students in Eaton Rapids, Michigan, February 2014. Courtesy *Lansing State Journal*.

With my wife, Kelly, Knox (*standing*), and Nash (*held by me*),
September 2019. Ianni family.

Coming out of the tunnel before a game at the Breslin Center, November 2011. Courtesy Hondo S. Carpenter Sr.

# 9

## ON THE BANKS OF THE RED CEDAR

LONG BEFORE I ACTUALLY ATTENDED Michigan State and played basketball for the Spartans, I felt at home on the grand campus. I loved crossing over the Red Cedar River on fall Saturdays, stopping mid-bridge to watch the water flow beneath me. The leaves were turning red and orange along the bike paths, tailgaters grilled burgers and brats near the stadium, and green-clad football fans streamed from all directions toward the Spartan Stadium gates.

MSU's campus in the fall is one of the greatest places on Earth. I thought that when I was a boy, and I still think it today. I've traveled to a lot of college campuses throughout the country, and I still say that there is no place like East Lansing on a sunny fall Saturday.

By the time I was in elementary school, the bobcat in the Ohio University arena was a fading memory. My mascot was Sparty. Every home game, I sought out Sparty as he roamed the stands flexing his muscles, busting out some dance moves, and waving to the Spartan faithful. It wasn't just *nice* to see Sparty. Every game, I *had* to see Sparty and give him a high five. It was an absolute requirement. And not just at football and basketball games, either. My family went to a lot of MSU volleyball games at Jenison Field House. Dad sometimes had to attend for work, Mom had a few former players on the Spartans' team that she liked to watch, and Allison sometimes helped as a ball girl during the matches. There was a storage room door in Jenison's western corner at the end of one stretch of bleachers, and Sparty always emerged from this door. Once I figured out Sparty's entrance, I started breaking off from my family and grabbing a seat near that storage room. I was on a stakeout. The second Sparty pushed open his door, I leaped down from the bleachers and rushed across the indoor track to greet him.

"Hi, Sparty!"

Sparty always offered me a high-five or a fist bump.

"How are you doing, Sparty!"

He gave me a thumbs-up. Then he put his hand to his ear, and I knew what that meant:

"Go Green!" I yelled, and he clapped his approval. Then he marched past me, out onto the floor.

\* \* \*

Wardcliff Elementary staged a school-wide talent show every year, and in third grade, I decided to enter.

"What are you going to do?" I remember my teacher asking.

"The Spartan Fight Song."

This was not unheard of. Okemos isn't far from campus, a lot of the school district's parents graduated from Michigan State, and many Okemos residents work for the university. The previous year I'd seen a girl play the fight song on her violin.

"How are you going to do it?"

"Sing it."

"By yourself?"

"Yes."

"Do you know all the words?"

Better than anybody.

The night of the talent show, parents and families filled the Wardcliff gymnasium. The other performers and I checked in, and our teachers reminded us of our order. All those rows of folding chairs, all those eyes on us . . . and I wasn't jittery at all. I didn't have the social awareness to be nervous.

On stage, a boy solved a Rubik's Cube really fast. A girl sang the Celine Dion song from *Titanic*. There was a speed-chess player, and a piano player. And then it was my turn.

From the opening words, I just belted it out:

> On the banks of the Red Cedar,
> There's a school that's known to all;
> Its specialty is winning,
> And those Spartans play good ball.

By the second line, every person in the audience was clapping along on the beat, just like they do with the Spartan Marching Band after a touchdown.

> Spartan teams are bound to win
> They're fighting with a vim
> Rah! Rah! Rah!

They kept clapping, and when the "Rah! Rah! Rah!" line came they shouted it with me, just like the 75,000 fans do at Spartan Stadium. To be honest, I almost giggled. Through all of the other acts, the parents and grandparents had sat politely and silently until applauding at the end. But for me? They were showing me boisterous support—during my song! I smiled and kept on singing. When I reached the last two lines, the whole gym joined in:

> Fight! Fight! Rah, Team, Fight!
> Victory for MSU!

\* \* \*

That same year, I met my future coach for the first time. I'd followed my dad down to the court after a game, and from there we went through the tunnel to the locker rooms. Dad led me to the coaches' locker room.

"You need to be quiet in there," Dad warned me. "Coach is probably still doing his post-game show for the radio."

Dad was right. When we entered, Coach Izzo was still answering questions into a microphone. The Spartans had won, and I could tell that Coach and the hometown radio guys were all in a good mood. (One of the broadcasters, Gus Ganakas, had served as MSU's head coach in the 1970s before Jud Heathcote—Tom Izzo's mentor—took over the program.) Dad silently pointed me to a couch.

After he finished the radio interview, Coach Izzo shook hands with my dad.

"Antonio was getting those rebounds tonight," Dad said.

"Yeah, he was good."

Dad praised certain players—Antonio Smith, Morris Peterson—and Coach Izzo agreed, but he also noted the mistakes. "We gotta get a little better there," he said a few times.

Coach then turned to me. "Who's this guy here?"

Dad said, "Tom, I'd like you to meet my son, Anthony."

We shook hands. "So, Anthony," Coach said, "do you like basketball?"

"I love it."

"Where are you going to play?"

"Michigan State."

He grinned. "All right. That's what I like to hear. Are you a good student?"

"Yes."

"You listen to your teachers and do your work?"

"Yup."

"Keep it that way. All right?"

I started tagging along with Dad onto the court and into the locker room whenever I could. We'd step onto the floor, and I always had two thoughts. The first was, *Man, this is so cool!* But the second thought was, *I should get used to this, because I'm go-ing to play on this court and run out of the tunnel with my team one day in a Spartan jersey.*

\*   \*   \*

I didn't have to wait until college to fly in an airplane with the Spartans. I did it as a fourth grader.

It was mid-February, more than halfway through the season. Michigan State had won ten straight games, and we were in first place in the Big Ten. The Spartans had a tough road game in Minneapolis, against the Minnesota Golden Gophers. Michigan State and Minnesota were both ranked that Saturday. Dad and I flew out on the team's chartered plane the day before the game.

At the Minneapolis airport, Dad pointed to the idling bus. "Go ahead and get on, Ant," he said. "Pick some seats for us. I'll get our bags and be there in a minute."

I stepped on. I was only ten years old, but I was five and a half feet tall. Most of the players had already grabbed seats near the back. Some of the guys stretched their long legs out across the aisle. I plopped down in the front row. A few of the players gave me funny looks, but I didn't think much of their glances.

Coach Izzo and my dad were the last two to get on. When Coach boarded, he saw me, shrugged his shoulders, smirked, and walked on past.

Dad came up the bus steps. "Anthony," he snapped, "what are you doing?"

I was confused. "Sitting in our seats."

"That's not where you sit."

I had no idea what Dad was talking about.

Dad strode past me to the middle of the bus, where Coach Izzo had sat.

"Tom, go up and take your seat," Dad said. "Anthony will move."

"Don't worry about it."

"Go on and sit up there."

"It's OK."

I didn't know whether to stand up or stay where I was. I think some of the players were quietly watching, too, waiting to see whether Coach would kick the kid out of his seat. Eventually, Coach Izzo came and took the seat next to mine, and Dad settled in six or seven rows behind us.

"How's school going this year?" he asked.

"It's going really good."

"What subject do you like the most?"

"Reading."

"That's a good choice."

The bus rolled out of the airport and onto the highway. Coach Izzo asked me about my basketball season, and we talked about Minnesota's team. The Golden Gophers' best player that year was a senior forward named Quincy Lewis. Coach Izzo and I agreed that the Spartans needed to stop Lewis.

I looked out the window and saw a giant stadium with a bubbled gray dome. "Is that where we're playing?"

"No, that's the Metrodome. That's where the Vikings play, and the Minnesota Twins." I didn't like the Twins—they beat the Detroit Tigers a little too often.

"Our game is in Williams Arena. You'll see it here in a minute."

The bus crossed the Mississippi River, turned on to campus, and came to a stop at the arena. The players went straight to the locker room and changed for the nighttime shootaround. Dad and I followed the tunnel out to the court, and I claimed a chair at the end of the team bench. When Coach Izzo emerged, he walked toward me and gestured for me to stand.

"Hey! Uh-uh. You stole my seat, and you're not out of the doghouse yet. You've got to come out here and do work now."

"I'm sorry."

"You have to be a ball boy. You're in charge of rebounding and passing it back to the guys."

I was already wearing basketball shoes, sweatpants, and a Michigan State sweatshirt, so I was dressed to play. I stood near the hoop, waiting for the players. Soon enough they arrived. "Right here," they called, clapping for a ball, and I started pushing bounce passes their way. I kept my place near the basket, catching the balls that swished through and rebounding the shots that missed. Every time, I tossed it right back to the shooter. Tempting as it was to put up a shot or two myself, I knew I wasn't allowed. I had a job to do—help the players get ready for an important road game. I couldn't believe I was sharing the court with these guys! Every player on the floor was a hero of mine. This was the team I dreamed of joining one day. Antonio "Big Tone" Smith gave me a high five. Then Mateen Cleaves did. More high fives, from Charlie Bell and Morris Peterson.

We stayed in a hotel that night and then went back to the arena the next day for another practice before the evening's game. I was the ball boy again, and I got another round of high fives from my heroes.

At lunch that Saturday, I ordered a hamburger. When it arrived, I did what I always did with a hamburger: I took it apart. I worked my way through the burger item by item, starting with the top bun, then the pickles, then the onions, the lettuce, the meat, and finally the bottom bun. Gus Ganakas watched me with fascination.

"Does it taste good that way?" he asked.

"Yes."

Gus died in 2019. I got to know him well in the last twenty years of his life—he was still broadcasting for the Spartan Sports Network during my playing days. When he and I meet up in the afterlife, I'm sure he'll tease me about taking Coach Izzo's bus seat, and he'll ask me if I still eat hamburgers one item at a time.

I can't remember why, but Dad had to give up one of our tickets in the first row behind the bench, so Dad sat in one of the empty time-out chairs at the end of the MSU bench. I was among team parents and school donors. I actually knew some of the parents and looked for them at every game. Mateen Cleaves's mom and Antonio Smith's mom gave the biggest, warmest hugs.

That night's game was televised nationally on ESPN, and the packed arena knew it. The Minnesota fans were loud and crazy from the opening tip-off. Williams Arena's nickname is "The Barn," and the crowd's roars bounced off the rafters and the high old ceiling and doubled in volume. I was on my own in that seat. Mom wasn't there to cover my ears or escort me to a quiet corner in the concourse. The Barn doesn't have a quiet corner. Whenever Minnesota scored, the cheering echoed and surged and pummeled my ears. But I was old enough to handle it—and even to enjoy it a little. I scanned The Barn, studying the banners hanging from the ceiling. I felt independent. I could see Dad, a row in front of me and at the end of the bench, but I could take care of myself.

Midway through the second half, things didn't look good for us. Minnesota had the lead, and it seemed like they were going to keep it. With less than seven minutes left, Quincy Lewis—the same guy Coach Izzo and I had worried about on the bus ride the day before—drained a three-ball to give the Golden Gophers a ten-point lead. The Barn went nuts, and I clapped my palms over my ears. I was sure it was over. I started to cry. The seat next to mine was temporarily empty, so Dad joined me.

"You have to keep believing," Dad told me. "Don't give up on your team."

"Stay positive," he instructed. "We're going to win. You'll see."

Sure enough, the Spartans fought back. Almost as soon as Dad said we'd win, Mateen drove the lane and made a layup, cutting the deficit to eight. We kept clawing back and actually took a one-point lead. Then, with twenty seconds left, Charlie Bell dunked it for a three-point lead! Minnesota rushed up the court . . . and drilled a three-pointer to tie it. A flurry of action. The clock kept ticking. MSU darted right back down the court, Mateen Cleaves carrying the ball most of the way. From the top of the key, Mateen drove to his right and, with only a second left, banked his layup off the glass. It went in! The Spartans won!

The bus ride back to the airport was upbeat. We'd beaten a ranked team—on the road!—and we were pulling away from the rest of the Big Ten. I sat next to Dad, but not in the front row.

"The front row is *always* the head coach's seat," Dad reminded me.

\* \* \*

I made guarantees to everybody I knew that I was going to play basketball for Michigan State one day. Classmates, family, teachers, and Coach Izzo himself—I'd declared it to all of them. But did *anyone* think it could happen?

Probably not. Sure, I was tall, but when I was twelve, there wasn't much to my game besides my height. If I didn't have any skills to go with my height, I wouldn't be playing at *any* college, let alone Michigan State. Other people knew that, but I didn't.

There was something else I still didn't know about myself, either: I was autistic. Autistic kids didn't play team sports. Autistic kids didn't go to four-year universities. I was the kid who freaked out during fire drills. I was the kid who cried during gym class. In kindergarten I had smelled toys and growled at classmates.

A future Spartan? Me?

If this makes you think of another underdog's story, you're not alone. In the 1960s there was a kid who vowed to play football for Notre Dame, even though the odds were against him. He wasn't autistic, but he was small, and he struggled academically. He had lots of doubters, and people teased him. They shook their heads at how ridiculous his dream was. The kid's name is Daniel Ruettiger, but the world knows him by his nickname: Rudy.

People have called me "the Rudy of Michigan State basketball." I think it was Ray Weathers who first said it. Ray played basketball for Michigan State in the mid-1990s and then played a lot overseas. He also had a short run in the NBA with the Phoenix Suns. Ray had stopped by a practice one day during my first year at Michigan State. He liked to visit with Coach Izzo and some of the other guys he knew, and also get his own workout in. Ray was watching our starters go against me and the rest of the scout team. Our job was to replicate the play and the strategies of MSU's next opponent. We were supposed to get physical with the starters and knock them out of their game mentally. Sometimes this meant I had to block the lane and take a charge from Draymond Green, letting him smash me to the ground. This was dirty work, but somebody had to do it. The starters had to be ready.

I didn't know Ray was watching me. I was just busting my butt, hustling during a routine practice like the Big Ten championship was at stake. My freakish intensity caught Ray's eye. "That guy's like the Rudy of MSU basketball," he told Isaiah Dahlman, one of my teammates, who later repeated it to me. Since then, people in my family have picked up on it, as have my friends.

"Rudy's got nothing on you, A.I.," they tell me. Or they'll call me "the A.I. Rudy."

I've lost count of how many times I've watched *Rudy*. Sometimes before a big presentation, I'll listen to the movie's soundtrack to get focused and fired up. I think about the kids in my audience. Who is the next Rudy out there? Who out there in the gym or the auditorium is taking their seat, dreaming big but dealing with doubters? I want *those* kids to be inspired. I want *them* to be the next Rudy. Rudy had his turn. I've had my turn. Now it's theirs.

# 10

## "DO THOSE IMPRESSIONS"

ATHLETICS WASN'T THE ONLY THING passed from one Ianni generation to the next. Another passion of mine also came straight from my family: the Three Stooges. From Grandpa Nick to his sons, and from my dad to me, we all loved watching the Three Stooges. When I was growing up, Dad and I often caught them on AMC, and for a few different Christmases, I received Three Stooges DVDs. I think I was the only kid at Chippewa Middle School who found the Three Stooges even remotely funny. Nobody—not my friends, and not the kids I thought were my friends—wanted to watch the Three Stooges for even a minute.

Curly was always my favorite. He could create an incredible range of odd noises, and he accompanied them with hilarious snaps and hand gestures. I started trying to mimic Curly's noises and movements. "Why, *soy-tan-lee*," I'd say. "Nyuk, nyuk, nyuk." I raised my voice's pitch in an effort to match Curly's.

I did my best Curly a few times in school, and boys noticed. They laughed, which thrilled me. This was my chance to be the cool kid! I could rise through middle school's social ranks by impersonating Curly.

In the halls between classes, guys started requesting performances.

"Hey, Ianni, do those impressions again," they said. "From the comedy group you like so much."

And I'd launch right into Curly, flinging my hands around. "Nyuk, nyuk, nyuk."

The boys laughed. For a long time, I interpreted their laughter as a sign of approval. I assumed it meant that I belonged. That I was one of them. That I had a lot of friends.

Looking back, my guess is that they thought I was "retarded." It's a word I hate, but it's probably the word that was in their heads—and the word they said out loud as soon as I walked away. I think the word "retarded" should be banned altogether. It shows terrible disrespect for people who are developmentally disabled or who have special needs in some way. Such people have done nothing to deserve their challenges, just as my parents and I did nothing to deserve mine. The boys who were mocking me must have thought everyone was supposed to meet their definition of "normal." I say the world would be a boring place if we all had the exact same abilities.

The full weight of their ridicule finally dawned on me in high school. One night after dinner Dad and I were chatting about something, and he said, "Why, soy-tan-lee," the way Curly did. I hadn't said it myself in a few years. The middle school memories came back to me, and I realized in that moment that no one had been laughing *with* me. It wasn't my Curly impersonation they'd laughed at. It was *me*. I felt my whole body tense up, and my stomach got queasy. It was devastating, to realize in an instant just how much those kids had been belittling me.

*Hey, Ianni, do those impressions again.*

As if they liked me. As if I were one of the cool guys.

This was what it meant to be autistic in middle school: to be humiliated and to not even know it.

*       *       *

Sometimes, though, I recognized mockery for what it was.

When I was in eighth grade, my sister's AAU volleyball team had a national tournament in Atlanta. My family traveled often for Allison's volleyball—she was a year away from college, and she needed to face the best competition in the country to get herself ready. I didn't mind the trips. It was a thrill to watch my sister dominate. Allison destroyed her opponents, which made me proud to be her brother.

I was still a middle schooler, but I was taller than most of Allison's team, and I was old enough to want to impress them.

One of the girls was celebrating a birthday during nationals, and the whole team gathered in her hotel room to have ice cream and cake. I tagged along with Allison.

We sang "Happy Birthday," and I attempted my own rendition, with a goofy voice and a bad sense of pitch.

After the song, Allison's teammates started peppering me with questions about the middle school dating scene. I confessed who my biggest crushes were. They egged me on, and I talked about the girls in my grade with as much swagger as I could manage.

"Oh, I'm *sure* she likes you back," one girl said.

"Definitely," said another. "You should ask her out."

"You should try to kiss her."

Every single thing they said was sarcastic. They were being cruel, and this time I knew it right away.

Allison put her plate of cake down. "You guys need to grow up," she snapped. "Just because he doesn't get what you're doing doesn't make it OK."

The room went silent.

"Let's get out of here," Allison said to me. "You don't need to take this crap anymore."

Allison and I wandered down to the hotel lobby. Sadness and anger swirled inside me.

"Are you OK?" she asked.

"Not really."

"Ant, if you ever sense that someone is making fun of you, if you can tell they're not being nice, I don't want you to take it. Don't go along. You're better than they are."

"OK."

"I mean it," Allison said. "You're stronger than they are."

She guided me back to our room. My parents were there, and Allison recapped what had happened at the birthday party.

My parents didn't freak out or rush out of the room, ready to attack Allison's teammates. They knew Allison was looking out for me. That was all the protection I needed.

A few minutes later, Allison's phone rang. It was one of her teammates. Allison listened for a minute. Then, she offered me the phone. "She wants to talk to you," Allison said.

I trusted Allison. If she was handing me the phone, I should take it.

"Hello?"

"Anthony, I just want to say that I'm really sorry about the way we treated you. We weren't being nice."

"OK."

"I don't know why we acted like that. We didn't mean anything by it."

"All right."

The next day, between volleyball matches at the nearby convention center, most of Allison's teammates found me and offered similar apologies. Allison had stood up to them, and it had made a difference.

\* \* \*

I was the tallest kid on my eighth-grade football team, but because I was lanky (thanks to another growth spurt), some guys assumed I was soft. One kid in particular—a boy who also went back and forth between offensive line and tight end—really started to target me, day after day.

"Hey, Super Soft!" he'd say. My face quivered. I knew if I said anything back, I'd explode, or cry, or both. And I knew he could see that in my face. "Softie," he'd call me. He never called me Anthony. Just "Softie." Other boys followed his lead and slung the same insults at me. "Softie." "Super soft."

"Nobody on this team likes you," he said.

"That's not true!"

"Nobody wants you on this team 'cuz you're so soft. Nobody wants a softie on the team."

My friends told me to keep my head up and ignore it, but how could I? It was continuous. Even during games, when a team should be at its most united, he was jabbing at me, trying to get me to crack.

A few games into the season, I told my mom I wanted to quit.

"You're not going to quit," she said. "Nobody in our family quits in life. If things don't get better, you don't have to play next year. But you can do this. You can finish the season."

I listened to my mom and tried to ride it out, but each practice was another day of taunts, another afternoon full of teasing. And my tormenters knew that each insult was hitting its mark. My eyes revealed that they were winning. I was collapsing inside, and quickly.

I started trying to make myself gag before every practice. "I'm sick," I'd tell my mom. "I just threw up. Call the coach and say I can't go to practice."

Sometimes this worked and sometimes it didn't.

Whenever Dad asked how practice was, I'd say, "It was OK." I was afraid if I started talking about the bullies, I'd cry my eyes out.

Night after night: "How was practice?" "It was fine."

Finally, one night the truth came out. I told Dad everything that the bully and his followers had been saying, everything I'd been enduring. The words came out slowly. Tears formed in my eyes.

Dad's expression was fierce. I think he was resisting the impulse to walk out the door and go fight my battle for me.

"Son, you're one of the toughest guys that I know. Tomorrow when you go to practice, show your teammates how tough you are. Give that guy a good licking with those shoulder pads of yours."

Violence is *not* how my family solves problems. Beating up other kids—whether they've invited the retaliation or not—isn't allowed in my house. Dad told me to deliver a clean, if powerful, hit. "You've got skills," he said. "You've got technique. Use them to your advantage."

The next day at practice, I waited for my moment. We started with stretching and running and some other stuff. Finally, we lined up for tackling drills. I wanted to be matched up against the guy who refused to call me anything but "Softie." Other days I would have avoided him. Instead, I cut in line a couple of times, seeking him out. I wanted to be matched up against him. I made it to the right spot in line, and then we were face to face, maybe ten feet apart, waiting. He cradled the ball, ready to run toward me. When the coach blew the whistle, I exploded toward him, lowered my shoulders, and popped him good. He landed on his back and I landed on top. You could have heard a pin drop on the practice field that day.

I stood and trotted to the back of the line without saying a word.

Some of the bully's followers approached me the next day. They apologized for the name-calling. Besides the hit, they said, putting up with their harassment showed toughness.

The bully backed off after that, and I stopped gagging myself before practice. Not only did I finish out my eighth-grade season, but I played in ninth grade, too, before deciding to focus on basketball.

Technically, this wasn't autism-related bullying. It was just plain old bullying. That didn't make it OK, of course. Scars are scars, no matter how or why you got them.

\* \* \*

One place where nobody picked on me was in Mrs. Hall's classroom. Nobody took advantage of my naivete and demanded Curly Howard impressions, or called me "Freak" or "Green Giant" because of my height. It was the safest, most calming room at Chippewa Middle School.

Mrs. Hall was a special education teacher, and all three years I had her one period a day for "Resource Room." Resource Room was like a study period, except that every kid in there was part of the special education program.

I still didn't know I was autistic, but I knew that I needed extra help in school. I kept up with my homework just fine, but tests were another story. Frequently the questions didn't make sense to me. Let's say my language arts teacher had the class read an article about Jane Goodall, and we had to answer multiple-choice questions at the end of the passage. One of the questions might look like this:

1. What is the author's purpose in writing this article?
    A. to entertain the reader with stories about chimpanzees
    B. to inform the reader of the importance of wildlife conservation
    C. to encourage travelers to visit Africa's natural wonders
    D. to describe the work and life of Jane Goodall

I could make a case for every answer. The article mentioned chimpanzees, and protecting wildlife, and Africa, and Jane Goodall. They were *all* right. How was I supposed to pick one? And then, what about that word "purpose"? Purpose means a lot of things. You can do something "on purpose." You can go somewhere with a "specific purpose."

It was like the ducks on the pond all over again.

Trying to answer a question like that made me want to punch my own head. But, Mrs. Hall could always calm me down. "This room is your safe place," she reassured me.

I started taking my quizzes and tests in Mrs. Hall's Resource Room. She crossed out one or two answers so that I didn't have to deal with so many options swirling around in my brain. Mrs. Hall often read the questions aloud, pausing to explain words like "purpose."

In middle school I often felt completely alone. Academically, socially, physically—you name it.

Except in Mrs. Hall's Resource Room.

Every kid in the class was in the same boat. We all needed extra help and extra time. Not everyone was autistic. Students with a variety of disabilities were in there. Most of the kids, I never found out what their learning disability was. Really, it didn't matter. Maybe in other classrooms your peers could make you feel uncool for asking questions and requesting help, but not in Mrs. Hall's room. We all had each other's backs. Resource Room felt like family. It was a safe place to struggle and be vulnerable.

Mrs. Hall must have sensed that school was a source of anxiety for most of us. Everything about her room put us at ease. She had couches where we could stretch out and read, and there were computer stations where we could work on assignments from other classes so that we didn't feel so behind all the time. Mrs. Hall put out snacks for us—always a great way to put students in a good mood. She hung a Michigan State flag in her room, and when March Madness came around, we used her whiteboard to follow the brackets. Mrs. Hall turned on the radio sometimes, and you could feel the stress leave the room.

Whenever we had a fire drill, I was sent to Mrs. Hall's class ahead of time. She and I left the building early, and she took me across the street and far from the noise. "See, you can barely hear it from here," she said.

I agreed. "Right, barely."

Mrs. Hall said I could come to Resource Room whenever I needed, even during other times of the day. "If other kids are bothering you, just come in here," she said. "They won't follow you in here. They won't pull that stuff in my room."

I took her up on that offer—a lot. Even during lunch.

We were playing basketball in the gym one day during lunch period. I was dribbling the ball with my back to the rim. "Michigan State is down by a point with ten seconds to go," I announced in my broadcaster's voice. "Ianni has the ball for the Spartans. The game is on the line. Ianni could win it for Michigan State."

Before I could even take my heroic shot, a few boys strolled over to the baseline.

"Hey, Ianni," one called out. "You know you're never going to play for Michigan State, right? It's nice and all that you pretend you're playing for them, but don't get your hopes up."

"I am going to play for Michigan State!"

"Be realistic. I'm doing you a favor."

I dropped the ball, left the court, and headed straight for Mrs. Hall's room.

"Don't listen to them," she said. "They don't know what they're talking about. They're not trying to be realistic—they're just being mean."

"Yeah."

"Do you believe in yourself?"

"Yes."

"And I know your parents believe in you. And I believe in you, Anthony."

\* \* \*

I was fortunate in many ways. I had good teachers who respected my special needs and made adjustments. I had fellow special education students who put supporting one another ahead of being cool. And I had parents who read my IEP closely and made sure it was respected on a daily basis. Having extra time to work on tests and assignments in resource room is known as an "accommodation." My parents made sure that I had all the accommodations I needed, and they monitored my classes to guarantee that my IEP was followed to the T.

Few students—no matter their academic abilities or social status—look back on the middle school years with fondness or nostalgia. They are tough years for most kids. They were definitely miserable for me. I take no pleasure in revisiting them.

There is consolation, though, and it is this: I go to middle schools a lot now. I speak with groups of students all the time, in gyms and auditoriums and classrooms. There are kids in those audiences who are longing for kindness and respect. There are autistic students in those crowds. And gifted students. And bullies. And victims of bullies. And students who are combinations of those things—a person can be both the bully and the bullied, both autistic and gifted. When I talk to those kids, I speak as someone who endured a lot of pain. If sharing details from my hardest years can make another kid's time in middle school less awful, I'm OK with that. More than OK with that.

# 11

## "WE WANT TO TELL YOU A STORY"

OUR HOME HAD A ROOM on the first floor, to the right of the entrance, that was cut off from the rest of the house. The walls were painted a soothing green, and its window looked onto the front yard. My parents put a computer desk, a comfortable recliner, a couch, and our smaller TV in this room, and we called it our den. By middle school, I was claiming the room more and more, and the rest of the family gradually surrendered it to me. Often I did my homework in the den, and on nights when all of our practices and games and Dad's events prevented us from having dinner as a family, I ate in there. Mom and Dad started calling it "the Cave," because it was where I went to hibernate. I stretched out in the recliner, flipped on the TV, kept the volume low, and retreated from the world and all of its stimulus and stress. It was my place.

One August night about a week before I started my life at Okemos High School, I was in the Cave, worn out after a long football practice in the summer heat. Allison was already gone. She was more than two thousand miles away, playing college volleyball in California. How was I supposed to figure out high school without her help? Allison had always been around to give me pointers. I knew we could call, and there was no doubt that my sister still had my back, but it wasn't going to be the same. I was scheduled to have classes in places like "Lower A" and "Upper B." How was I going to make it from one room to the next without arriving late or getting completely lost? I didn't care for *small* changes, and this was not a small change. The first few times we talked cross-country, I taunted Allison by telling her I was turning her room into a video arcade. I crowed about how wonderful it was to be an only child. "Would you pretend you miss me for a five-minute phone call?" she complained. The truth was, I missed Allison a ton. Often I went into her empty room and sat on her bed, wallowing in her absence.

Two middle schools fed into a single high school in Okemos, so things were about to get a lot bigger. I braced myself for the crowds and the strangers. I was already well over six feet tall, but my height meant nothing. I feared I would feel small and disoriented.

"Anthony," my dad called from the living room. "Why don't you come in here? We'd like to talk to you."

I had no idea what this was about, or what was coming.

I sat alone on the couch. Mom sat in a nearby chair, and Dad stood near the fireplace. Dad has always been a stander. It's one way he takes charge of a situation.

Mom went first. "We want to tell you a story," she said. "This goes back to Ohio. You had some difficulties when you were a toddler, and we took you to some different doctors. We had a lot of tests done. It took a while, but when you were four years old, you were diagnosed with something called pervasive developmental disorder. Sometimes people say 'PDD.' It's a form of autism."

Mom described the trip to Children's Hospital in Columbus, and parts of it came back to me in flashes. I'd forgotten all about that day.

My parents spoke calmly. There were no tears. This wasn't bad news. It was just something I needed to know.

"When you started kindergarten," Mom continued, "we already knew you were autistic, and we shared that with the

school. You had a tough time in kindergarten. So, some therapists and psychiatrists did more tests, and then they met with us
and made some predictions about you."

"What did they predict?"

"Well, they told your dad and me that, because of your autism, we shouldn't expect you to do much in life. They said you'll
just barely graduate from high school. You won't go to college."

"They also said you'd never play sports," Dad said.

That seemed like an absurd prediction. *Me*—not play sports?

Mom said, "And your living situation when you're an adult—
they speculated it would be something like a group home."

I made tight fists with my hands. I clenched the ends of my
shorts. It was like I was getting ready to punch the wall, or tear
my clothes.

"Why would they say that about a five-year-old?"

My parents couldn't answer.

"I'm pissed," I said. "They don't know me. They don't know
what I'm capable of."

Although they stayed laid back themselves, Mom and Dad let
me be pissed off. I think they were happy to see me pissed off,
pleased that I was offended. That meant I was going to fight the
predictions. I'd show the people who tested me just how wrong
they were.

"So, what is it about me that makes me autistic?"

Mom gave me a slew of examples: how I used to misunder-
stand her directions with toys and clothes, how I wigged out in
Target, my outbursts in elementary school, my struggles with
expressions like *raining cats and dogs*. "There is a reason you
don't like fire drills," she said.

"It's the autism?"

"Right."

Dad said, "Remember how much the Breslin Center used to
upset you?"

"Yes."

Dad was right: I'd been miserable at the Breslin Center—but I'd buried those memories.

I asked, "When I was confused about Meijer having a face, was that because of my autism, too?" Years earlier, we'd been on our way to Meijer when Mom mentioned that the supermarket was getting a "facelift." It baffled me. How could you lift a store's face? *Where* was Meijer's face?

Mom laughed. "That's a perfect example."

I was quiet.

"Is there anything else you want to ask us?" Dad asked.

"No." Finally, I released the grip on my shorts. "No, I'm good. I just want to go sit and process."

The diagnosis made sense. For a few years I'd suspected I had some kind of learning disability. There must have been *some* reason I was in Resource Room. There must have been *some* reason that quizzes didn't make sense to me, even though I did all the homework. If you had asked me whether I had a learning disability, I would have said yes, I probably did. But if you had asked me to get more specific, I couldn't have. I had a learning disability. End of story. That was it. Did it get more specific than "learning disability"?

Apparently it did.

Although I immediately agreed with the diagnosis, I *hated* the predictions. How dare they say that about a five-year-old?

I returned to the den, closed the door, and turned the TV back on. ESPN had a baseball game going, but I couldn't focus. After a minute I muted the game.

A group home?

I'd show them just how wrong they were. I'd shut them up. I would do more than graduate from high school. I'd go to Michigan State, and I'd play basketball there, and I'd graduate from college, too. I was going to set high goals for myself, and I would achieve them.

\* \* \*

So, I started freshman year with a chip on my shoulder. I had things to prove and people to silence. Not that I got off to a brilliant start. My freshman year of high school was no less crushing for me than middle school had been. I was still the Freak. I was still the Green Giant. Boys mocked me, and girls all but sprinted away from me. In gym class, guys laughed at the way I dribbled a basketball, and they made fun of the way I ran. (I was a gawky runner. My arms flapped, and my legs waddled. Some people are born runners, but I've had to work a lot on my form. The one year I joined the track and field team, eighth grade, I ended up throwing the shot put. I had some good results, including a sixth-place finish at the all-league meet, but the main reason the coach assigned me to shot put was that I couldn't run.)

"Why do you wear those shirts, Ianni?" boys said of my Michigan State shirts. "Michigan State is terrible." (MSU's football team had finished 4–8 the previous season.)

"I'm going to go there."

"No, you're not."

The next day, they targeted me again: "Are you actually wearing a Tigers shirt, Ianni? They're worse than Michigan State." The Tigers were finishing one of the worst seasons in the history of baseball, but my family believes in loyalty. I was raised to stand by my teams through thick and thin. Grandpa Nick and my dad have no patience for fair-weather fans.

"Why do you wear basketball shorts every single day, Ianni?" kids chirped. "You look stupid. You think you're good at basketball or something?"

"I'm going to play basketball for Michigan State."

"Give me a break. There is no way you're playing there."

"I am, too!"

"But you're terrible."

"You're wrong," I stammered. "You're wrong."

I never had a good comeback ready. Whenever I tried to dish it back at them, I said something stupid and made it worse. I walked away on the brink of tears.

\* \* \*

Geoff Hall was born near Detroit. (He isn't related to Mrs. Hall, my middle school Resource Room teacher.) His family moved a lot when Geoff was young because of his dad's work in sales and distribution for Pepsi. He spent his elementary school years near Green Bay, Wisconsin. His family relocated to Okemos as Geoff and I were entering sixth grade. We grew closer during eighth grade—I remember playing dodgeball in gym class with Geoff. He was one of the best pitchers on the baseball team, so it was no surprise that he could whip a dodgeball at people with speed and accuracy. Geoff had a cannon.

By the summer between middle school and high school, Geoff had become my best friend. We played football together on the freshman team, so we had practices together throughout August. I started spending as much time at his house as I did at my own. We shot a lot of pool in his basement, and Geoff almost always won. Then we'd play HORSE in his driveway, and that was my game. Some days Geoff pulled out his hockey net with a goalie target stretched across the front. We aimed for the holes in the corners from different spots on the driveway—the hockey version of HORSE. Geoff played travel hockey, so I almost never beat him. We played a lot of video games in Geoff's basement, too, and those could go either way: *NBA Live*, *Madden Football*, and pro wrestling games.

The first time I met Geoff's parents, his dad shook my hand warmly and said, "How you doing, Big Fella?" Geoff's mom gave me a big hug, and when I left she gave me another hug *and* a kiss on the cheek.

"Mom, stop it!" Geoff said, embarrassed, but I didn't mind one bit. I loved the idea of having more family in my life—it meant that Geoff was my brother.

I started calling his mom "Mama Hall." And his dad rarely addressed me as anything but "Big Fella." I overcame my fear of spending the night at friends' houses, and I slept as well at Geoff's house as I did at my own.

Something else connected Geoff and me, too: we both received special education services. Like me, Geoff had Resource Room throughout middle school and high school. Our schedules never lined up, though. We shared a few other classes, but never Resource Room.

On a Saturday shortly after high school started, Geoff and I were at his house, doing our usual things: watching MSU football, playing video games, and shooting pool.

We were standing at opposite ends of the pool table when I decided to open up. "I found out something about myself," I told him.

"What?"

"You know how I'm in Resource Room? Well, I found out what my disability is. My parents told me that I'm autistic."

Geoff hadn't gone to Wardcliff Elementary. I tried to describe what I was like there: looking out the window for Cloud Nine, hiding under a table so I wouldn't miss *Iron Will*.

"And I still hate fire drills," I said. "I can't stand them."

Geoff shrugged. "Guess what? I've got a learning disability, too. You're autistic, and I have comprehension issues. Reading is harder than it should be. I misinterpret what I read. So, it's not a big deal. It's OK."

I'd unburdened myself to the right person.

More than ever, Geoff was my brother.

* * *

Geoff's house may have been a safe place for me, but the halls of Okemos High School weren't getting any easier. Day after day, guys ridiculed my Tigers and Spartans shirts. They rolled their eyes at my tongue-tied attempts to defend myself.

"Why don't they ever stop?" I whined. Geoff and I were walking from one class to the next. "What did I do to them? I'm so sick of it."

Maybe it's strange to imagine a six-foot six-inch guy crying about being bullied, but I didn't have the emotional toughness to go with my size.

Out of nowhere, Geoff grabbed my shirt collar and slammed me up against some lockers. I may have been tall, but I was a twig, and Geoff was muscular.

"It's not about what they think, it's about what you think," Geoff barked at me.

Students gave us strange looks. Was this going to be a fight? Weren't those two guys buddies? Traffic slowed around us.

"If you're wearing a shirt you think is good, wear it," he snapped.

"But I'm sick of the comments. It's every day. What did I do to them?"

"Who cares? It doesn't matter what they think." He still had me by the collar. "This shirt you're wearing, and whatever shirt you wear tomorrow, and the next day—if your opinion is that it's a good shirt, that's the only opinion that matters. And that goes for everything you say and do. Man, stop worrying about what anybody else thinks."

Geoff released me and started walking to class, ten feet ahead of me, like he hadn't even seen me that hour.

I trailed after him, stunned. What had just happened? He was supposed to be my best friend.

Pretty quickly, I realized that that's exactly what he was.

*   *   *

If I wanted a spot on the MSU roster, I'd have to start playing like I was worthy of it. My game needed to change, and fast. In middle school, basketball had been fun, but I hadn't approached the game with an eye toward improvement. I didn't worry about fundamentals like footwork and dribbling. I let my height, not actual skill, set me apart from the other guys on the court. If I wanted to show how wrong those predictions were—that I would never be an athlete and would never go to college—then I needed to start putting in the time and effort.

As soon as the freshman football season ended, I started rushing to the gym right after school every day. No team had the gym until at least thirty minutes after school got out. That half hour became my half hour. I shot free throws. I worked on my hook shot. I improved my post moves. I paid attention to my feet. Weekends and off days, it was more of the same. Mom had a key to the Okemos High School gym, and Dad had a key to the Breslin Center's auxiliary gym, so between the two, I had all the practice space I needed. And I took advantage of it.

I also benefited from having two college athletes for parents. When Dad took me to the Breslin to shoot, Mom came, too. She brought schoolwork along: assignments to grade, and plans for her next week of lessons. But before long she put her papers down and scrutinized my play.

"Why did you do that with your pivot foot?" she'd call. And I'd try the shot again.

"Don't bring that ball down," she'd say a minute later. "Keep it up. Above your head! Look at your elbows. What are you doing with your elbows?"

Mom had played against Michigan and Michigan State. She'd been part of Ohio University's coaching staff. Who was I to argue with her? Mom appreciated what an asset a good hook shot could be. When my hook shot was off, and everything I put up was clanking off the rim, Mom knew what correction needed to be made.

* * *

Guys were going to get cut. That was a fact. When two middle schools feed into one high school, you have boys who played on their eighth-grade team get cut from the freshman team. I didn't want to be in that group.

To be honest, I didn't fear getting cut. I was far and away the tallest kid from either middle school. I seemed a likely starter, but I knew the coach wouldn't hand me the spot on a silver platter. I had to bust my butt in practice every day and earn my place in the starting five.

I started all season, and we won a lot of games. One of our most memorable contests, though, was actually a loss. We were facing East Lansing, one of our local rivals, and we trailed by sixteen going into the fourth quarter. Instead of giving up, we fought back, and we dominated the final eight minutes. Everything I shot seemed to go in that quarter, and the same went for our guards. I finished the game with twenty-eight points, and the majority of those points were in the fourth quarter. We came back, only to lose by one point. Despite the loss, we realized as a team—and I realized as an individual—just how much we were capable of.

When we played Grand Rapids Ottawa Hills, I matched up against a taller player for one of the first times in my life. He had a few inches on me, and I had to figure out how to deal with that. I managed to score thirteen points, grab my share of rebounds, and defend him well enough. I emerged from that game with a lot of confidence. If I wanted to play high-level basketball, I'd have to get used to playing guys my height. In middle school I was the anomaly, but from now on, most teams would have an Anthony Ianni. Could I handle that?

If I wanted to be anything on the basketball court, I would have to.

# 12

## AAU

I HAD NEVER PLAYED FOR a team outside of Okemos. Okemos city rec leagues and Okemos school squads were all I knew. But if I was going to improve as a basketball player, that had to change. Once my freshman season ended, Dad started looking for an AAU team. "AAU" stands for "Amateur Athletic Union." AAU teams aren't affiliated with any high schools. Most elite players join AAU teams so they can square off against other top players. This prepares them for bigger and faster competition, and it also gets them noticed by recruiters. College teams across the country send talent scouts to the big AAU tournaments to find their future stars. Promising athletes join AAU teams by the time they're in fifth or sixth grade. There are even teams for seven-year-olds. I was fifteen, and I'd never played in an AAU game.

Dad feared that the wrong team could push me backward—permit bad habits and destroy my growing confidence. Some AAU teams loaded themselves with stars who played only for themselves, and some coaches all but encouraged selfish offense and undisciplined defense. I didn't know that, but my parents did. There was only one person to turn to for advice: Tom Izzo. Coach Izzo knew the various AAU teams and coaches in Michigan, and Coach also knew about my autism. Dad asked Coach Izzo what he thought, and Coach made some calls and lined up a tryout for me at a high school gym in Kalamazoo, about eighty minutes southwest of Okemos, for a team called the Michigan Mustangs.

As my parents and I drove toward Kalamazoo, we didn't know what to expect. One of my Okemos teammates, Tyler Stewart, was trying out, too. But everything else about the team was a mystery.

Actually, I'd heard about one guy: K.D. Bell. Basketball analysts ranked K.D. as one of the top freshman guards in Michigan. I worried that compared with him, I would look terrible.

"Go out there and just play," my dad said. "Show them what you can do. That's all you can do today."

We pulled up to Kalamazoo's Loy Norrix High School and found the gym. We spotted the coach and went to introduce ourselves.

"Do you have a nickname?" Coach Anthony Stuckey asked me.

"No, not really."

"Tell me your last name again."

"Ianni."

"I can't pronounce that. And nobody's calling you Anthony. There's already one Anthony on this court: me."

Coach Stuckey left it at that, and he started practice.

My parents took seats in the bleachers near Tyler Stewart's parents. If Mom and Dad worried about Coach Stuckey neglecting fundamentals, they didn't worry long. First we ran. Then we ran some more. Coach Stuckey put us through footwork drills, rebounding drills, and three-man weaves. It was an old-school, back-to-basics practice—exactly what my parents were looking for.

K.D. intimidated me. Not with trash talk or bullying, but with his game. The hype around him was real. K.D. slashed quickly through traffic, and he dribbled like a pro. He was strong and athletic. Was there really a place for me on the same team?

Afterward, Coach Stuckey waved Tyler and me over, and he gestured to our parents to join us. "I'm keeping both of you," he said. "I like what you guys bring to the table."

Then Coach Stuckey addressed me directly. "Now, about that nickname."

I waited.

"How about 'A.I.'?"

No one had ever called me that before. I loved it instantly.

"Yeah, Coach. You can call me A.I. That'd be cool."

I immediately thought of Allen Iverson. This was the spring of 2004, when Iverson was in his prime with the Philadelphia 76ers. Iverson had a few nicknames, and A.I. was one of them. My new coach wanted to call me A.I.? This was a good start!

Iverson was one of my favorite NBA players to watch, even though our games couldn't have been more different. He was small—he was listed as exactly six feet tall, but that may have been generous. He was a flashy dribbler who shot from anywhere. He had moves that could fake out opponents so bad they'd fall on their asses. His drives to the basket—through players a foot taller than he was—were sometimes reckless, often creative, and always fun to watch. My game, to the extent that I had one in ninth grade, was based on my size. I was tall, I could rebound, and I was learning how to post up and make shots from ten or fifteen feet out.

The other A.I. and I also had very different personalities and off-court styles. He wore cornrows and sported countless tattoos, and critics labeled him a thug. I followed rules, craved structure, and came from a comfortable subdivision and a high-achieving school district.

But I didn't care about those differences. He was a brilliant player. And if my new coach wanted to call me "A.I.," was I OK with it? Hell, yes!

I didn't know it then, but "A.I." had been applied to me once before. One of the kindergarten reports about me indicated that I was "AI."

Autistic impaired.

That's what "AI" means to people in the world of special education.

Whoever filled out that document never could have imagined what lay ahead for those two letters. By the time I was a junior at Okemos High School, the whole building called me "A.I." My teammates and coaches started it. The entire student body chanted it at basketball games. Teachers dropped "Anthony" in favor of my initials. Throughout the world of AAU basketball I was A.I. And it had nothing to do with being impaired.

A person who is impaired is weakened or damaged. I get why they wrote that. Autism did weaken me back then. I trailed my classmates in so many ways. But was I going to let autism weaken me permanently? Was I going to stay impaired forever? No way. Being autistic has made me stronger, not weaker. Because I'm on the spectrum, I can help others. I serve as a role model for those who want to dream but face obstacles.

Am I autistic? Proudly.

Am I impaired? Not even close.

\* \* \*

We played in our first tournament—in Midland, Michigan—a few weeks after that first practice. Okemos is halfway between Kalamazoo and Midland, so my parents and Tyler's invited the whole team to Okemos the night before our first game. After practicing in Kalamazoo, our team carpooled to Tyler's house for a team dinner. By then I'd learned my teammates' names. Cornell, an eighth-grader, was the youngest of us. Sid, one of our guards, talked a lot of trash, but it was way more funny than mean. David came from Muskegon, and Austin was from a small town called Cedar Springs. Mikel and Tommy had grown up in Kalamazoo with K.D. Half of the guys would be staying at Tyler's house and the other half at mine. It was just what Coach Stuckey wanted. "We're going to play as a team, and we're going to get to know each other as a team," he'd said. Tyler lived in Cornell Woods—the same subdivision that Geoff lived in. The houses were large, with bay windows and groomed lawns, and they all had attached garages.

When Cornell saw the sign announcing the subdivision's entrance, he said, "They knew I was coming! The neighborhood's named after me."

The garages surprised him, though.

"Mrs. I.," he asked my mom as we parked in Tyler's driveway, "do all houses in Okemos have garages like this? You know, big and connected to the house?"

"Most of them, I guess."

"That's not how it is in my neighborhood."

It was one of the first times I realized that Okemos was better off economically than a lot of other communities. Now I know that the issues extend far beyond attached garages, but that's when the differences first hit me.

We played three games our first day in Midland. In the morning game I came off the bench and scored four points. I didn't start in the afternoon game, either, but Coach Stuckey played me a lot, and I finished with ten points. That evening, we warmed up for our third game and then huddled. Coach Stuckey started pointing at guys. "All right. It's K.D., Sid, David, Austin, and A.I. You guys are gonna start this game."

I was starting at center for the Michigan Mustangs.

\* \* \*

Coach Stuckey pushed me, but he did it with patience. We were running our offense one practice, and a pass came to me in the post. The guy guarding me defended aggressively, and I froze. Coach Stuckey blew his whistle.

"You should have used a drop step, A.I.," he barked. "Drop step there, and you've got a high-percentage shot."

I gave him a blank look.

"You know what a drop step is?"

"No."

"That's OK. I'm glad you said so."

Coach Stuckey showed me how to catch the ball with both feet planted so I could "drop" either leg. He demonstrated how to fling my leg back so that it all but wrapped around the defender's leg, pinning him to the baseline and giving me a clear shot.

Coach Stuckey ran the shell drill often. The offensive players spread out around the perimeter and toss the ball quickly from player to player. The defense has to adjust fast, shifting their coverage constantly. Every single pass, the defense moves. After a while, this gets exhausting. The players on defense start reacting to the ball more slowly. They don't make it all the way to the spot they're supposed to hit. That's when Coach Stuckey would explode: "Defense, you're trying to take shortcuts! A.I., you look lazy! There are no shortcuts here. Nobody on this team takes a shortcut. If you take shortcuts on the court, you're gonna try to take shortcuts in life. And you'll learn the hard way that shortcuts don't work out there. You gotta dig and get to your spot fast, A.I. That goes for all of you. No shortcuts, you understand? Now do it again, and do it right."

Coach Stuckey knew that I needed more mental toughness, too. In basketball, everybody screws up: a bad shot, an ugly turnover, a dumb foul. The key is to put it behind you immediately. Make up for it. This is easier said than done. Mental toughness is like every other aspect of the game: it comes with practice.

The Michigan Mustangs had traveled to Cleveland for a tournament. One game, we trailed by a point with ten seconds to go. We had the ball, so we'd get one last shot. Coach Stuckey called for me to inbound the ball to K.D., who was going to be cutting sharply. If I timed the pass right, K.D. would have a good lane for a game-winning layup.

I misread K.D.'s cut and mistimed the pass. My pass sailed behind him, bounced across the empty court, and rolled out of bounds. K.D. stared at me. *What the hell kind of pass was that?* I'd just blown the game.

We had no choice but to foul now. They made the first free throw but missed the second, so we trailed by two.

We rushed down the court, looking for a last shot, but they fouled K.D. before he could get a look. It wasn't a shooting foul, so we got the ball underneath the basket with two seconds left. Coach Stuckey called time out.

"We're gonna run line," he said in the huddle. "We're gonna run it for A.I. Line up straight, and then move quick to the corner and open up that lane for A.I."

"Are you sure?" I said. I couldn't believe my coach was trusting me like this.

"Yeah, I'm sure. You're gonna tie the game for us."

Now it was K.D.'s turn to put it in my hands—and he was still pissed at me.

The whistle blew, my teammates bolted, and the lane opened. K.D. passed it perfectly, and I went up for the shot. The defender hit my wrist, my shot went in, and the ref called the foul.

Tie game. Half a second left. And I was going to the free throw line. I looked at Coach Stuckey, and he gave me a wink.

I stepped to the free throw line, gave the ball a few bounces, and took the same shot I'd taken thousands of times after school in the Okemos gym.

It went in. Game over.

K.D. gave me a big chest bump and smiled. "You're lucky."

"I know."

Not many coaches would have called the play for me, but Coach Stuckey did.

\* \* \*

I continued to rush to the gym every day after school. I worked on the drop step, like Coach Stuckey told me to. I also practiced hook shots more and more. I wanted the hook in my arsenal. When done right, a hook shot is deadly because it's almost impossible to defend. The shooter puts so much of his body between the ball and the defender that the shot can't be blocked. I practiced hundreds and hundreds of hook shots, mostly in the ten- to twelve-foot range. Both of my parents have pretty good hook shots themselves, so they observed and gave me pointers. I also watched videos of NBA players with legendary hook shots, especially Kareem Abdul-Jabbar.

Coach Stuckey had another shot for me to work on: the dunk.

For a big guy, I wasn't much of a dunker. That's because I didn't jump well. Coach Stuckey ordered me to start jumping rope: three sets of one hundred each day on both feet, three sets on my left foot, and three sets on my right. That's nine hundred jumps a day. "If you improve your jumping," he said, "you'll improve your whole game. Your quickness, your footwork. Everything else will follow."

In warm-ups before AAU games, most of my teammates threw down dunks, but I stuck to layups. I was afraid to dunk and miss.

"You need to dunk, Ant. Coach is right," Dad nagged on our way to one tournament. "You can't be afraid to miss. Never have a fear of failure. If you miss one, you miss one."

Warming up, I thought about dunking—everybody else was—but my first few trips through the line, I stuck with layups.

"What are you doing, Ant?" Dad snapped from the sideline. "What did I tell you? You gotta dunk it."

Anger surged through me. *Get off my back. Don't tell me how to play.*

I grabbed a ball and got in line. My next turn, I went at the hoop with ferocity. I took a running jump and absolutely *flushed* it. It was the most convincing dunk of my life.

Back in line, Austin laughed. "Is that all it takes?"

*  *  *

One day in May of my freshman year, I was called down to the athletic office. When I got there, the athletic director's secretary handed me a letter. It was from Indiana-Purdue Fort Wayne. The letter said they were interested in having me play basketball for their program. The letter came with a questionnaire asking me about my family, my grades, my favorite subjects, and my off-court interests.

I hurried back to history class with my letter. Geoff happened to be in that class, and I showed him immediately.

"That's awesome!" he said. "Do you think you'll go there?"

Nothing against IPFW, but I wasn't too tempted. I had a feeling there would be other letters. Sure enough, a few days later I had to stop by the athletic office again. The second letter was from Valparaiso.

Fortunately, nothing about the letters surprised my parents. "Do your best on the court and in the classroom, and let the recruiters come to you," they said. They'd just gone through the recruitment circus with my older sister. Recruiters had crowded the bleachers at Allison's tournaments and had paid special attention to her. One afternoon I had opened the mailbox and had found letters for her from Maryland, UCLA, and Penn State. Three major programs in one day! Allison had traveled around the country—Utah State, Auburn, Georgia, and Pacific—for on-campus visits, and coaches visited our house.

I called Allison in California, and she said the same things my parents did. Those two letters, she said, were the first of many. "Don't get wrapped up in the hype, Ant," she urged. "Keep taking care of business."

\* \* \*

Taking care of business meant hustling in practice, jumping rope at home, working on my hook shot and my drop step and my free throws after school, and battling the best players in the region at AAU tournaments. I had grown a few more inches my freshman year, and was approaching my eventual full height of six feet nine inches tall. I was still a big player, even by basketball standards, but I wasn't freakishly tall. Other teams had their big men, too. One game I matched up against a kid who was seven foot one. I held my own against him and finished the game with more confidence in my abilities than ever.

My freshman year at Okemos High School ended in June, but the AAU season continued for another month. We finished our schedule with a national tournament: the Super 64 in Las Vegas.

We faced stiff competition in Las Vegas. College scouts crammed the venues' bleachers, so the country's most talented players and AAU teams all showed up. The Mustangs got knocked out well before the finals, bringing our season to a close.

After our last game, I met with Coach Stuckey in the hotel lobby. We found some empty couches and sat down. "You're one of the hardest-working kids I've ever had the privilege of coaching, A.I.," he said. "Now, listen to me. You are varsity ready. If you want it and you believe it, then a spot on the varsity team is yours."

The idea had never occurred to me. Skipping JV and going straight to varsity as a sophomore?

"I want it, Coach."

"Then here's what you do. Every day, you wake up, you look into your mirror, and you tell yourself that you're going to be better today than you were yesterday. You stick with the jump rope. Calf raises. You take no shortcuts. You do all that, and *nobody* is going to take your spot on the Okemos varsity basketball team next year."

# 13

## #44

JOHNATHON JONES WAS ONLY A year ahead of me in school, but when I was a freshman, the difference seemed much greater. I was just a kid, and he already was a legend in the making. He quarterbacked the varsity football team while I played on the freshman squad. JJ didn't just start for Okemos's varsity basketball team: he provided leadership. JJ didn't shout or hoot much. He led by example, with his work ethic and his competitiveness. He exuded calm, even in tense situations.

As a freshman, I watched the varsity games from the stands. (The ninth-grade team played hours before varsity, to half-empty gyms with no student section.) I also caught some of JJ's games at AAU tournaments. He played for a Lansing-based team, in the division a year older than mine. There was a lot of hype around JJ in Okemos, and I saw that he was as good as advertised. I couldn't wait for him to be my teammate.

That summer a lot of guys regularly showed up for open gym at Okemos High School. Basketball season was months away, but everybody held high expectations—of a league championship, and more. The JV players scrimmaged against each other on one court, and the guys who assumed they would play varsity took the next court over. I showed up for the first open gym not knowing which scrimmage to join. Coach Stuckey had urged me to go grab my place on varsity, but when I entered the gym, I drifted toward the JV court. Those were the players I knew, my teammates from the previous season.

We hadn't been scrimmaging long when JJ interrupted our game and waved me over. "Your butt's over here," he ordered.

I knew it wasn't my place to argue, so I silently followed him back to the varsity game.

"You're playing with us now. Got it?"

*　*　*

Later that summer, Dad received an email from his brother Rob, who lived in Texas. "Look what I found," Uncle Rob wrote. "So cool! So proud of Anthony."

Next was a link to "Michigan Rivals," which followed prep sports across the state. The website rated high school basketball players by grade and position. I skipped over the seniors and the juniors, and I skipped over the guards. Finally: sophomore centers.

I was number one.

Before Uncle Rob's email, I didn't even know these rankings existed—and now I discovered I was the top-ranked sophomore center in the state of Michigan.

It was a thrill to see my name on that list, and I let myself enjoy it. But the work wasn't done. Far from it. I hadn't played one game of varsity basketball yet.

"It's nice to be recognized," Dad cautioned me, "but rankings don't mean much right now. It's too early." (He said the same thing my senior year of college, when Michigan State put together some good wins and we shot to number six in the country. "It's way too early in the season for that number to mean anything," Dad stressed. "The only thing that matters is the last team standing.")

Dad was right. But try telling that to kids at school. That September, word quickly spread that I'd been rated Michigan's top sophomore center. Suddenly, kids who'd bullied me for years eased up. Guys who had duped me into thinking my Three

Stooges impressions were funny now showed me some reluctant respect. A few months earlier they had mocked me for my wardrobe. Now they found ways to give me props. As if I would forget the last four years. As if none of their cruelty had registered or meant anything.

The first week of school, I reunited with friends and acquaintances I hadn't seen since June. "Hey, Ianni," they said.

"Call me A.I.," I told them.

"A.I.?"

"Yeah. A.I. It's what my basketball team calls me."

My friends quickly made the switch, and word of my new nickname spread.

That fall, my Resource Room period fell late in the day. I liked having it in the afternoon. I tried to complete all of my assignments during Resource Room so that I didn't take any work home. Did I rush through the assignments at times? Yeah, I did. When questions didn't make sense, especially in math and biology, I clutched my head and exhaled heavily. My Resource Room teacher, Mrs. Shafer, recognized my distress signals. She sat next to me and asked if I was OK. I confessed how stressed I felt and admitted that I was ready to wig out.

"This assignment is too tough," I complained. "And this other one is supposed to be easy, but I tried this supposedly easy one, and it's hard, too."

"Only one assignment at a time, OK? Let's do the hard assignment first, and forget about the others for now." She turned my geometry book toward her and scanned the page. Mrs. Shafer broke the first problem into small steps and walked me through each. Then she did the same with the next problem. I began to relax.

My difficulties in math may surprise some people. Many people on the autism spectrum, especially people who have Asperger's or another type of high-functioning autism, have success in math. But not me. The autism community is a diverse one, and if you start making assumptions about any of us—like assuming math comes easily to me—you're going to get it wrong.

Mrs. Shafer hung a Muhammad Ali poster in the Resource Room. This Ali quote was on it: "Champions aren't made in gyms. Champions are made from something they have deep inside them—a desire, a dream, a vision. They have to have last-minute stamina, they have to be a little faster, they have to have the skill and the will. But the will must be stronger than the skill."

I reread that poster a lot. *Champions aren't made in gyms.* I wasn't sure how it applied to me, but I sensed that it did.

Most Resource Room students had the same accommodations when it came to tests. Our teachers allowed us extra time, and Mrs. Shafer often read the tests to us. I don't think anyone else in Resource Room was on the autism spectrum, but I couldn't say for sure. We didn't talk about our disabilities with each other. Geoff was still the only classmate who knew I was autistic.

Even with Mrs. Shafer's help and accommodations, tests didn't go well. To be honest, I hurried through my reviews the night before a test. Sometimes I even rushed through the tests themselves. When it was a test that didn't affect my grade, like a state-issued standardized exam, I raced through the bubbles lightning fast. Why prolong the misery?

One evening I came home from school with two bad tests in my backpack: a C-minus and a D. Mom asked to see them.

We sat at the dinner table with the two tests between us. "I know you studied for these," she said, "so why didn't you do well on either one? Did you not study enough?"

"I don't know."

"Did you only study the night before the test?"

"I don't know."

"This isn't good enough, Anthony. You need to do a better job on your tests."

I pushed against the table with rigid fingers. "Tests are just really hard. Having autism makes me a bad test taker. I don't know what else you want me to do."

Mom's voice rose. "Don't you ever pull that autism card with me. I've seen you have good test scores. Look at how you've done on history and geography tests. So these grades—" she pointed at my C-minus and my D—"that's on *you,* not on the autism. And don't you ever again try to use your autism as a crutch. Once you start making something a crutch, it *stays* a crutch, and you're not going down that road."

\* \* \*

Sophomore year was the first autumn in years that I didn't play football. I didn't miss it for a minute. Dropping football freed my afternoons to work on basketball. The varsity football coach called and encouraged me to go out for varsity that year. Now that I was six foot nine, he said, the starting tight end spot was mine for the taking. I thanked him for the offer, but declined.

Friday nights that fall I went to all of the Okemos home games, but I could sit in the bleachers with Geoff and my other friends, rooting for our team but still free to goof around and have fun. We cheered for JJ, who quarterbacked the Okemos team, and for Mike Emerson, another basketball player who also shined on the football field. Afterward, we grabbed some Taco Bell or some junk food from Quality Dairy (a Lansing area mini-mart) and spent the night at Geoff's house, staying up late in his basement, playing wrestling video games and shooting pool.

Athletically, it was a mellow autumn for me, but I knew the pressure was coming: varsity basketball.

Coach Dan Stolz was nothing like Coach Stuckey. I'd spent the spring and summer adjusting to Coach Stuckey's vocal approach. Coach Stuckey put his emotions right out there for the whole gym to see. He shook his fists, and when we screwed up he leaped like he was still in his playing days: "K.D., come *on*!" he blurted after one bad turnover, almost hitting the rafters. "What was *that*!" Coach Stuckey yelled, but he yelled because he wanted us to be better. He patted us on the back as often as he yelled.

Coach Stolz, by contrast, was chill. He kept his emotions in check. He didn't storm along the sideline. Instead, he crouched. (His demeanor came in handy with calmer sports like golf and tennis, which he also coached.) Coach Stolz never let go of his clipboard—he took a cerebral approach to basketball. He respected his players, and he respected the game.

Tryouts exhausted me. My running wasn't pretty, but I kept up well enough with the other big guys. Coach Stolz called out drills, and I recognized all of them. I executed my shots and defended with confidence. *It's your spot*, I kept telling myself, remembering my orders from Coach Stuckey. *Don't let anyone take your spot on varsity.* I utilized my post moves, especially my hook shot. We scrimmaged, and I seized my share of rebounds and put-backs. My jumping still wasn't going to blow anyone away, even though I'd spent the summer skipping rope. But at least it was better.

When I missed a shot, I tried to forget it instantly. *Make up for it*, I told myself. *Get a block. Draw a charge.* I remembered the game in Cleveland, how I'd thrown away the ball and the game seconds before playing the hero. That's the beauty of basketball: it offers plenty of opportunities for redemption.

With one day of tryouts left, Coach Stolz pulled me aside after practice.

"I'm going to put you on varsity, A.I.," he said.

"I won't let you down, Coach."

"We still have another day to go. Don't tell anyone yet that you're on varsity."

I was happy and proud, but I didn't run around the building whooping with joy. I'd been preparing for this all summer with the Mustangs. I'd come to expect this for myself. I'd made varsity. So what? Making the team didn't mean I'd play. I hadn't contributed to a single victory yet.

"You got a number in mind, A.I.?"

"I was thinking 42."

For years I'd planned to wear 42 for Okemos. That number had belonged to Mark Kissling, the guy who shot baskets with me after practice when I was still an elementary school kid waiting for my mom's volleyball practice to finish.

"Sorry," Coach Stolz said. "I already promised that to Tyler."

Coach Stolz intended to have Tyler Stewart start the year on the JV team, where he would get a lot more playing time, but then bring him up for the playoffs.

"You want 50?" Coach Stolz said. "You want 44? That isn't taken."

"Yeah, I'm good with 44."

That night, Dad told me what his number had been at Dexter High School: 44. And Mom's number, I learned, had been 22—exactly half.

I didn't get my first choice, but I ended up getting the number I was supposed to wear. I kept it for the rest of career—high school and college. I wore 44 with pride, feeling the connection between my parents and me.

My number, incidentally, was right next to Rudy's number at Notre Dame. He wore 45.

\* \* \*

The same year I started high school, Okemos joined a newly created conference called the Capital Area Activities Conference, or CAAC. From the start, the conference looked like a powerhouse basketball league. Sure enough, Lansing Everett High School won the CAAC title that year and proceeded to win the state championship. Everett's lineup included Goran Suton, who played for Coach Izzo at Michigan State, and Derick Nelson, who signed with Oakland University. Of course, Lansing-area basketball fans and Michigan State supporters are quick to point out Lansing Everett's most famous alumnus: Magic Johnson.

The bottom line was, if you could hang with the best in the CAAC, you could hang with anybody.

Coach Stolz started me the second game of the season against nonconference opponent Holly, a rural district about fifty miles to the east. My first varsity start also happened to be my first varsity double-double: ten points and ten rebounds. I thought that performance would guarantee me the starting spot, but Coach Stolz saw something in my game that worried him. Ugly running. A lack of mental toughness. Immaturity. The kid capable of autistic outbursts still lingered inside me. In the locker room, I could be sensitive. When guys teased me for being the team's kid brother and gave me a hard time about my sprints being half stork and half penguin, I retreated to a corner and put a towel over my head. "Can you tell them to back off," I quietly asked JJ or Mike Emerson. Nobody meant any harm, and soon most of my older teammates had taken me under their wing, but Coach Stolz probably was asking himself a fair question: If A.I. can't handle affectionate teasing from guys who care about him, how will he deal with the pressures of a road game—and an opposing gym's booing and jeers?

Our team ate together the night before every game that season. Each family took its turn hosting. My mom and JJ's mom partnered up, so when the team ate at my house, JJ's mom helped out, and vice versa. They laid out the pasta, chicken, steaks, salads, and pies together. Twice a week, all winter long, the fifteen players and their families came together like this. I started thinking of the entire team as my brothers, especially Mike and JJ. Parents grew close, too. If we gathered at a house with a finished basement, the parents claimed the dining room for themselves, and the other players and I took our food downstairs. Every dinner felt like a family reunion.

We picked up some good wins to start the season, but after the Holly game, my playing time dwindled.

JJ often gave me a ride home after practice that year. One night I told him, "I'm ready to play anywhere, anytime."

"Yeah, I know."

"I don't know why Coach isn't using me more. Those run-and-gun teams, like Sexton and Everett, they don't scare me. I played against big and fast teams all summer in AAU."

JJ turned into my subdivision. "That's why I talked with Coach Stolz about you. I told him you can handle it. That you're not just a project player. I said we're not just grooming you for next year. We need you this season."

We rode in the dark.

"Something else, A.I.," he continued. "I know what's going on with you. I know about your autism. And it's cool. Your mom told my mom. I got your back, OK?"

A few days later, I had one of the worst practices of my life. Nothing went right in a single drill. By the end, I was fighting tears. JJ and my other teammates must have seen my face quivering. I barely said a word to JJ on the ride home. An hour after he dropped me off, my phone rang.

"You OK, A.I.?"

"No. I was terrible today."

"What do you mean, you were terrible? What made it a bad practice?"

"I wasn't making anything."

"That's how it goes. Everybody has practices when they don't make shots."

"And I kept missing assignments. Offense, defense, everywhere."

"You're fine, A.I. That's why it's called practice. You screw up in practice, and you learn from it. Just don't do it in a game."

I exhaled. "I won't."

The camaraderie our team had extended beyond the court, the bus, and the team dinners. Even in the school's halls, the older guys treated me like a brother. They waved me over to join their conversations. They put their arm around my shoulders. They insisted I walk with them. I was headed to Resource Room and they were going to honors and Advanced Placement classes, but that didn't matter. Not when you're family.

In the middle of the season, we hosted an important game against Lansing Sexton. I didn't start, but Coach Stolz used me as one of his first substitutes. The game got chippy, and we ended up losing. After the final buzzer, JJ crossed the court toward our bench in an agitated daze. The Sexton players celebrated and their fans cheered, while JJ ignored everyone around him. He accidentally bumped into one of the referees. The ref immediately signaled a technical foul and ejected JJ from the game, even though the game was already over. The ejection meant JJ would have to sit a game.

JJ served his suspension when we played East Lansing on the road. With JJ watching from the sidelines, Bobby Albers and Ivan Parker stepped up, and we pulled off the victory. We were in a joking mood on the quick bus trip home. JJ said, "Dang, A.I., sometimes you get the ball and look like you're surprised it's in your hands. Like you're scared of it, man."

"No, I'm not."

"You gotta shoot that ball. Can't be afraid to make your move and put it up."

"If you don't shut up," I said, "I'm going to make sure you get suspended again."

The comeback made no sense. Why would I get my own teammate suspended? *How* would I get my own teammate suspended?

Trash talk is a part of most sports. On team buses and during practice, trash talk is a good way to get guys laughing and have fun. I didn't always catch the wordplay and the sarcasm, but I'd laugh, anyway, so I didn't stand out or look stupid. During games, players try to get in their opponents' heads by talking smack. *You don't even belong out here, man. We're gonna mop the floor with you. You can't shoot, man. You ain't got nothing.* Two guys from my AAU team, Sid and Mikel, were particularly clever and jabbered constantly. They used goofy voices and tossed in rap lyrics. It drove the other teams nuts.

I knew better than to try.

\* \* \*

Lansing Everett was defending its CAAC trophy and the state title that season, but Everett had lost its stars to graduation, so the CAAC title was up for grabs. We wanted it. But we weren't alone.

Another school to join the new conference was Holt. Like Okemos, Holt is a suburb of Lansing. Like Okemos, Holt had a talented basketball team with a good shot of winning the CAAC title. We were in each other's way.

The conditions were perfect for a rivalry.

We faced each other twice that season, first in Okemos and then in Holt. The first match-up went to overtime, and Holt pulled out the victory on our court. The second contest went to *triple*-overtime, and we beat them on their court, 93–87. The win wasn't enough to put us ahead of Holt in the league standings, though. They won the CAAC title, and we finished in second, a game behind them.

With the regular season behind us, it was time for the state playoffs. A fresh start. If we were good enough to almost win the CAAC, we were good enough to make a deep playoff run. And who did we draw in the first round?

Holt.

After two overtime games that season, Holt and Okemos had grown to dislike each other. Fouls were a little harder. Insults were sharper. We'd wanted the conference title, and they'd snatched it from us. We saw an opportunity for payback.

Unfortunately, Holt beat us in the playoffs, 72–58. Our season was over.

We watched Holt win one game after another, making it to the state championship game, where they faced Romulus at the Breslin Center. Holt led by eleven points early in the fourth quarter, only to see it dwindle to a one-point lead with less than a minute to go. They held on to win, 65–62. Holt had won the state championship. We had beaten them, *in their gym*, but they were the ones to hoist not only the CAAC trophy but also the state championship trophy.

We had let an opportunity slip away.

It wouldn't happen again.

# 14

## FAMILY

I RETURNED TO THE MICHIGAN Mustangs for another spring and summer of AAU ball, but my focus was already on Okemos's next season. Our two starting big guys, forward Drew Yancey and center Peter Sauer, were graduating. I knew I had to step up. Most of the teams in our conference had at least one talented player who was close to seven feet tall. I needed to be that player for Okemos.

That spring, more recruitment letters arrived from colleges. They weren't serious offers. They weren't guarantees. They were just letters of interest that included the usual questionnaires. One letter came from the University of Michigan.

"Take a look at this," I said, showing one of my buddies in class after retrieving the letter from the athletics department. He was a University of Michigan fan and insulted MSU whenever he could.

"Would you really go?"

I shrugged. "If that's the best offer, what am I going to say?"

"I can't believe it."

I thought of the one U of M fan in my family: Grandpa Nick. He would have gotten a kick out of that letter.

Another piece of mail arrived that spring: an invitation to the Adidas Top Ten All-American Camp. My AAU performances had earned me the invite to the three-day showcase in Atlanta.

I didn't want to go.

My apprehensions began almost as soon as I opened the envelope with the big Adidas logo. Who would my roommate be? What if I said something dumb in front of him? What if I didn't understand what other people were saying? What if the other players made me look bad? What if they timed our runs?

I was comfortable sleeping at Geoff's house, but Geoff was my best friend. The Adidas camp was a hotel room in Atlanta with a kid from some other part of the country. Who knew what expressions and slang they used where he was from?

I was asked to join a prestigious basketball camp, and all I could do was dread the hotel room.

"It's nice I made their list," I told my dad, "but I don't know. It's the best guys in the country, playing in front of a ton of college recruiters. That's a lot of stress."

"What about your tournament in Vegas last year?" he said. "That had the best competition in the nation, with colleges watching every game. You handled that. Think of this as Vegas all over again. This is a good opportunity to face guys who will play at the college level and let recruiters see you, too."

I didn't admit my other fear: that I didn't want to room with a stranger and misspeak in front of him.

We flew to Atlanta a night early, and I stayed with my parents the first night. I didn't want to leave their room, but camp rules said I had to. I planned to be extremely careful when I spoke.

My roommate was a guy from Utah named Brady. He was easy to talk to—about sports, our hometowns, our school teams. We watched *SportsCenter* together and flipped through channels when nothing good was on ESPN. I relaxed, but not completely. We were getting along; I didn't want to screw it up with a stupid comeback. What if he joked that Michigan State wasn't that good? How would I answer?

The court was more relaxing than the hotel room for me. We started with shooting drills and ball-handling drills, and I knew all of them from Coach Stolz's practices. I breathed a sigh of relief when I scanned the agenda and saw no timed runs on our program.

The camp put me on a team with eight other players, and we scrimmaged a lot. Our coach was from Philadelphia. He showed us some plays that we had to learn quickly. When he told me explicitly what my movements were, I was fine. If I wasn't a key component of the play, though, and he didn't deliver the instructions directly to me, I felt a little lost.

There were definitely some guys there who were a level above me, but I made some shots and displayed a variety of post moves for the colleges.

And I avoided saying anything ridiculous.

\*   \*   \*

My Resource Room period shifted to the morning my junior year. I preferred having it in the afternoon, but I could live with it. Often I did my work on the floor in Mrs. Shafer's room, with my back against the wall near her whiteboard. Mrs. Shafer didn't mind, as long as we were comfortable and used our time well. One of my favorite classes was social studies. Once I learned a date, it stuck. World War I began in 1914 and ended in November 1918. The Japanese attacked Pearl Harbor on December 7, 1941. President Kennedy was assassinated in Dallas on November 22, 1963. Movies locked in the information even more, whether it was a documentary or *Forrest Gump.*

From the first day of school, I had basketball on my mind. I wanted a conference championship. To avenge our losses to Holt. I wanted to play in the state's final four in the Breslin Center. I wanted to be the best basketball team in Michigan. But, a week into my junior year, more than a month before we even could hold our first practice, my season almost ended.

Coach Stolz was my gym teacher that year for a class called Team Sports. He took us outside on those first sunny days of September.

Ultimate Frisbee today, he said one morning.

I'm not a great runner, and I'm not much of a leaper, but one thing I can be in an ultimate Frisbee game is a big target with good hands. In some ways the game was a repeat of the volleyball tournament in middle school. Some of my teammates and opponents were content to let the game happen around them. Win or lose—it didn't matter. But I was as competitive as ever, and when a high pass zipped my way, I jumped for it like it was a crucial fourth-quarter rebound.

My friend Ben Burmeister had been running for the same pass. He saw me jump and tried to put on the brakes, but he lost his footing and crashed into my legs. The collision completely undercut me, and I flipped in the air. I landed hard on my arm, and my shoulder popped out of its socket. I stayed on the ground, unable to move.

Coach Stolz remained as calm as ever. When he saw me lying on the ground, he may have feared that I was seriously injured, that our team's chances of a state championship were threatened, and that my own future in basketball could be jeopardized, but nothing in his face or his voice indicated worry.

"Take it easy, A.I.," he said. "Once you can sit up, we'll have your mom come get you and have this looked at."

Coach Stolz must have known it was bad, but he sounded like I'd done nothing more than stub my toe.

The X-ray indicated that I had broken and displaced my humerus—a bone in my upper arm. I underwent a fifty-minute surgery that night, and I threw myself into physical therapy immediately. I knew what was at stake. The original prediction was that I wouldn't return to the basketball court until January or February. That was no good. I'd miss half the season or more, and then when I finally returned, my game would be completely off and I'd be useless out there.

I reported for gym class every day, and every day Coach Stolz saw his starting center in a sling. If he was worried, he didn't show it. "You're going to be fine, A.I.," Coach said. "You're going to come back better and stronger than ever."

Fearing I had completely let down my coaches, my team-mates, and my school, I worked my tail off in rehab that fall. I pushed that arm and shoulder; I followed the therapist's every instruction. I could feel it getting stronger. October came and went, and basketball tryouts approached.

Two days into tryouts, my doctor gave the verdict.

Completely recovered.

I was cleared for every aspect of the game: not just shooting, but rebounding, guarding, physical contact, the shoving and colliding that goes on underneath the basket. Miraculously, I wouldn't miss a beat.

\* \* \*

Once tryouts ended and the season approached, we resumed our team dinners. JJ's parents hosted one of the first gatherings, and they urged parents to attend, too. The adults drank beer and wine in JJ's living room while we played Ping-Pong and video games in the basement. This team seemed even more like a family than the previous year's. Every one of those guys felt like a brother to me.

This was going to be JJ's year. We all could sense it. JJ had a chance to show he was one of the best players in the state. We expected him to break school records and become Okemos's all-time leader in points, steals, and assists. I wanted a lot of those assists to go to me. JJ and I could become the Kobe and Shaq of Okemos. JJ was Kobe Bryant, the brilliant guard with all the moves and a ton of creativity. And I was Shaquille O'Neal, the big presence inside whose hands were always ready for a pass or a rebound. If JJ got in trouble driving the lane, he could dish it off to me, and even if the pass was near my ankles, I'd bail him out with a deft catch and a quick post move.

We won the first few games of the season, but Coach Stolz and his assistant, Carter Briggs, weren't thrilled with my play. They felt my opponents pushed me around too much. Other teams' big guys had more upper-body strength than I did, and they used it to their advantage. I had stronger legs than a lot of my opponents did, but I wasn't using them.

Coach Briggs was six feet eight inches tall and solidly built. He had played basketball for Lansing Community College and Central Michigan University in the 1980s. Briggs had a variety of post moves in his arsenal, but he also shot well from three-point range. He was at least twenty years older than us, but he loved to take the floor against us and go one on one. And when he burned you, believe me, he crowed about it. Briggs still had great moves, and Coach Stolz assigned him to work with me and our other bigs.

Briggs guided me threw hook shots and up-and-unders the way Mrs. Shafer helped me tackle math problems: by breaking them into tiny and manageable chunks. He gave me an exact number of steps to take for each move, and an exact number of dribbles. When I pressed for more details—big steps or little? straight steps or diagonal?—Coach Briggs answered patiently. He wanted me to get it right as much as I did. We were all in this together. We were family.

The whole state of Michigan—coaches, sports writers, college recruiters—knew we had a great team. And Okemos High School knew that the whole state knew. The building buzzed with energy. Everyone sensed we would win and win and keep on winning. Fans packed the bleachers for every home game. Their craziness made each contest feel like a cross between a playoff game and a party. Our fans' costumes and chants and cheers boosted us. They were part of the family, too.

I have seen the movie *Hoosiers* probably a hundred times. It's one of my favorites. It's right up there with *Rudy*. In most ways, our story that year had little in common with the Hickory Huskers, the team that Gene Hackman coaches in the movie. The Huskers barely have enough guys to form a team, their season is full of instability and controversy, and they are underdogs for their entire playoff run. The one connection I see between the movie's Hickory Huskers and my real-life Okemos Chiefs is that each team brought a community together. Our fans generated so much energy for us that season. Students developed wardrobe themes for each game: Hawaiian night, white-out, maroon-out, and so on. One of my favorites that season was toga night. I'm not sure how there is a direct connection between wearing a toga and firing up your team, but it worked in Okemos. My parents and my teammates' parents generally stayed away from the lunacy of the O-Zone, preferring to sit on the other side of center court, near our bench.

The kids in the O-Zone developed chants for each player announced in the starting lineup. When Denny Means was introduced each game, the Okemos faithful thundered, "Denny! Means! Business!" For JJ, it was "J-Train!" ("J-Train" was a carryover from football season. JJ was our starting quarterback that year, and he earned the nickname after a long touchdown run.) For me, every game they roared, "A! I! A! I!" They shaped an "A" and then an "I" with their arms. We weren't just playing for ourselves. We were playing for the entire student body, and all of the staff, and our entire town. If we could win that state championship, it wouldn't just be for ourselves. It would be for everyone.

\* \* \*

Every aspect of JJ's game was clicking. He drove with confidence, hit jumpers, drained threes, the works. He drew so much attention from defenders that it freed up the rest of us to play our games and make our baskets. Whenever teams paid too much attention to JJ, he distributed the ball to the rest of us, me included.

One game I attempted an up-and-under—a move where you pretend to go up for a shot, get your defender off his feet or at least on his toes and then pivot and swing under his outstretched arm for a layup. My up-and-under failed miserably, and the defender blocked my shot. At our next time-out, Coach Stolz pulled me aside. "Do you know why the up-and-under didn't work, A.I.?"

"No."

"You didn't sell the fake. Your 'up' wasn't big enough. Watch me. Watch how far I go, and how fast."

Coach Stolz demonstrated a perfect up-and-under.

I asked, "So I should take the fake up here, this high?"

"Go an inch or two higher. There. And it has to be fast. Sell the fake."

There is no one way to coach an autistic athlete. There is no one way to coach *any* athlete. Breaking a move down into small and logical parts worked for me. But so did Coach Stuckey's more animated approach. Coach Stolz showed he cared through patience and quiet respect. Coach Stuckey jumped and yelled. I absolutely knew both men cared about me. That's what mattered.

\* \* \*

Holt was the twelfth game on our schedule that season. We would be playing them in late January, in their gym. We won our first eleven games that season. So did Holt. Two undefeated teams. The season was only half over, but whoever won would,

for the moment, take sole possession of first place in the conference. The winner also would send the message that it might be
the best in the state.

For me, playing Holt meant facing Paul Crosby.

Paul was Holt's big man inside. Like me, Paul was a junior. I
was a few inches taller than he was, but he weighed at least forty
pounds more than I did and could outmuscle me. We paid attention to Holt's results, and our coaching staff watched Holt's
films. Paul was having his way inside. In the days before the
Holt game, Coach Briggs spent a lot of time with me, preparing
me for Paul Crosby.

"He's got more upper body strength than you, A.I.," Briggs
said, "but you've got stronger legs. You need to use them. They're
your leverage."

Coach Briggs worked me over. He banged against me and
made me defend shot after shot.

"Paul Crosby loves the baseline," Briggs said. "You've got to
anticipate that. When you know he's gonna go baseline, you've
got to get there first. Plant your feet and draw the charge. Set
yourself, and let him knock you down. He wants that baseline,
A.I. Don't let him have it."

After school that Friday, we boarded the bus for the short trip
from Okemos to Holt. I wasn't looking out the window as we
pulled into Holt High School's parking lot. Then I heard intense
banging. People were pounding on the side of the bus. What
was this? Had Holt's student body come out to harass us? Our
team swarmed to one side of the bus and looked. The crowd,
we realized, was on our side. They were supporters! Half of
Okemos was in the Holt parking lot. They'd come hours early,
and they were banging on the bus as a sign of encouragement.
As we inched through the crowd, I noticed lawn chairs and barbecue grills. Then I smelled the burgers and the brats. It was
twenty degrees out, and they were tailgating. Our community

had come together, for us. At that moment, I fully appreciated what this team meant to our town. We couldn't let them down.

Unfortunately, we did.

We had a ten-point lead in the fourth quarter, but against Holt, there is no such thing as a safe lead. They made basket after basket in the final eight minutes, and we couldn't do anything. I threw everything I had at Paul Crosby, but he still found ways to score. So did their guards. Our lead disappeared. Holt tied the game, and that's how it stood as the clock ran out. We headed to overtime. The third Okemos-Holt game to go to overtime in the last four match-ups.

Holt pulled ahead in overtime, and they stayed ahead.

Our first defeat of the season.

They were in the driver's seat now.

We didn't let the loss derail us. We won the next game, and the next, and the next. We started a new winning streak, and we waited for our rematch with Holt.

Then, Lansing Everett did us a huge favor. A week and a half after our loss to Holt, Everett went into Holt's gym and won a close one, 70–67. This changed everything. If we took care of business one game at a time and then beat Holt when they came to Okemos for the scheduled rematch, the CAAC title would be ours.

And that's what happened. At the end of February, when we faced Holt in our gym, we still had one loss, and so did they. Whoever won would take the CAAC and would be favored to go all the way to the state championship game.

So much hype surrounded the game, and so many people called Okemos High School about tickets in the days leading up to the game, that the Breslin Center contacted our athletic director and offered to host the game there. Our athletic director came to our team and asked us what we thought.

We don't want to make it to the Breslin floor that way, we said. When we play in the Breslin, we told him, we want to be in the state semifinals and finals. No shortcuts.

The game would be played in our gym.

Tickets sold out long before game time, of course. Normally when Okemos hosts Friday basketball games, the three teams—freshman, JV, and varsity—play back to back to back. Our coaches and our athletic director feared that the gym and parking lot couldn't handle the swarm of three contests, so the freshmen played a day early. JV still played right before we did. JV games usually happen in a half-empty gym, but because people wanted to get there early and claim their seats, the Okemos and Holt JV teams battled in front of a full and rowdy house. Our young guys loved it.

Once the varsity game started, our gym got even noisier and even crazier. The O-Zone was rocking, and we fed off of them. Holt's strategy was to shut down JJ. They focused on him all game, which meant our other starting guard, Ivan Parker, had a little bit of breathing room. Ivan scored ten for us. Bobby Albers, one of our starting forwards, also benefited from Holt's stop-JJ-no-matter-what approach. Bobby scored fourteen that night. I contributed nine points. We built a second-half lead, just as we had the first time we played Holt. And we let it slip away. Again. An eleven-point lead became a one-point deficit with a little over two minutes to go.

But the last two minutes went our way. We got the rebounds. We made the right passes. We drained the free throws. Final score: Okemos 56, Holt 49.

Our fans, who had been going nuts from the opening tip, somehow increased their volume as the final seconds ticked off. The CAAC title was ours.

\* \* \*

Allison came home from California that winter. She'd had some conflicts with coaches at the University of the Pacific, and a scholarship position had opened at Michigan State. Allison lived at home for a month until her apartment near the Breslin Center became available. She came to all of my games, and often she brought some MSU volleyball teammates.

When I started high school, teachers knew me as Allison Ianni's younger brother. I couldn't match her popularity or her academic success. I didn't lead the way she did, and I didn't try. One report, though, assumed I did. This was written at the end of my freshman year:

> Review Anthony's schedule for his sophomore year making certain that he is not overloading himself with many demanding academic classes. This examiner is concerned that Anthony seems to feel that he has to follow the same track as his older sister who did not have any specific learning difficulties and was, in fact, quite a gifted student and athlete. Anthony's parents, along with his teacher consultant and school counselor, should help him to understand the nature of his disability and appreciate the many gains that he has made throughout his academic career so far.

Why would they write this? Why would I want to stop pushing myself? Why would I want to settle for "the many gains" I'd made? I was just getting started! And if they thought my parents would encourage me to lower my expectations, they did not know Mom and Dad.

I knew I wasn't Allison. I don't remember thinking I had to sign up for all the advanced classes she'd taken. I never tried to match her legacy. But as the basketball team entered the postseason, I wanted to do one thing that Allison hadn't done: bring home a state championship for Okemos.

Not surprisingly, a few games into the playoffs, we collided with Holt.

We were playing the Rams for the sixth time in two years. Three games had gone to overtime. Four of the games had league-title ramifications. This was the second meeting in the playoffs. The rivalry was fever pitch now. For me, it meant another battle down low with Paul Crosby. Coach Briggs worked me hard in the days before the third Holt game, especially on defense. He wanted quick feet. He wanted my hands in Paul's face. Every point Paul scored, he'd have to earn.

Because it was the playoffs, we faced off in a neutral location, the Don Johnson Fieldhouse in Lansing. This was a short trip for both schools. This probably goes without saying by now, but I'll say it anyway: our supporters sold the place out.

We played the most perfect first quarter of our season and established a 22–4 lead. The eighteen-point lead didn't last. Holt came back, and so did Paul Crosby. Defensively, I threw everything I had at Paul—my forearm never left his body, and we fought for position on every play—but he found ways to score. Their guards started finding the basket, too. Our lead shrank to nine, and then five, and then it was gone. Holt took the lead early in the fourth quarter, 36–35, but we countered with a three and never surrendered the lead again. With the seconds ticking down, Holt rushed up the court trailing by four. They heaved a desperation three. The shot clanked off the rim to my teammate Ivan Parker, whose momentum was carrying him out of bounds. Leaning, Ivan passed to me, and I dribbled away from traffic to kill the last few seconds. The buzzer sounded, and I chucked the ball toward the rafters. We'd done it! JJ sprinted to our bench and raised his hands to our crowd. I followed him and did the same. We gave as many high-fives as we could. It was pandemonium in the O-Zone. Building security swept in to prevent our fans from storming the court.

We were two wins away from the Breslin Center.

Next we faced Dexter, my dad's alma mater, and a district where Grandpa Nick had once been superintendent. We won that game, 56–48. One game away from the state semifinals in the Breslin Center.

Northview, a suburban Grand Rapids school, was our next opponent. Our season almost ended that night, one win short of the semifinals. We trailed late, but Mike Emerson hit a three-pointer with five seconds left to force overtime. The extra time was ours, and we got out of there with a win, 55–47. We were on our way to the Breslin.

The semifinals and finals were held on back-to-back days in late March, on a Friday and a Saturday. We were excused from classes and we traveled as a team from school to the Breslin Center. We'd gotten there the way we wanted to.

Our semifinal opponent was Orchard Lake St. Mary's, a school from Detroit's northern suburbs. Orchard Lake's star was junior guard Kalin Lucas. (Kalin and I became teammates at Michigan State a few years later. Another future Spartan, my Okemos teammate Mike Kebler, also played in that Okemos-St. Mary's game.)

The game was a battle. We went on a 13–5 run in the second quarter, but we still only led by a point at halftime.

In the third quarter we extended our lead, going up 35–28. Then, Kalin Lucas took over for St. Mary's. No matter what defense we threw at him, he found ways to score. Ivan Parker often had the thankless task of containing Kalin, but we mixed it up and put other guys on him, too.

It was back and forth. We'd score on one end, and Kalin Lucas would score on the other. St. Mary's held a one-point lead with a little over six minutes to go. Thanks to Holt, close games didn't rattle us. We'd been here before.

The next few minutes we couldn't retake the lead, but we stayed close. With three and a half minutes to go, JJ went up for a dunk and was fouled hard. He made his free throws, and that gave us the lead. It was a lead we refused to surrender. After Mike Kebler made a free throw with four seconds left, we led 57–53. St. Mary's rushed up the court and hit a three as time ran out. The basket only changed the margin of victory. We'd won, 57–56. One game to go.

# 15

## INSTANT CLASSIC

EVERY GUY ON THE OKEMOS team lived within fifteen minutes of the Breslin Center. Door to door, Okemos High School and the Bres are only five miles apart. We could have driven ourselves to the semifinal game or gone with parents. But we were family, and we traveled together. For the semifinal, our pep band led us through the school parking lot to the bus, rocking our fight song, and the Okemos police escorted us to the arena. The next day, for the championship, police cruisers ushered us again. In elementary school I had wanted just one kid to have my back. Now the pep band, the student body, the police, and the entire community of Okemos had my back. Everybody had everybody's back.

We entered the championship game as the favored team. We'd been ranked number-one in the state for a month, we'd lost only once all year, we'd defeated defending champs Holt twice, and we'd just stopped one of the state's best players in Kalin Lucas.

Saginaw Arthur Hill was playing the role of underdog. They'd already lost six times—though, in fairness, they had lost to good teams. Their coach had deliberately scheduled several tough non-conference games. They weren't highly ranked, but they had a player we worried about: junior forward Darquavis Tucker. Dar was explosive. He dunked ferociously and nailed big-time shots. He played aggressively on defense and forced turnovers. Saginaw Arthur Hill also had Tommie Prater, a six-foot-two-inch guard who played a physical game, shot well, ran a dangerous fast break, and created chances for his teammates.

We told ourselves it was just another game: play like we'd played all year, and prepare the same way. Coach Briggs had stretched with me before every game that season. Today was no different. He helped me loosen my legs, back, and shoulders. The same stretches as always, in the same order.

I didn't take the opening tip. I was the tallest guy on the court from either team, but there is more to winning a jump ball than just height. Timing is a big part, too, and I couldn't time my jumps well. So Bobby Albers went to center court for the toss-up.

We scored the first points when JJ zipped a long pass to Ivan Parker as Ivan cut down low, but Saginaw countered with a three. My turn was next. I put back a rebound and made another layup soon after, and we quickly built a 9–5 lead.

We had a size advantage over Saginaw, and we intended to use it. Our game plan was to get the ball to me in the post as much as possible. So far, it was working.

Then, Saginaw went on a 12–1 run, and suddenly we were down 17–10.

Every time we came close to tying in the game, Saginaw countered with a big basket of their own. And the points weren't coming from Dar Tucker or Tommie Prater. Sophomore La-treze Mushatt nailed one three-pointer after another in that first quarter for Saginaw. We trailed 23–18 entering the second quarter, and Mushatt had scored fourteen of their twenty-three points.

Early in the second quarter I made another basket under-neath, closing the gap to 23–21. After Saginaw created a few more turnovers and scored again and again on the fast break, they led 34–25. Saginaw's lead never reached double digits, but it kept coming close.

We entered this championship game with a record of 25–1. We had played in the lead for most of the season. We weren't used to playing from behind, but it didn't scare us. Our motto that year was "No plays off." It meant we approached every play on both offense and defense with complete intensity, whether we were losing, tied, or winning big. We were down by nine. So what? No plays off. No letting the tiniest amount of doubt or discouragement creep in.

JJ hit a three late in the first half to cut the lead to four, 36–32. Saginaw got another basket before the half ended, and we went into the locker room trailing 38–32.

One of the great things about our team that year was how balanced our attack was. JJ usually led the scoring for us, but the number-two scorer could have been any number of guys. Ivan Parker shot the three well and also could put the ball on the floor and drive to the rim. Bobby Albers had a clutch jump shot, and he was fantastic from the free-throw line. Mike Emerson could do a little bit of everything: hit threes (like he had against Northview to force overtime), make jump shots, and drive the ball. I had my big nights, too. Ivan and JJ would feed me the ball in the post for hook shots and short jumpers, and I put back offensive rebounds for points. Every game had a new hero. We had plenty of depth. Guys who came off the bench for Okemos would easily have started elsewhere. That caused no resentment on our team. Players didn't gripe and neither did parents. We were committed to winning. The state championship was what mattered.

JJ opened the second-half scoring with two free throws, but Arthur Hill countered with a basket of their own. On our next possession, Ivan Parker drove the lane, drew the defenders, and dished to me. I put in the layup and was fouled. I made my free throw to complete the three-point play, and now we were only down by three: 40–37.

The game's biggest stars—Saginaw's Dar Tucker and our JJ—then traded three-pointers, and we trailed 43–40. Saginaw had a mini-spurt to extend the lead to eight, but we countered with a mini-spurt of our own, and their lead was again cut to three. I was having a great game—seventeen points now—but that didn't matter. Only the championship mattered. I would have been content with two points, as long as I was contributing to a win and a state title.

Saginaw brought the ball up, but JJ stole it and scored on the fast break: 51–50. The O-Zone went nuts.

On Saginaw's next possession, Latreze Mushatt attempted a three. In the first quarter, it seemed like he drained a three-ball every time we got close. Would he do it again?

Mushatt missed, but JJ fouled him on the shot. Mushatt went to the free throw line for three, but he only made one. Saginaw now led 52–50.

Our next trip up the court, Ivan Parker fed JJ as he was cutting underneath for a layup. Tie game. Even more insanity from the O-Zone.

Saginaw regained the lead on free throws. We inbounded the ball with 5.9 seconds left in the quarter. JJ rushed the ball up court. Saginaw guarded him closely, assuming JJ would look to shoot. The tight defense didn't matter. JJ dribbled, created some space, and drilled a three just before the buzzer. We led 55–54. It was our first lead since early in the first quarter.

Saginaw's Dar Tucker opened the fourth quarter with a three, and just like that we were behind again.

The fourth quarter was back and forth. Neither team could put together a run. Bobby Albers hit a three for us. Dar Tucker dunked for them. Tommie Prater drove the length of the court for them. JJ countered with a three for us. Saginaw stole one of our passes. JJ drew a charge and got the ball right back.

With a minute and a half left, JJ launched a long three-pointer. Swish! That pulled us within two. JJ now had thirty-one points for the game, and he wasn't done.

After JJ's triple, we called timeout and set up our defense. We intensified our pressure, hoping to cause a turnover, and it worked. Arthur Hill knocked it over their own baseline. Our ball. The clock showed 1:19. We had a chance to tie the game or take the lead with a three.

On our inbounds play, Bobby Albers broke away from his man. The defender grabbed Bobby. The ref called the hold, and Bobby went to the line. He made both, and the game was tied.

Coach Stolz sat me for the next possession. He wanted my teammate Kyle Miller on the floor. Saginaw was putting an all-guard offense out, so we needed Kyle's speed and tenacious defense out there. I never liked sitting, but it gave me a chance to catch my breath and maybe notice something in our opponent that I'd missed when I was on the floor.

Saginaw missed the shot, but grabbed the offensive board for the put-back. Saginaw Arthur Hill 70, Okemos 68. The clock showed 48 seconds.

Our next possession, JJ didn't wait. He saw a lane and drove to the hoop almost immediately. He missed but was fouled. Two free throws.

The first free throw rattled in.

The second: in.

Tie game, 70–70.

Saginaw got the ball back with forty seconds left. They let the clock run down. Twenty-five seconds. Twenty. Fifteen.

We did everything we could to keep the ball away from Dar Tucker. With three seconds remaining, Darmarkis Carroll took the shot from fifteen feet out. Miss. Somehow, with time running out, he ended up with his own rebound and put it up again. Off the rim. We were going to overtime.

Neither team scored in the first two minutes of overtime. Then JJ and Latreze Mushatt traded jumpers. I got the ball in the post on our next trip down. My back was to the basket, and I shielded the ball from my defender. It was time for my hook shot. I sank it, and we regained the lead, 74–72.

Saginaw missed on their next possession. With a minute and a half left in overtime, we had the ball and a two-point lead. Things were looking good.

In basketball, though, fortunes can change fast.

JJ controlled the ball, killing clock. When he attempted a pass, Saginaw anticipated it. Steal. They drove for the basket but missed the layup. We knocked the rebound out of bounds, and Saginaw kept the ball.

The ball went to—no surprise—Dar Tucker, who drove, spun, created separation, and floated it in to tie the game.

The clock showed 32.8 seconds, and we had the ball.

We ran the clock down. We spread out and tried to give JJ room to find a lane, but Saginaw was having none of it. His man was all over him, forcing JJ back nearly to midcourt. With four seconds remaining, JJ created enough separation to launch a shot from just beyond the free-throw line. It hit the back of the rim, but the rebound deflected all the way out to Okemos's Bobby Albers at the three-point arc. Bobby hurriedly put it up. He beat the buzzer, but the ball banged off the backboard.

Still tied.

In the second overtime, Dar Tucker made a free throw to give Saginaw a one-point lead. At the other end, Bobby Albers fed me inside for an easy layup, and now we were up by one, 76–75.

Saginaw missed their next attempt. With three minutes to go, we had the ball and a one-point lead.

Tommie Prater fouled me with 2:52 on the clock. I made both free throws, and now we led 78–75.

Two minutes later, we still clung to a three-point lead. Saginaw started up the court with just forty-four seconds standing between us and the state championship.

Rather than attempt a three, Dar Tucker drove the ball on us. He made it and drew a foul. He sank his free throw, and suddenly the game was tied again.

We could play for the last shot again, just as we had in the first overtime. JJ carried the ball for us, starting up the right side. He crossed midcourt and made his way to the left side of the court, letting the seconds tick down.

Then, with 17.4 seconds left, came one of the most controversial calls in the history of Okemos basketball.

The ref blew the whistle on JJ for a five-second violation. The call was that JJ was being "closely guarded" for five seconds straight and he didn't pass the ball, drive past his defender, or have the defender back off.

I have watched the video—almost everyone in the world of Okemos basketball has—and I say the ref made two mistakes. First, he didn't restart the count when JJ's defender backed off. Second, the ref is supposed to count the five seconds with five arm waves, from his chest outward. His arm waves look rushed.

Terrible call or not, the ball went to Saginaw with seventeen seconds left.

Dar Tucker dribbled on the perimeter. We double-teamed him and forced him to his left. Somehow he went to the outside, found a lane, made his cut, and put the ball in with 4.5 seconds left.

We had a glimmer of hope left. We called timeout and set up our play. They knew we'd try to get it to JJ on the inbounds pass, so they covered him tightly. We tried a trick play—JJ dashed across the baseline, received the pass out of bounds, and became the inbounds passer himself. He hurled the ball down court, but Saginaw intercepted. We fouled Damarkis Carroll, who made both free throws. Now it was 85–81.

We hit an uncontested three as time ran out, so the final score was 85–84.

To this day, I have such a mix of feelings about that game. I am proud of what we accomplished that season. I am honored that we got to be a part of one of the greatest games in Michigan high school basketball history. And I am happy that I showed up for my team that game, finishing with twenty-three points and nine rebounds.

But the double-overtime loss was devastating. We were so close. Okemos had never won a state championship in basketball since its promotion to Class A. This was our chance to give something to the school and to the town. Everyone had come together—the O-Zone, the parents, the teachers, the community—and we were supposed to end the run with a victory. And we almost . . . *almost* did.

As for that controversial five-second call? It still infuriates me.

# 16

## STILL AUTISTIC

Anthony tended to talk to himself quietly as he walked around the room looking for a book to read. He was then joined by two other boys who came up and sat near him while he was reading. From time to time, Anthony shared information about the book that he was reading. Anthony continued talking out loud even when the teacher had begun to give directions.

*From an evaluation conducted when I was in third grade*

YOU CAN SEE HOW EASY it is to forget that I am on the autism spectrum. The drama of a sports season can do that. In fact, basketball has always benefited me that way. Working on my shots, playing games, trying to help my team—those things require so much focus that there is no room in the mind for anything else. My struggles with language went away. My social limitations didn't matter. No wonder the gym was my happy place. You don't have to be autistic to experience this. Any athlete who is in the zone knows what this is like. The task at hand consumes you, and whatever stresses and problems you're dealing with momentarily disappear. But only momentarily.

Some of my odd behavior was innocent enough. I liked talking in the shower. I'd stand in our upstairs bathroom shower, doing a play-by-play of an Okemos basketball game.

*Johnathon Jones with the ball, bringing it up court. Jones to Parker, who tosses it back to Jones. Quick pass from Jones to Ianni in the low post. Ianni makes a move. He puts up the hook. It's good. Two more for Ianni. What a hook shot! Was that Kevin McHale or Anthony Ianni?*

Inevitably I'd raise my voice as the imaginary game intensified, and sometimes my mom would knock on the door.

"Ant, everything OK?"

"It's all good, Mom," I'd call.

After a while, she got used to this habit.

Often I'd switch from the contest to the post-game press conference.

*A.I., you hit some crucial free throws down the stretch. Did you ever have any doubts about them?*

*Nope, not for a second. If you start thinking about how you might miss, you will.*

*Your free-throw shooting style is a little unusual. Do you want to talk about that?*

*Well, when I was first learning to shoot a basketball, my parents told me not to bring the ball down. When I grabbed an offensive rebound, I wanted to keep it above my head and put it back. If I brought it down to my chest, other kids could swipe at it. So I kept it above my head. That shooting motion kind of carried over to my free throws. It might look a bit unusual, I'll admit, but if it goes in, that's all that matters.*

*Speaking of your form, is it true that, because of how you shoot jumpers, your teammates call you the white Rasheed Wallace?*

*Well, not everybody calls me that, but one or two guys do.*

I could go on and on. I loved holding press conferences at full volume in the shower.

When I showered in the locker room, I had the same inclination: to conduct an "interview" at my usual volume. I fought the urge. It wasn't easy, but I managed to do it.

When guys started trading insults during practice, I tried to stay out of it. When I had no choice but to say *something*, I had a fallback comment. It wasn't clever, and it rarely made sense:

Your mama.

Yup, that's all I had.

"A.I., you call that jumping? Your feet went like one inch off the ground."

"Your mama."

Or, "What kind of shorts are those, A.I.? You wore those to school today? Ugh."

"Your mama."

It wasn't the best counterpunch, but the alternative—trying for something quick and witty—would have been worse.

I never mentioned my autism to any teammate other than JJ—and he heard it first from his parents, not from me. But the guys may have suspected *something*. Maybe they made their own diagnoses. Maybe the word "autistic" even occurred to some of them. Others probably just figured that I was slow, or that there were some loose wires between my brain and my mouth. I don't know. And the theories and the diagnosing went beyond the players. Some parents must have suspected autism.

One home game during my junior year, the O-Zone was conducting its usual pregame rowdy cheers. When the public address person announced me as the starting center, the student section did its usual "A.I." chant, complete with arm gestures. A woman sitting near my mom was horrified.

"That's awful! Don't they know that stands for 'autistically impaired'?"

My mom turned around.

"Those are his initials," Mom said flatly.

If the woman didn't have suspicions about me, would she have been appalled by my nickname? I don't think so. How did the woman even know me or know how I talked and acted? To this day I have no idea.

If I could track her down, though, I would tell her a few things. First, I love the nickname. It is part of who I am. My nickname indicates belonging. It says I am a part of a community. Second, I am proud to be on the autism spectrum. Yes, I try to suppress some of my *behaviors* that go along with being on the spectrum, in order to play by the usual rules of social interaction and not make others around me too uncomfortable, but the autism itself is nothing to be ashamed of. Third, I am not impaired! If I'm being announced as the starting center for one of the best high school basketball teams in the state, am I impaired? No! If I have friends and classmates cheering for me and encouraging me to do my best for our school, am I impaired? No! If I'm on my way to college to get a degree and play basketball, am I impaired? No way!

\* \* \*

Fox Sports Detroit televised our championship game against Saginaw Arthur Hill. Often I was on camera. Sometimes it even focused on me, especially when I took free throws. The announcers said my name again and again that game. (In overtime, after the microphone picked up Coach Stolz calling me "A.I." during a timeout, even the announcers switched to my initials.) Never did they mention my autism. Never during the game would viewers at home have suspected I was autistic. In the heat of battle, I had no "tells." But when the game ended, the autism peeked through. The camera cut away from the celebrating Saginaw Arthur Hill players to show our defeated faces. Drained and deflated. Downcast eyes. And then there was me. I wept openly. It wasn't grown-man crying. It was kid crying. My lips curled and I made no effort to hide my blubbering face in a towel. I cried like I was back in kindergarten and another child had a toy I wanted. In that camera shot, if someone had challenged you to pick out the autistic kid, you would have pointed at me.

The camera missed what came next. Tyler Stewart put his arm around me and kept it there. Tyler had been playing with me for years, both for Okemos and in AAU ball. I never mentioned my autism to him, but Tyler must have had his theories. He knew me enough to know I needed that arm around me. I needed that consolation. That was the kind of camaraderie we had that year. In our most painful moment, the guy with the 4.0 grade point average sought out and comforted the Resource Room kid who'd never said anything wittier than "Your mama" all season.

* * *

The world of high school dating is difficult for just about everybody. Teenagers say dumb things around the people they're attracted to. Every high schooler tries to solve the contradictory advice: Don't be shy . . . but don't come on too strong. Be yourself . . . but be an edited, less awkward version of yourself. I struggled with nuances and missed social cues, so the dating world wasn't challenging—it was miserable. My crushes on girls were as strong as anybody's—maybe stronger—but my "game" left a lot to be desired.

In middle school, a lot of girls caught my eye. Some because they were cute. Others because they were friendly and interesting. But my freshman year of high school is when I *really* fell for someone for the first time. She was a year ahead of me. She played volleyball and basketball, she was cute, and she was warm. She became something like my obsession for the next two and a half years. The word "obsession" gets overused when it comes to high school crushes, but it applies in my case. I fixated on her. People on the spectrum are prone to this. When there is something we want—whether it is an action figure at Target or a relationship in high school—we don't drop it. It was innocent when I was six and *had* to give Sparty a high five at an MSU volleyball game. But it loses its sweetness when we shift the conversation to dating.

She and I were friends. We even went to the movies together a few times, and she agreed to be my date for Homecoming one year. But, she made it clear we were going as friends and nothing more. I was in the "friend zone." I fixated on this. How was I going to get out of the friend zone?

I went out of my way between classes to join her in the halls. I tried to walk with her every hour. Often I asked for a hug. During basketball practice, I talked all the time with JJ and a few other teammates about how much I wanted her to be my girlfriend.

"You gotta play it cool, A.I.," they told me. "Don't you know anything about playing hard to get?"

I didn't. What I knew how to do was to fixate. I knew how to smother.

Sometimes JJ and I lingered after practice, shooting a few extra free throws.

"You just need to play it cool and be yourself," he said. "Don't be chasing her around all the time. People like you for who you are."

His advice made sense, but I struggled to follow it. I continued to pursue her in the halls.

My senior year, after my first serious crush had graduated, I fell for another girl. She was also an athlete. Her parents had known my parents for years, so she and I had been around each other since we were little. She was good-looking, and I appreciated how kind she was to everyone around her.

She was a sophomore when I was a senior, so we didn't have any classes together, and under normal circumstances our paths would not have crossed often in the halls. But that didn't stop me. I took long detours to my classes to pass by her locker. I wrote a lot of letters to her, and I slid them in her locker when she wasn't there. Whenever I spotted her, I tried to talk to her as much as I could. On Valentine's Day I bought her a lot of candy, and on my game days I gave her one of my practice jerseys, hoping she'd wear my number in the crowd. At school I even looked for excuses to put my arm around her.

JJ had graduated, but Geoff was still around to give me basically the same advice: Play it cool. Be yourself. Don't smother her.

I am old enough now to appreciate how fixating on a girl and touching a girl can make her uncomfortable. I have learned enough about social cues to recognize some of my mistakes.

She and I did go to prom that year. When she said yes, she made it clear that she was excited to go with me, but that we were going only as friends.

I wish I hadn't been so obsessive, but I think it was a lesson I had to learn the hard way. High school kids on the autism spectrum experience the same attractions as the rest of the adolescent population. My advice is this: Don't get hung up on one person. Resist the fixation. Don't be mad or upset if that person wants to be just friends. I was in the friend zone a lot in both high school and college, and I hated it. Looking back, though, I realize it wasn't the end of the world. There are a ton of fish in the sea for all of us. Everyone in the world is meant to be with somebody, and eventually your paths will cross. When those paths cross, things will work out—as long as you're brave enough to be yourself. As my college years progressed and I stayed single, I worried that I would be alone and lonely for the rest of my life. That's when I met my future wife. She loves me for who I am. I have never tried to be anybody but myself around her. I am thankful that I learned how to do that, and I'm grateful to her that the real me is who she wants me to be.

# 17

## COMMITTED

WHEN MY OKEMOS TEAM WAS marching toward the state title game, I thought of myself as a basketball player, not as an autistic basketball player. And that's how I wanted the world to recognize me. My autism was still a fairly private matter. Geoff knew, and JJ knew, and my teachers all received paperwork indicating that I was autistic, but I wasn't going out of my way to share it with others. But on February 15, 2006, a week and a half before we defeated Holt to claim the league title, another basketball player who happened to be autistic made national news: Jason McElwain.

J-Mac played only one varsity game for his school in Rochester, New York, but he made it count. In the last four minutes of the one game in which he was promoted from team manager to reserve guard, he scored twenty points, mostly on three-pointers. The game footage went viral both on the Internet and on the news. I first saw it on *SportsCenter*. *He's like me*, I thought as I watched his highlight reel. *And he just went out and balled out for his one and only game. He didn't let his diagnosis stop him.*

I was in my recliner in the Cave when Mom came in and watched the segment with me. J-Mac down the right side of the court, beyond the three-point line, high-arc shot . . . in! Down the court again, another shot up . . . in! His bench went nuts. The gym erupted. With a second left on the clock, J-Mac lofted one final three-pointer . . . good! The student body stormed the court and lifted J-Mac on their collective shoulders. Mom and I both had goosebumps.

I said, "Can you believe there is somebody out there who is like me, and who loves basketball, too?"

"He is one inspiring young man. He didn't give up. Ever."

"Can you believe he's getting a moment like that?"

An autistic basketball player on *SportsCenter*: When was the last time that happened? I wanted to be next.

J-Mac and I have two different stories. We are at different places on the spectrum, and I'm almost a foot taller than he is. Still, what if we could have the same effect on others—to show them what is possible for people on the spectrum?

\* \* \*

A lot of colleges recruited Johnathon Jones. They made real offers—not letters of interest but guaranteed full-ride scholarships. When JJ played in the double-overtime game for the state championship, he still hadn't made his final decision. Soon after, he committed to Oakland University, north of Detroit. During our team banquet that spring, the juniors gave parting gifts and farewell words to the seniors.

"JJ, it's been an honor playing with you," I said when it was my turn at the podium. "And who knows? Maybe our days together aren't over. Maybe you and I will reunite at Oakland and play together one more time."

I winked directly at JJ, but not very secretively. All the other guys and their families saw me wink. At that moment, everybody assumed I would follow JJ to Oakland University. In fact, *I* thought I would be playing for Oakland. I'd had serious talks with them before my junior year began, and they had offered me a scholarship.

That spring, I switched to a new AAU team: the AFE Wizards, out of Dearborn Heights, near Detroit. We opened with some tournaments in the region, including in Fort Wayne, Indiana. Fort Wayne's Spiece Fieldhouse features eight basketball courts and beautiful facilities. Every game the Wizards played, no matter which court we were on, a guy in Grand Valley State University gear sat in the low bleachers. He seemed to be watching me intently. A few times I even noticed him talking with my mom.

We were driving back to Okemos after the tournament when Mom explained: "His name is Burt Paddock. He's an assistant coach at Grand Valley. He really likes you, Ant. He likes your game and he likes you as a person and as a teammate. He told me to tell you that they're going to keep an eye on you."

I was flattered, and I enjoyed the attention, but my preferences remained the same: follow JJ to Oakland, or play for Coach Izzo at Michigan State.

That summer the Wizards traveled to Las Vegas for a big AAU tournament. Oakland University was there, of course. *Every* university was there.

One evening in the hotel, Dad said to me, "Oakland doesn't look like it's going to be an option anymore."

"Why not?"

They had promised. They had made an offer. They couldn't change. I felt like I was flying back in time: to a day in elementary school when a girl promised to play with me then went back on her word, to an afternoon when Mom canceled a trip to the park because of supposed car problems.

Dad said, "They've been watching you play here in Vegas, and they weren't as excited as before. The other thing is, they've had their eye on a guy from Wisconsin, and they want to give your scholarship to him instead."

I was devastated.

"They said their offer was on the table until the fall."

"I know. Well, now it's off the table. They saw something they liked in the Wisconsin kid."

"They can't do that."

"Yes, they can."

"But what am I going to do?"

So much for playing with JJ again. So much for hinting to the Okemos faithful what my next step would be.

The difference between flattering letters of interest and firm offers was becoming painfully clear.

What *was* I going to do?

The school of my dreams, Michigan State, said I could walk on, but Coach Izzo couldn't offer me a scholarship. The University of Toledo was still interested in me. So were in-state rivals Western Michigan and Central Michigan.

One by one, each team proved problematic. Central Michigan stopped recruiting me after their head coach resigned. Western couldn't guarantee a full ride. I had some miscommunication with Toledo about scheduling an official visit, and it didn't end up happening at all.

Through it all, the only certainty was Grand Valley State. As soon as regulations allowed, Assistant Coach Burt Paddock—the coach who had watched me in Fort Wayne—started calling me. "How's it going, buddy?!" He exuded enthusiasm and friendliness, even over the phone. We chatted about sports and school and family. I could tell his interest in me was genuine. Coach Paddock invited me to campus in August for an unofficial visit. Grand Valley State is in Allendale, Michigan—twenty minutes from Grand Rapids and an hour and a half west of Okemos. My parents and I toured the campus and the athletic facilities. Coach Paddock introduced me to staff, including Dr. Damon Arnold, the basketball team's academic coordinator. Dr. Arnold told me his own story: he had dropped out of high school and had felt aimless. People figured he'd end up wasting his life. Somehow, he found the fire to try again. He made adjustments and discovered a passion for education. He returned to school, got his high school diploma, and kept going. Eventually he earned master's degrees from both the University of Idaho and Chico State University and a doctorate from Washington State.

People expected him to be a nobody, and now he was *Doctor* Damon Arnold. I could relate to this guy. He projected a tremendous amount of positive energy, and I could tell instantly that he cared deeply for all of his student-athletes.

"I know your story," he said to me. "I know a lot about you, A.I." I smiled gratefully. This was a guy I would keep no secrets from—about autism or anything else.

Doc added, "We're going to turn you into a hell of a student."

A few weeks into my senior year at Okemos, Coach Paddock surprised me. I was walking to lunch, and I noticed my principal standing in his usual spot in the middle of the cafeteria . . . talking with Coach Paddock.

"What are you doing here?" I said, laughing.

"I came to check out your school! I've heard good things about Okemos. I wanted to see it for myself."

We visited for a minute, but I was hungry. I led Coach Paddock to my usual table, with my usual group of friends. Their faces were easy to read: *Who is this guy and why is he sitting with us?*

I introduced Coach Paddock to the table, and he did the rest. He talked and asked questions and fit in like he ate lunch with us every day. Coach Paddock genuinely enjoys people and conversation. "Outgoing" doesn't begin to describe Coach Paddock. He is always smiling and laughing, whether he's answering questions from reporters, running a practice, or eating cafeteria food in a high school with a potential recruit.

Coach Paddock was winning me over, but there was still one problem: in my heart I was a Spartan.

My dad called Tom Izzo and asked him to meet with me and talk me through the decision. On a September evening

I drove to campus and parked near the Breslin Center as the sun was setting. I knew the Breslin Center well, but I was going somewhere in the building I'd never been: Coach Izzo's office. I moved through the hallways that night not as a fan, and not as Greg Ianni's kid, but as a basketball player. I still wanted to play for Michigan State, and I wanted Coach Izzo to hear it from me.

"So, what are you looking for, Anthony?" Coach Izzo asked after he'd offered me a seat.

"The bottom line is, can I get a full ride here?"

"That would be a real risk for me," Coach Izzo said. "I've taken chances on guys in the past. I've made some offers that were gambles, and they didn't pan out."

"But why not take a chance on me? I'm not going to be that guy who's gonna slouch or take plays off. I'm going to run through a brick wall for you. I'm going to go all out."

He nodded. "I know you would. At the same time, though, we've got NCAA rules to follow. I don't have any full rides to give," he said. "You can come here as a walk-on, and maybe you can earn a scholarship down the road."

"I guess if I'm going to go somewhere, I want to go on a full ride."

"Well, what else is out there? Oakland pulled back, right? Gave your scholarship to another kid?"

"Right."

"That's tough, but it's the nature of the business. Would you walk on there?"

"Probably not," I said.

"So what are your other options?"

"Grand Valley State. They have a full ride on the table."

Coach Izzo scowled. "If you don't take that offer, I'm gonna start yelling at you right now."

"I know, Coach," I said. "It's just that Grand Valley is Division Two."

"Here's the deal, Anthony. It doesn't matter if it's Division One, Two, or Three. You get to play at the next level. And you get to go after a championship at the next level. That's one of the best Division Two programs in the country and one of the best Division Two coaches in the country. You win a championship, and you get a ring, and nobody can take that away from you. It doesn't matter what division it is. Plus, let's not overlook this: you're going to get a hell of an education at Grand Valley. They are top tier when it comes to academics." Coach Izzo gave me a look that was both caring and stern. "Take the full ride. Take it."

*   *   *

A week later my parents and I toured Grand Valley again, this time on an official visit. The place felt more like home. The coziness of the campus appealed to me. Everything seemed close: the dorms, the on-campus apartments, the academic buildings, the athletic facilities.

*I could live here. I could play here*, I thought. *Grand Valley can be a home for me, the way Okemos is a home and Michigan State is a home.* When we passed the Cook Carillon Tower in the center of campus, I noticed a resemblance between it and Michigan State's Beaumont Tower. That seemed like a good sign.

That evening the coaches took my parents and me to Grand Valley's football game against Michigan Tech. From the opening kickoff I felt myself rooting for the Lakers. On their second possession, Grand Valley completed a long pass that put them near the end zone. A play or two later they scored on a reverse. The stadium roared, and Lakers fans rowed off the seven points—a tradition I'd never seen before, but loved.

Coach Paddock showed me to the student section after the first quarter and introduced me to a bunch of basketball players. "Enjoy the game, and have fun tonight!" Coach Paddock said as he left.

The student section chanted: "L-A-K-E-R you a Laker?"

The booming response: "Hell, yeah!"

It felt like 15,000 people were asking me that: Are you a Laker?

After the victory, some players took me back to their dorm, and they waved in friends—both guys and girls. The TV was on, and I paid more attention to whatever the movie was than to the college students around me. People asked me questions, and I gave two- or three-word answers. I'd needed years to figure out my place in Okemos schools. I'd needed big brothers like JJ and Mike Emerson. I couldn't throw myself into new friendships and a new scene in one night. I shrank into my spot on the couch as much as I could, hoping conversation could swirl around the room without my help.

Some guys go to off-campus parties on their official visits and meet more people, but chilling in a dorm room was plenty for me. I must have struck them as innocent and reserved—afraid to joke around. Eventually Justin Ringler, a freshman guard who was redshirting that season, drove me back to my hotel just off campus. On the bed sat a gift basket: energy bars, bottles of Gatorade, the basketball team's media guide, and a few "articles" cut out from USA Today. One headline was this: "Ianni signs with the Lakers." Below it was a picture of me on the court during an Okemos game. Another headline: "Ianni leads Lakers past rival." The article said I scored twenty-five points against Ferris State to help Grand Valley pull off a comeback win.

Sleeping alone in the hotel room that night, I sensed how close I was to independence. Life on my own. It was scary and thrilling at the same time. I still had a season left to play for Okemos and a senior year to enjoy. I wanted to savor the coming months, not skip over them. But my dream of playing college basketball had never felt more real.

Mom and Dad returned the next morning, and our Grand Valley tour continued. Up to that point, most of my interactions had been with Coach Paddock. On my official visit, I spent more time with the head coach, Ric Wesley. I could tell right away how competitive he was. Grand Valley had finished 27 and 4 the previous season and had won all eighteen home games. "We've got a great group of guys who work hard every day," Coach Wesley told me as we walked through the practice facilities. "We push them to the limit, and it results in winning. We won our first conference championship this past year, and we're primed to win another one this season. And when you get here, A.I., we hope to add a third in a row."

"Sounds good to me."

"Your skills and personality can bring something special to the team. We want to win, and we want to win with you."

Coach Wesley's office was the last stop on the official visit. When I entered, I saw spread out on his desk a collection of blue, black, and white Grand Valley State Lakers gear: jerseys, practice jerseys, warm-up pants, shoes. All of them with the number 44.

That gesture closed the deal.

Two days later I called Coach Wesley. "If you want me, you got me," I told him. "I'm committing right now."

\* \* \*

All of this happened before my final high school season even started. We had lost JJ, but plenty of guys were coming back. There was no reason we couldn't compete for another league title. Heck, there was no reason to count us out of another deep run in the playoffs.

I co-captained that team with senior Mike Kebler, who also had started the previous year. I felt honored that Coach Stolz and his staff saw me as a leader. It meant that they trusted me to make sure guys did everything the right way—practiced the right way, approached academics the right way, and played with pride. For two years I'd observed how JJ had led the team. He wasn't afraid to speak up and push guys, but first and foremost, he led by example. I tried to do the same thing.

I busted my butt in practice and tried to make everybody feel included in the locker room. I did more talking that season, but I don't think my autism hurt me in this regard. Maybe a few times things came out the wrong way, but I spoke my mind and tried to be as clear as possible, and I don't remember any problems caused by my autism.

We started the season strong, with five straight wins. But we lost our next two, including a conference match-up against East Lansing. A few games later, Paul Crosby and the Holt Rams defeated us in our own gym, 55–47. Later in the season we blew both payback opportunities: East Lansing beat us again, and so did Holt. It was one of those years, though, when anybody could beat anybody. East Lansing and Holt both picked up four conference losses along the way, and so Okemos finished the regular season in a three-way tie for first. Although we shared the title of champions, the honor lacked some of the luster of the previous season's accomplishment.

We won a few playoff games, including against East Lansing—our first win in three tries against them that year. But, Ann Arbor Pioneer eliminated us a few rounds before the state semifinals. We were denied another appearance in the Breslin Center. In my mind, we had the ability to win the league outright, and we had the players to get us back to the finals. Not everybody sees it this way, but I think we underachieved that season. Either way, with that loss, my career as an Okemos basketball player came to an end.

\* \* \*

A few months before graduation, Mrs. Shafer announced to the Resource Room that she was leaving and couldn't finish the school year. Her husband was taking a new job in southeast

Michigan, and they were moving right away. I couldn't believe it. Mrs. Shafer's Resource Room had been my refuge for almost four years. I couldn't imagine crossing the finish line without her there.

Over a few days she packed her boxes and shifted her duties to her replacement, a young teacher who had interned in the Okemos special education department. Mrs. Shafer deliberately left some items where they were. She said to me, "On the last day of school, I want you to take the Muhammad Ali poster with you. It's yours."

The gesture overwhelmed me. I thanked her over and over. "I'm going to have this poster up in my dorm room," I said, "and I promise I'll think about everything you taught me."

She gave me a big hug, and she hugged the rest of the seniors, too.

I felt like Muhammad Ali and Mrs. Shafer were telling me the same thing: that I could become a champion and do something special with my life.

\* \* \*

Graduating from Okemos High School was supposed to be my final achievement. College wasn't supposed to be in my future. Athletics weren't supposed to be in my life. Neither was independent living. And yet, all of those things were just around the corner. Okemos held its commencement ceremony in the MSU Auditorium, and as I waited for my name to be called, I thought, *I wonder if any of those doctors and psychiatrists are here today. I wonder if they remember what they told my parents all those years ago.* Whether they attended or not, I hope somebody told them, "Anthony Ianni just graduated from high school, and now he's going to college."

As I crossed the stage, Dr. Lanzetta, my principal, extended his hand. I ignored it and gave him a hug. Friends told me later that, between my height and my graduation gown, when I hugged Dr. Lanzetta, he completely disappeared. From the audience's vantage, I had just *swallowed* him in my gown. This got a lot of laughs.

"What was so funny?" I asked when I sat down.

# 18

## ON CAMPUS

AT SIX FEET SEVEN INCHES, Mike Przydzial stood out in the halls at West Bloomfield High School as much as I did at Okemos. In public places he drew stares. Przy committed to Grand Valley State shortly before I did. A local newspaper did an article on him when he made his decision official. Coach Paddock mailed the clip to me with one addition: he penned a speech bubble onto Przy's picture. It read, "A.I., I need a roommate."

I'd heard of Przy (pronounced to rhyme with "dizzy") and was vaguely aware of what he was doing for West Bloomfield's team. We'd actually faced each other once in an AAU game. My team won, but Przy played through a fever and still dropped a lot of points on us.

After I committed to play for Grand Valley, Przy's dad found my dad's contact info and emailed him. He sent his son's cell phone number to Dad and encouraged me to call Mike. I texted him almost immediately. *I can't wait to be a Laker with you*, I wrote. *We're going to do great things together!*

I spoke on the phone with Przy a day or two later. My parents and I were driving from East Lansing to Ann Arbor to watch my sister play volleyball against the University of Michigan. Przy called just as we were leaving, and we talked the whole time I was in the car. Before we hung up, I invited him to Okemos for a weekend. A few weeks later, Przy made the drive and met Geoff and some of my other friends, and he fit right in. *This is a guy I can trust*, I thought. *We're going to be great roommates together. And classmates. And teammates.* I knew it was an unrealistic wish, but I wanted Przy to transfer to Okemos for his senior year. He could play for us and join my social circle. After he left, people talked about him for days. It was Przy this and Przy that. I think my friends would have traded me away to bring Przy back!

We kept tabs on each other throughout our senior seasons. It was easy to root for each other, since we played in different conferences in different parts of the state. By the time move-in day came around in August 2007, Przy felt like a longtime friend.

Mom teared up as she said her goodbyes. For more than fourteen years, ever since my PDD-NOS diagnosis at Children's Hospital in Columbus, Mom had provided extreme levels of structure for me. She remembered the tantrums and the wig-outs. The Breslin Center games we left early. The Wardcliff Elementary days when she pulled me from class. Not to mention all of our perfect moments together, like singing in the car and the bear hugs. She knew every word in every IEP, and she'd made sure that my teachers did, too. Mom had taken the lead on our family's adjustments to my autism. Mom had coaxed me through my meltdowns. She had spent my entire life watching my environment. Now it was time to let go.

\*  \*  \*

"There's something you should know about me," I said to Przy a few days after we'd moved in. My Muhammad Ali poster already hung on the wall, and I'd found specific places on my desk and shelf for snacks, iPod, books, and binders. "I am on the autism spectrum. I was diagnosed when I was four."

Przy looked surprised. "So, what's hard for you?"

I explained my language issues—the trouble I had with sarcasm and idioms. I mentioned the fire alarms. I even confessed that I was shaky when it came to social cues.

"I wasn't supposed to make it this far," I told him. "A lot of experts examined me when I was in kindergarten, and they predicted that I wouldn't go to college or play sports or have much of a life."

"I wouldn't have guessed it," he said. "Really, I didn't notice anything that gave it away."

I explained that I'd matured enough to act like a "normal" person, but I still had my tics, if you knew what to look for.

"Is there anything I should do differently?"

"Just be you," I said. "Don't do anything different. But be ready. Sometimes you might say something that won't make sense to me."

The first few weeks of classes, I was the one who didn't make sense. Throughout high school I'd gone to bed around 9:30 and had gotten up at 6:30. I preserved that schedule during my first fall at Grand Valley. Przy was mystified. What kind of college freshman goes to bed at 9:30?

I never drank in high school. Not once. Even as I started college, I assumed I wouldn't touch alcohol until I was twenty-one. After all, that was the law. Laws and rules give the world structure, and I embrace structure in all its forms. Plenty of college freshmen throw structure out the window and use their new freedom to drink too much, eat too much, and stay up too late. None of that appealed to me. Parents or no parents, I planned to keep doing what I was doing.

I spent a lot of time in the dorm room that fall. I was shy— that was one of the most withdrawn times of my life. On weekends I stayed up later, but I didn't go out. Mostly I watched movies, followed sports, and listened to music. Through Facebook I kept in touch with my Okemos friends. I went back home for

Michigan State football games and Okemos football games. Przy made new friends, and he went out without me.

Finally, a few weeks before basketball season started, Przy took action. He and another freshman teammate, a guy from the Chicago area named Mike Balleto, came into the dorm room and announced, "We're going out tonight."

"We're getting you out of your comfort zone," Przy said. "We're not going to do anything insane. We're just going to chill out with people we know."

I nodded.

"A.I., you're in college now. You can take care of business and still have fun."

That night we went to one teammate's on-campus apartment and then another's. I nursed a Gatorade. I made friends. I laughed. By the time Przy and I got back to our room, it was almost 3:00 a.m.

After that, socializing became easier. Most weekends some guys from Grand Valley's football team hosted a bonfire. They rented a house a few miles from campus, out in the country. The athletes at Grand Valley were one big community, no matter what sport you played, so people from the football, basketball, soccer, volleyball, wrestling, and other teams all drove out to the bonfires. Thanks to Przy, I started joining that scene.

I hadn't shared a room since Allison had endured my lullaby tapes in the MSU apartment fourteen years earlier, but Przy was a good roommate. He was organized, like I was. We kept the room clean. We did laundry. He didn't touch what was on my desk, and vice versa. Przy showed me where he kept his car keys. He said I could borrow the car as long as I asked first and put gas in the tank when it got low.

Our suitemates, though, were another story.

We lived next to two other basketball players, Alvin Storrs and Toreau Brown. A bathroom linked our two rooms, and

Alvin and Toreau came into our room all the time. Toreau, especially, came and took food from my shelf without asking—sometimes as I watched.

"I didn't say you could have it," I sputtered.

"Thanks, A.I.," he said as he walked back through the bathroom.

Toreau took my iPod, too, while I sat six feet away on the couch.

"What are you doing?"

"I'll bring it back."

"No."

"I'll put some actual good music on it for you."

"I said no."

And then he left.

Another time, I was hanging out in the room when Alvin started tapping on the wall. I cut through the bathroom. "Do you think you can stop the tapping?" I said to him.

Alvin shrugged.

A minute later the tapping started again.

I yelled through the bathroom. "Hey, you need to cut it out."

Alvin came in, holding a pencil. "I *need* to?"

"I told you not to tap on the wall."

He whacked on my wall a few times, looking me right in the eyes.

It was the Easter egg hunt with my cousins all over. Alvin and Toreau shouldn't have pushed my buttons—and I needed to handle it better when they did.

\* \* \*

Coach Wesley had called a team meeting to take care of some beginning-of-the-season stuff: team rules, workout schedules, road-game policies—things like that. Coach Wesley also wanted us to start bonding as a team.

"We want everybody in this room to get to know each other a little better," he said. "We'll go around the room, and I want you to share with your teammates something that nobody else would know about you."

We took turns, up and down the rows of desks. As it came closer to me, I thought, *You know what? I'm just going to open up about it.*

I hadn't planned to share my autism diagnosis with the whole team. I sure didn't have a rehearsed speech ready. But I told myself, *You're in college now. You need to solve your own problems. If you ever have communication problems with these guys, they should know why.*

And so I shared my story: the diagnosis at the age of four, the doom-and-gloom IEP meeting when I was in kindergarten, the outbursts in Target, Cloud Nine, all of it.

"They said I wouldn't be here at all," I told my teammates. "They predicted that my autism would keep me from playing sports, and from going to college."

My struggles weren't over, I added. Autism still made some things hard for me. But here I was in college and playing a sport.

The two reactions I remember the most were L.J. Kilgore's and Tommy Fellows's.

L.J. was our starting point guard. As I finished, I saw two things in his face. The first was disbelief. Like, there was no way I could be autistic. He had an image of autism in his mind, and I didn't match it. The second was respect, both for overcoming what I had and for letting down my guard enough to talk about it. Tommy's reaction was more a mix of care and curiosity. Tommy was a fifth-year senior. He'd played basketball for Holt High School, but since he was four years older than I was, we'd never faced each other, and his playing days predated the Okemos-Holt rivalry. Tommy was studying coaching and education at Grand Valley. Because of his education classes, he knew more about impairments and learning disabilities than my other teammates.

"If there is ever anything you need from me, let me know," Tommy said. "I'm there for you."

He asked me a lot of questions: about what bothered me, about the things that used to set me off and cause wig-outs, about the hardest parts of school. He was a teammate, a friend, and an educator all at once.

*   *   *

I've never been a good test taker, and every staff member in the Okemos Schools knew it. Frequently my IEPs read like this: "He does better on daily assignments than he does on tests. He also has difficulty with social and interpersonal skills."

And like this: "Anthony at times may think that he understands the material being discussed, but test scores show gaps in understanding. This is evident in the comparative religions class where Anthony has scored below a 60% on both tests thus far this year."

And like this: "Anthony has struggled on the reading quizzes in his nonfiction class, where the quizzes are looking at reading comprehension. His highest quiz score was a 64%."

So when I took my first test in a college class, I didn't expect a great score.

But I really *bombed*.

In high school I could cushion my grade by doing all of my homework assignments. If I turned in all of the daily work, as well as all of the papers and projects, I could do poorly on the tests and still earn B's. Often I kept my grade point average above a 3.0. But that was high school.

At Grand Valley, I didn't have assignments or projects to bump up my grade. It was *only* tests. My grades were based on what I was worst at.

When my first test came back, it was well under a 50 percent.

Another test, another class: the same thing happened.

I called Mom. "I failed," I told her. "I keep failing these tests, and that's all we get is a test score. We don't get homework points. I'll never pass college."

"You'll figure out a way through it," she said. It was on me, not her, to solve this.

I knew I had to show my scores to Dr. Arnold, my academic coordinator. He'd vowed to make me a "hell of a student."

"College isn't one test, A.I.," Doc said at our next weekly meeting. "College is a long road. There will be obstacles, and you'll overcome them."

"But it's always been this way with me and tests," I protested.

"I know. I know how it is with you. But you can't tell me you didn't make any mistakes preparing for those tests."

I was silent.

"You made mistakes. That's OK. Learn from them."

Doc told me to prepare more for tests, and to start preparing sooner. "We have a lot of resources here," he said. "If you don't use resources, that's on you. Professors have office hours. Go to them before the test and ask questions. You'd be amazed at how much professors will share, if you bother to see them and ask. Plus, we have tutors. Sign up for one well before the test—well before—and start preparing. Tutors are here for a reason."

Doc reminded me that I had permission to record all lectures. "If a professor's explanation flies over your head, listen to it again in your room. You can even replay it for a tutor."

Doc was right. Help was out there, but I had to make the first move.

"Utilize every single thing that is available. Keep charging forward every day, A.I.," he said. "Always moving forward."

\* \* \*

Our workouts started in earnest, and they could be brutal. Running and more running. Lunges. Pull-ups. Squats that killed my knees. The sets seemed endless and cruel. After one tough conditioning session, Tommy Fellows saw the defeat on my face and offered to drive me to dinner. If Tommy was hurting, too, he didn't show it. He reminded me of the Fonz from *Happy Days*: a cool guy who didn't let anything faze him.

When Tommy and I entered the cafeteria, I asked him, "What did Coach mean when he told us to eat a rainbow?"

Coach Wesley hadn't done much yelling. He struck me as closer to Coach Stolz than to Coach Stuckey. But he had a dry sense of humor that I struggled to catch. When he told us to eat a rainbow every day, I wondered whether Coach Wesley wanted me to eat more Skittles.

Tommy said, "A rainbow is a salad. With lots of colorful vegetables. Carrots and peppers."

I grinned. "Got it."

One joke solved. How many left to go?

# 19

## THE STREAK

CALLISTUS EZIUKWU WAS ENTERING HIS senior season that fall. "Bean" was expected to be one of the best players in the conference that season—even one of the best Division II players in the country. Like me, Bean played center. I'd see little playing time—Coach Wesley planned to keep Bean on the floor as much as he could, and who could blame him? This switch from starter to reserve didn't bother me. I expected it my freshman year.

I knew that when practices started, I'd often go up against Bean. *You're going to get your butt whooped*, I said to myself, *but it will be good for you. You probably aren't going to take the starting spot from Bean, but you can make sure he remembers you as the toughest guy he ever faced in practice.*

The differences between high school and college basketball are immense.

Coach Wesley drew up more plays than I was used to, and more complicated plays. He created a variety of looks for our defense, and he expected us to learn them all, fast. Scrimmages felt like a fast-forward version of anything I'd played before. The ball flew around the court in a blur, and players seized positions and dashed through lanes before you could blink. College ball is way more violent, too. Near the basket it's nothing but shoving, hip-checking, banging, and flying elbows. In high school, elbows generally were accidental. In college, elbows were almost as much a part of the game as dribbling and passing.

I battled Bean nearly every day, and most days he schooled me. He was so quick and so smooth—I'd never faced a player that good. He could do everything and go everywhere. If I anticipated that he'd try the baseline, the way I did against Holt's Paul Crosby, Bean took the middle and dunked on me. Even when I knew he'd use an up and under, he sold his fake so hard I bought it.

As our first game approached, Coach Wesley and Coach Paddock told me I might not play at all; they were considering redshirting me. If I didn't step onto the court and didn't go on road games, they could save my eligibility for later, when I would be a fifth-year senior. A few other freshmen, including my friend Mike Balleto and my suitemate Alvin, had already accepted their redshirt status. Upperclassmen who had redshirted their freshman year—including Tommy Fellows—told me that it wasn't so bad, and that they were glad they'd done it. It was a good way to learn the team's system, improve as a player, and save your eligibility for a season when you would start—or, at the very least, play a lot more minutes. But I didn't want that. I wanted to play. Even if it was only four or five minutes a game, I wanted to contribute. I wanted to be Bean's clear backup.

The decision was the coaches', not mine. All I could do was tell them how I felt. Several times that fall I pled my case to Coach Paddock. "I can have a role this season," I told him. "At the end of the day, it's your decision. I know that. But I want you to know I'm against it. I don't want to be redshirted."

I didn't just want to play. I wanted to travel. Basketball was all I had that fall. I was too shy to find friends beyond the team. I pictured Przy and the rest of the team bussing to Ohio or the Upper Peninsula for a long road trip without me, and it frightened me. What would I do while they were gone? When I went to the cafeteria, I went with basketball players. When I hung out and joked around, it was always with teammates. If they left me behind, who would I eat with or talk to?

\* \* \*

For the first time in my life, I wanted Michigan State to lose.

All fall I'd rooted for Michigan State's football team. The Spartans had a new coach that year: Mark Dantonio. My dad had told me that Coach Dantonio brought a lot of intensity to the program. "I think he's going to take the team to new heights," I said, and Dad agreed. The Spartans opened the season by beating two smaller schools, the University of Alabama–Birmingham and Bowling Green. These games were at Spartan Stadium, and I went back home and sat in my usual seat with my family for these games. Next MSU defeated Pitt, Grandpa Nick's old team. For their fourth game of the season, they traveled to South Bend, Indiana, and beat Notre Dame 31–14 to maintain their perfect record. Things were definitely looking up.

Grand Valley is a funny place. The student body roots for the Lakers, of course, but just about everybody also roots for a second college team: either Michigan or Michigan State. Students from southeastern Michigan tend to support Michigan, whereas people from the Lansing and Grand Rapids areas are more likely to back Michigan State. Among the people I knew, the split was about fifty-fifty.

The Spartans lost four out of their next five, but the losses were all close and against respectable teams. They lost by three on the road against Wisconsin, and a few weeks later, they lost 24–17 to the best team in the country at the time, Ohio State. In the past, these down-to-the-wire defeats would have unraveled me. I would have cried. The outbursts and wig-outs that still lurked inside me would have tried to come out. But instead I turned off the TV and went to practice, or to work out, or to Grand Valley's own home football game, or I ventured off campus with Przy and some other friends, and I was OK.

But on Friday, November 2, 2007, I wanted Michigan State to go down.

My Grand Valley team was facing Coach Izzo's Spartans in the Breslin Center for a preseason exhibition contest.

I don't know if Michigan State underestimated us or not. They shouldn't have. Grand Valley had been to Division II's Elite Eight the previous spring, and most of the guys from that team had returned. What's more, this exhibition was a rematch, and Grand Valley had almost pulled off the upset the previous year.

We—and by "we" I mean Grand Valley—fought toe to toe with the Spartans all game. We trailed by two with fifteen seconds remaining, but Justin Ringler scored for us to force overtime.

After an extra five minutes, we were still tied. (I don't know what it is about me playing double-overtime games in the Breslin Center.)

Bean scored eight points in the second overtime to help us pull away, 85–82.

My handshake with Tom Izzo after the game was bittersweet. I was happy to see him and proud that our team had won, but I have so much admiration for Coach Izzo that I *never* want to see him lose, not even when I'm wearing the opponent's uniform.

"I'm still here for you, A.I.," he told me. "You ever need anything, you call me."

The Grand Valley coaches told us to savor the victory. Exhibition game or not, we'd just beaten one of the best programs in the country. The bus ride back to Allendale was a fun one that night, with a lot of laughing and celebrating.

To start the regular season, we faced Columbus State in Orlando in Disney's Wide World of Sports Division II Tip-Off Classic.

Not surprisingly, Bean scored our first six points of the year, on a layup and two dunks.

Seven minutes in, Columbus State took a 12–10 lead. They held it for almost twelve minutes, at one point leading 26–20. We pulled ahead 29–28 on a three-pointer from guard Jason Jamerson with five minutes left in the first half, and we never let go of that lead. We built a sixteen-point lead in the second half, and the final score was 83–71. Przy played six minutes, mostly at the end of the first half. Thirteen seconds after he went in the game, he recorded the first steal of his college career. A few minutes later he tipped in an offensive rebound, and he had his first points.

The next day we beat Stonehill College, and the day after that we defeated Barry to win the Division II Tip-Off tournament. We received a trophy, and three games into the season, we were already champions. What a start to my college career! I was disappointed that I hadn't contributed to the victories or even played a minute, but I knew the coaches still hadn't decided whether to redshirt me.

Collectively, we quickly shifted our focus to the future. The trophy was nice, but our team had much more to accomplish.

Our winning streak continued a week later when we played our first home game of the season, against Missouri–St. Louis. We built a sixteen-point lead in the second half, only to let it dwindle to four. We eventually won 62–53. Callistus Eziukwu led all scorers with seventeen points. Przy didn't see any action, and neither did I.

Mom had come to Allendale for the game. (Michigan State's football team was hosting Penn State that day, so Dad had to stay in East Lansing and work.) It was a new experience for her, too, watching me stay on the bench, but I'd warned her that Coach Wesley still hadn't decided whether to save my eligibility for later.

"Just keep busting your butt every day, Ant," she said. "On and off the court. Do that, and everything will take care of itself."

A few days later, on November 20, Kalamazoo College came to Grand Valley for a Tuesday night game. Kalamazoo College was a division below us and not expected to win. My old AAU and Okemos teammate Tyler Stewart was on the Kalamazoo team, and I looked forward to seeing him. During pregame warmups, Tyler and I chatted at half court. It was a little weird, wearing different uniforms. We'd been on the same teams for so long.

Grand Valley scored the first fifteen points of the game and never looked back.

Just over ten minutes into the game, when we held a 26–16 lead, Coach Wesley sent me into the game. With that, I knew I wouldn't be redshirted.

A few minutes later, Kalamazoo attempted a three-pointer. It clanked off the rim, and I hauled down the rebound—my first as a college player.

I was still on the floor with five minutes left in the half. We had the ball, and I moved to the low post and called for the ball. It came to me, and I put up my go-to shot: the hook.

I gave the shot a little too much, and it hit the back of the rim.

Late in the game I was back on the floor. I drew a foul and went to the free-throw line. It was my chance to score at the next level.

The first was a miss. So was the second.

Less than a minute later, I drew another foul. Two more free throws. I made them both. They were low-pressure shots—the two points gave us a 91–48 lead—but I'm not sure there is such thing as a low-pressure shot when you're trying to score the first points of your college career.

After blowing out Kalamazoo, we traveled to Rensselaer, Indiana, to face St. Joseph's. The game was tight throughout. With six minutes remaining, we were deadlocked: 49–49. I'd played a minute in the first half, grabbing a defensive rebound and going one for two from the free-throw line. Justin Ringler scored the next four points for us, on a layup and two free throws, and we kept the lead for good.

We improved to 7–0 by blowing out Marygrove College, 95–39. In the second half, I tried a short jumper and missed, but I grabbed my own rebound and put it in for my first field goal as a Laker. Late in the game, I put in two more layups, so I finished the game with six points, three rebounds, a block, and a steal.

The wins kept coming for us: we traveled to the Upper Peninsula and beat Lake Superior State and then came back to Allendale and won a string of home games. We traveled to Indiana and beat the University of Indianapolis. We bussed to Ohio and beat Tiffin University. After going back to the Upper Peninsula and beating Northern Michigan University, we were a perfect 15–0.

* * *

Somewhere in this chain of victories, we all had to take our final exams for the fall semester.

Dr. Arnold found tutors for me, and I studied more than I ever had. I used the Disability Support Services office to lock in my accommodations. Somebody from the DSS read each exam for me, and we did this in a quiet room without other students in it. I also was allowed extended time on each exam.

Often, the reader read a question, and I had questions of my own. What did the exam mean by this word or that phrase?

"I can't really help you there," the reader said.

This was different from Okemos High School. At Okemos, when one of the special education teachers read a test for me, they could answer my questions. They could explain what each item on the exam was really after. Heck, my anatomy teacher,

Mrs. Tandoc, even stayed after school one afternoon and gave me a test orally. She conducted the test one-on-one, as if it were nothing more than a conversation. But now I was in college, and all the reader could do was read.

Sometimes my struggles with testing frustrated me. *Why can't I just be a normal student?* I saw friends study so much less than I did, and they'd have more to show for it. *I go to every class, and I sit in the front row every time, and I study, and I meet with tutors and an academic coordinator, and I go to the DSS to have my test read to me in a private room, and I still can't get a good score. Why can't my grades be like everybody else's?*

\* \* \*

After we defeated Northern Michigan we stayed in the Upper Peninsula, traveling west through the snow to Houghton to play Michigan Tech. We won that one, too, 71–54.

We kept winning. After beating Gannon University, we were 20–0. That was one of the closest games of the season. They hit a three-pointer with a minute and a half remaining to pull within three, but we held on and won, 64–58. Other games were blowouts. We played Tiffin twice in the span of ten days. We beat them 90–61 and 86–45. We beat Ferris State by thirty-four. The final score against Ashland: 84–58.

I entered most games but usually only played a few minutes. In the tight games, I didn't leave the bench. This didn't bother me much. What mattered was winning. Bean was an All-American. My role was to give him the toughest battle I could in practice. I boxed him out, threw elbows, got physical, and gave him everything I had. There was a chance he would play in the NBA next season, and I wanted him to remember me. One thing was certain: I would remember him. He continued to amaze me. Everything he did—every post move, every defensive stance, every shot block, every move of his feet—was done with more skill than I'd ever seen up close. When we scrimmaged against each other, I often tried my hook on him. Entering college, I'd thought of my hook as indefensible. But Bean swatted it away time and again.

I thought of *Rudy*. Rudy knows his role. He accepts that he is a practice player and that his job is to get the starters ready. He practices with a fierceness that goes beyond his teammates' intensity. I tried to do the same thing my freshman year. I gave Bean everything I had. Unlike Rudy, though, I had another purpose besides preparing Bean for game day: I wanted to get myself ready for my sophomore season, when it would be my turn in the starting five.

\*   \*   \*

We finished the regular season still perfect and claimed the Great Lakes Intercollegiate Athletic Conference title. We marched through the GLIAC tournament, beating Hillsdale College and Lake Superior State in our first two games and defeating Findlay to win the tournament championship. In the final, we built an eighteen-point lead early in the second half, but they mounted a comeback. With sixteen seconds remaining, they pulled within two, but we held on to win 73–67.

Next was the NCAA's Division II tournament. Grand Valley had advanced to the Elite Eight the previous season, when I was still in high school. This time we hoped to go all the way.

We started with a win against St. Joseph's, 69–52. Next we slipped past Northern Kentucky, 62–58. We trailed late—one of the few times all season we hadn't led. The game was tied with eight minutes to go when Northern Kentucky hit a three-pointer. Pete Trammell hit a three for us to tie it, but they answered with a three of their own to retake the lead. We still trailed a few minutes later, 50–47. It was back and forth from there. Jason Jamerson put us ahead with two free throws and then a three-point shot, but Northern Kentucky answered yet again with a triple of their own. Justin Ringler put us ahead 54–53 on a basket from the paint with two minutes remaining, and we never relinquished the lead.

In the Sweet Sixteen we faced a familiar opponent: Findlay. We'd defeated them in early December, 82–60, and we had won a much closer contest in March, 73–67. In the tournament we beat them a third time, 75–58, to advance to the Elite Eight. Our record was 36–0.

We traveled to Springfield, Massachusetts, to play Winona State for a spot in the Final Four. We were behind for much of the first half but had a late spurt and took a 29–24 lead into the locker room at the break. Coach Wesley used his bench sparingly. There was no way I was getting into this game. As long as we won, I didn't care.

Winona State quickly tied it up in the second half and then pulled ahead. Eight minutes into the half, they had a 44–34 lead. I didn't lose hope. There was still a lot of time left. Every time we scored, though, Winona State had an answer. We closed the gap to four on a Bean dunk, but Winona State scored the next seven points. We got within six on a Jason Jamerson triple, but never came any closer. Final score: Winona State 67, Grand Valley 54. Our season was over.

Two games later, Winona State upended Augusta State in the Division II national championship game to claim the title we'd been shooting for all season.

# 20

## SOPHOMORE SLUMP

IN MIDDLE SCHOOL WHEN PEOPLE called me the Green Giant and the Freak, I unraveled. Nobody called me those things at Grand Valley, but students still stared at me. It happened to Przy, too, since he was only two inches shorter than I was. The looks multiplied whenever Przy and I walked together.

One lunch after the season ended, Przy and I took our trays to a table in the cafeteria. One student after another looked up from their meals and glanced at us. "I'm sick of this," he said.

I was, too, but I also was experiencing some relief. People were staring at me for my height, but they weren't staring *only* at me.

"Watch this," Przy said.

"What are you going to do?"

"Just watch."

Przy returned to the line for drinks. He got another bottle of Gatorade, walked to the center of the dining area, came to a halt, and bellowed, "What? Hasn't anyone in here ever seen a tall person before? We're tall. So what? Grow up."

He unscrewed the cap on his Gatorade, took a long drink, savored the stage, and then came back to our table.

\* \* \*

Moving out of the room I'd shared with Przy in Pickard Living Center was not a big emotional moment; we'd already signed a lease for an apartment together in the fall, along with our teammates Justin Ringler and Mike Balleto. I headed back to Okemos and took a job on an MSU paint crew for the summer.

About the time I moved back home, one of my former English teachers emailed me. Ms. Freeman explained that her classes were reading a book called *The Curious Incident of the Dog in the Night-Time*. The novel's narrator is a young man on the autism spectrum, she said. The class was also watching *Rain Man*. Ms. Freeman thought her students needed a better sense of how diverse the autism population was, and she asked if I'd be willing to speak to her classes. I didn't hesitate.

The whole time I attended Okemos, I acknowledged being autistic to two students: JJ and Geoff. Otherwise, it was my secret. That was about to change.

What a thrill it was that morning to return to my old stomping grounds and pass through those halls. I still had many friends in the building—guys and girls a year or two behind me in school. My senior year I'd hung out with everyone from seniors to freshmen. I'd talk to anyone in any hall, from any social group. A basketball player two years behind me named Travis Bader called me "The People's Champ." Travis was like the little brother I never had. Travis and I spent a few summers playing basketball at a neighborhood park for hours every day. (Travis loved to put up three-pointers as much as I loved to shoot the hook. After high school he played at Oakland University, where he set the NCAA record for three-pointers in a career.)

In the two years I had Ms. Freeman, I don't remember a day when she was angry or low-energy. She always smiled and taught with vigor, and it spread to the rest of us. Ms. Freeman loved Shakespeare and other books, and she encouraged students to volunteer in the community and be good citizens. We laughed a lot in her room.

For three class periods, I talked the whole hour. I explained to the students how my parents learned I was autistic, the awful forecast they received when I was in kindergarten, and how I continued to use the negative predictions to motivate myself. Ms. Freeman asked questions to keep me talking: Did autism make it harder to be a student-athlete in college? How did the spectrum work? What was the toughest part about being autistic in high school? Would I always be autistic? What did I think of *Rain Man*, since Dustin Hoffman's character, Ray, was so different from me? (People I know in the autistic community have mixed feelings about *Rain Man*. Some appreciate it for daring to create a main character who is autistic. They say Dustin Hoffman's portrayal gets *some* things right about *some* autistic people. Others worry that viewers will assume *all* autistic people are exactly like Raymond Babbitt—that we all have the same exceptional skills and the same impairments. Personally, I can see where both sides are coming from.)

"You did such a great job!" Ms. Freeman said afterward. "Will you come back again next year?"

"Without a doubt."

\* \* \*

When the fall semester started, I had a class in my schedule that I hadn't seen since high school: math.

I'd avoided it for a year, which seemed wise at the time, but now I was rusty. After a few weeks, I was wishing I'd taken it right away. The professor encouraged us to work in small groups. On my parents' advice, I tried partnering up with the smartest people in class. I asked around, especially in the cafeteria, and I found classmates who played football, volleyball, or women's soccer—and also happened to be 4.0 students who excelled in math.

When we worked together, I admitted how hard it all was. They explained things to me, and I told them to slow down. I couldn't handle more than one new idea at a time. My brain didn't sail along through the equations as fast as theirs did. When I was younger, it was my teachers and parents who figured out my weaknesses and came up with accommodations. I was a sophomore in college and almost twenty years old. It was time to advocate for myself.

I signed up for more tutors that fall, and I got better at signing up three days, four days, even a week ahead of time. When a class required a PowerPoint presentation, I requested a tech tutor. When I had to craft speeches for a public speaking class, I asked for writing tutors. I had to give a speech about my hometown, and I nailed that assignment, since I took such pride in being from Okemos. When we had to talk about a favorite athlete or other celebrity, I described Allen Iverson and his toughness—how he could score forty points in a game despite a broken hand or damaged ankle.

I did homework at our apartment without disruption as Justin, Przy, and Balleto all had girlfriends and spent a lot of time with them. When Balleto was home, though, you knew it. He was the life of the party wherever he went. He had a goofy laugh that started high and dropped to a lower pitch. Whenever he laughed, I started laughing, too, even if I had no idea what was funny to him. When Balleto had an opinion, he dug in his heels. We could be arguing about pro wrestlers or about cereal, and he treated it like a life-or-death issue. The day we moved in, he taped a giant Michael Jordan poster in our living room.

"Balleto, I know you love MJ," I said. "I know he's your Chicago guy and all, but he can't take up the whole wall. We need some Allen Iverson up there."

"Nope. It's not moving. Michael is God."

"Come on, Balleto. It's the whole wall."

"It stays."

"What about Larry Bird and Doctor J?" Balleto had put up a corny poster of the rivals pretending to choke each other.

"That stays too."

Balleto cooked more than the rest of us. Sometimes the smells of pasta and grilled chicken filled the apartment, and he made enough for everyone.

The apartment was a typical college guys' apartment: it could turn into a pigsty. We let the dishes pile up in the sink—and then pile up some more. I was as guilty as the others. If my parents hoped that my precise Thomas the Tank Engine arrangements meant I'd be a neat freak even in college, they must have been disappointed the first time they saw our kitchen.

\* \* \*

The team had lost some key players to graduation, including Bean. He'd won our MVP award the previous spring, and also was named the Lakers' most valuable offensive player. Bean remains one of the top scorers, rebounders, and shot-blockers in the history of Grand Valley State basketball. Those would be huge shoes to fill. I knew that. But I also saw the graduations, seven in all, as an opportunity. It was time for me to step up and be the Lakers' starting center. I looked at the other guys who entered Grand Valley with me: Przy, Mike Balleto, Alvin Storrs, Toreau Brown. I saw us as a kind of Division II Fab Five. We could carry the team, and do something the University of Michigan's Fab Five never did: win a national championship.

I'd spent the previous year battling Bean on a daily basis. If that didn't prepare me for the starting job, what would? Coach Wesley had recruited a new center named Nick West, but I doubted they would start a freshman. I had all the tools they were looking for in a center: I rebounded. I could play defense and block shots. I knew our offensive system. My hook shot kept getting more reliable.

One thing I didn't do well, though, was run.

Coach Wesley put a lot of stock in preseason workouts. He wanted to see who was fast and in shape.

Conditioning began with a two-mile run. Guards had to do it in less than twelve and a half minutes, and forwards got thirteen. Big guys like me had to finish in less than thirteen and a half. My first attempt the previous season, I'd taken about fifteen minutes. I did it again, and again, and again.

"Size is no excuse," Coach Wesley snapped at me. "When I was at Iowa State I had a guy who was bigger than you, and he ran it in twelve and a half minutes."

*Give me a break*, I thought. *I'm not him, I'm me.*

Back when I was in kindergarten, if I couldn't have a toy I wanted, I threw giant tantrums. Some remnant of that still lingered in me. When the coaches timed my run, and I sensed that I was going to come up short, I wanted to wig out. My brain was torn between exploding and shutting down. Shutting down seemed like the better path, and that's what I did. *Great. I failed.* I kept my outburst buried, but to everyone else—especially Coach Wesley—it looked like I just didn't give a damn.

The second morning of running, everyone had to show up at 6:30, but only the guys who missed their time had to run the two miles. By the third and fourth runs, the whole team had to wake up early just to watch me drag myself around the track for two miles. Some guys started to get pissed at me, but Balleto told them, "It doesn't matter how many times A.I. has to run this. If we're out here next week, then we're out here next week. We're all gonna be there for him."

Alone on the track, I busted my butt for the first few laps. Then another lap. It hurt, but I kept pushing. As I finished my first mile, Coach Wesley called, "Six-thirty." Good pace. I had seven minutes to run the second mile. But I was running out of gas. My teammates had spread out around the track as a show of support, but most of them were barely awake and a little resentful. If I missed my time and made them get up early again, they'd kill me.

As I began my seventh lap, I heard from the far end of the track, a hundred yards away, "Come on, A.I.! Come *on*! You got this!" It was Balleto. He sounded crazy hollering like that, but he didn't care. He wore a hideously bright orange polo shirt and a pair of black shorts—he looked like he was going straight from my run to the golf course. I fed off of Balleto's energy and gasped across the finish line with a few seconds to spare.

We had other running drills, including gut checks. These were three down-and-backs in the gym in thirty-three seconds. Then it was six of those in a row, with only a short break in between, and we had to finish all six in less than thirty-three seconds each. Inevitably I'd be the last guy to lug myself across the line—sometimes in thirty-three seconds and sometimes not.

*I don't think Shaquille O'Neal could manage this in thirty-three seconds,* I'd think. *Would they bench Shaq if he didn't make all his gut checks?*

I've never been the fastest guy on the court, but I thought I was fast enough to start. Coach Wesley didn't see it that way. Reading social cues is a weakness for me, but my guess is he thought I either was out of shape, or had a bad attitude, or was too slow to play the game at the college level, or some combination of those things. I disagreed, but I wasn't the coach.

To make matters worse, Coach Paddock was gone. Coach Paddock had recruited me and had always shown the most faith in me. The spring after my freshman year, Davenport University, a nearby business school, had offered him its head coaching position.

Instead of facing Michigan State again, we opened the season with an exhibition game against Utah in Salt Lake City. Not only did I not start, I didn't even play. At the half we trailed 26–16. That's right: we had managed only sixteen points in the first half. Most of last year's offense had graduated, and we were feeling it.

We started scoring in the second half, but so did Utah, and we lost 59–44.

The loss didn't count on our record, but it still gave us something to think about. The previous year we had beaten Michigan State in the preseason, and then had come close to pulling off a perfect season. The flight back from Salt Lake City wasn't as jovial as last year's bus ride from East Lansing.

* * *

By coincidence, we hosted Coach Paddock's new team, Davenport University, to start the regular season. When I saw him across the court watching his players warm up, I wanted to dash over and grab him and drag him back to our side. It didn't seem right that he was wearing another team's colors and coaching a different bunch of guys.

Toreau Brown and Przy both started, but my vision of a Division II Fab Five stopped there. We were neck and neck with Davenport for most of the first half. They went up by a few, and then we led by a few. They took a one-point lead late in the first half, but Justin Ringler sank two free throws to give us the lead before the break. Przy looked like he might be having his breakout game, which I was thrilled to see, but in the first twenty minutes, I hadn't stepped on the floor.

We never gave up the lead in the second half. Gradually we pulled away, thanks in large part to Przy's nineteen points— many of them coming from free throws.

With 1:14 on the clock, we held a 75–62 lead. Finally, Coach Wesley put me in. Twenty seconds later, I caught a pass in the paint and put in the layup for my first points of the season.

After the game, I chatted with Coach Paddock.

"You know I love you and I'm still here for you whenever you need anything, A.I.," he told me. "Keep busting your butt on the court and in the classroom."

* * *

Next we hosted Lake Erie College. The game looked like it was going to be a blowout—we led 37–20 at the half, and Przy opened the second-half scoring to extend the lead. After Przy's short jumper, though, the wheels started to come off. Lake Erie slowly chipped at the lead for the next several minutes. The lead dwindled to ten points. Then seven. Then three. We missed jumpers. We missed three-pointers. We missed layups.

We led by one.

With under eight minutes remaining, Lake Erie hit a three-pointer to pull ahead, 51–49. A minute later we trailed 56–51. We scored the next six points to retake the lead, and from there it was back and forth. We eked out the victory, 65–63. Alvin Storrs scored our final points from the free throw line.

I hadn't played a second.

Afterward, I called my dad. "I don't know what I'm doing wrong," I said. "I don't have a clue. Nobody is telling me."

Dad said, "Make your practices your games. Be that intense. Play so well in practice that they *have* to play you."

So that's what I started to do. *Game time*, I'd say to myself before every drill and every scrimmage. *This one counts.* I tried to embarrass my teammates. I didn't have anything against them, but Coach Wesley needed to see how wrong he was about me. I wanted him to watch me dominate.

Our third game of the regular season, we hosted St. Joseph's. Like with Lake Erie, we built a decent first-half lead and went into the locker room up 38–25. I played six minutes in the first half, scoring four points and collecting three rebounds. I made a bucket just before the buzzer, and when the half ended I sprinted from one end of the court to the other, touched the end line, and ran back. It was my way of saying, *This is how I make my time. Scoring in a game counts more than a thirty-three-second gut check in practice.* I admit it was cheap. Coach Wesley clearly agreed. When the second half started, I was back on the bench. Just like the previous game, we had a second-half letdown, and we almost gave away the lead again. We held on and won, 75–72. As the game tightened up in the final twenty minutes, Coach Wesley kept me where I was: in my seat.

\* \* \*

Przy and I may have been brothers off the court, but we could get violent with each other in practice. We went head-to-head a lot, and elbows often flew. Still, Coach Wesley didn't think I was physical enough. "You here to play basketball or become a ballerina?" he asked. He didn't really want to know whether I was a center or a dancer—I'd learned that much about sarcasm. But there is a fine line between angry sarcasm and lighthearted sarcasm. I couldn't tell which side of the line Coach Wesley was on.

"You taking the scenic route to your spot?" he asked me another practice. I'd been slow on a defensive switch. Was he pissed off, or gently correcting me with a joke?

Our next game we beat Indianapolis handily, 79–55, but I did little to contribute to the victory. I played five minutes, didn't score, got two rebounds, and picked up three personal fouls. The one consolation that game was that I was happy for my friends. Alvin, Toreau, and Przy all played well and put up points.

After wins against Ferris State and Tiffin, we were 6–0, but Ashland defeated us in their gym, 68–67, on a buzzer beater. I was one of the first guys off the bench against Ashland and ended up playing ten minutes, but I only managed two points on a layup in the first half.

A game later Findlay came to our fieldhouse and ended our home-court winning streak. They beat us soundly, 68–47. Findlay was picked to win the Division II national championship that year. They were strong in every facet of the game: tenacious on defense, deadly on offense, quick to box out, accurate from three point range. I played twenty minutes that afternoon but barely touched the ball. Their team of veterans included a ferocious defender named Lee Roberts. He was their big man, and he made it tough for us to create any kind of offense in the paint.

After Findlay humiliated us, Coach Wesley was looking to make some changes. Maybe I'd finally get my chance to start. The day before our next game, against Hillsdale, Coach called for gut checks. We had to make six in a row. My time was good enough on four out of the six. In front of the team, Coach Wesley snapped at me: "I don't know how I can play you. You're not making your sprints." He waved his clipboard at me. "Look. Here's the list. I had you in the starting five, but if you can't make an effort in sprints, I'm not gonna start you."

And he didn't. Instead, he went with true freshman Nick West—the guy I hadn't worried about all summer. To be fair, Nick was a strong, athletic player. He was tough on defense. And he made his sprints. Nick and I were friends—on his official visit the previous year, Nick had stayed with Przy and me in our dorm room. I'd liked him from the start, and when he joined the team, I was happy to explain to him how practices and workouts were going to go. Occasionally I borrowed Przy's car to give Nick a ride. We were jockeying for the same starting spot, but I didn't want that to poison our friendship.

Even though I didn't start against Hillsdale, I played twelve minutes and scored eight points. I also grabbed three rebounds and had a block and a steal. We won by twenty-two.

In January we went on the road and lost two more, to Lake Superior State and Ferris State. Nothing seemed to fall for me against Ferris State. I shot one for five from the floor and one for three from the free-throw line.

We finished January with six straight wins, but started February by losing road games to Findlay and Hillsdale. Two weeks later Lake Superior State came into our gym and beat us, 80–70.

Our record at that point was 17–7, but it felt worse.

# 21

## RELEASE

MY FRESHMAN YEAR, COACH WESLEY had an obvious starting center in Bean, and senior Nick Freer was clearly our best
power forward. Coach didn't have any hard decisions to make
with those positions. My sophomore year was trickier. Coach
Wesley didn't think any big guys, including Przy and me,
stepped up enough to be an undeniable starter. We had our
strong games, but we weren't like Bean, who had a great game
every night. I thought Przy was consistently good, but he had
just nine starts that season.

Coach Wesley experimented. He tried starting Toreau at
power forward instead of small forward. He played Przy at center instead of power forward. Przy could shoot off the dribble
and nail three-pointers, assets that went unused when he played
center. Sometimes Coach Wesley pitted me against freshman
Nick West in practice, and other times against Przy. Nick and
Przy went head-to-head, too. I hated the uncertainty. What was
my role on this team? Did I even have a role?

My fuse got shorter, and so did Przy's. We threw more elbows
against each other and pushed harder. One open gym I caught
him in the mouth, and he retaliated the next play by slamming
me in the ribs. The following practice, the first time we bumped
under the basket, he said, "Don't give me any cheap shots today."

"Dude, it was an accident."

"Whatever. No cheap shots."

We stayed pissed off through practice, but we forgot about it by the time we returned to our apartment. It happened on the court, and it needed to stay on the court. That's what made Przy a brother to me: we could fight and then move on.

A lot of coaches cut back on conditioning drills by mid-season. You don't want your players so drained from sprints that their tanks aren't full for actual games. Fortunately, this happened at Grand Valley, too. If I was scrimmaging instead of running gut checks, I thought I had a better chance to prove myself.

In mid-February I had the best game of my college career. Coach Wesley played me for twenty minutes against Michigan Tech, and I scored eleven points and pulled down six rebounds. We led throughout and won 69–59. Afterward I was optimistic about both the team and my place on it.

The next game I played nine minutes. The game after that: six.

Findlay won the regular season conference title that year. They still had a perfect record going into the GLIAC tournament, just as we had the previous year. We entered the twelve-team tournament seeded fourth—behind Findlay, Lake Superior State, and Hillsdale. We opened the conference tournament with a win at home against Ferris State. The game was tied 23–23 at the half, but we pulled away in the second half. I played four minutes. I had one rebound and one blocked shot, but no points.

In the tournament semifinal we faced Lake Superior State. This was our third contest against them that season. Lake Superior had won the previous two games, once in their gym and once in ours. This third battle would be on neutral ground: Findlay was hosting the tournament semifinals and finals. By this point, Nick West had emerged as Coach Wesley's clear starting center. Nick was playing well over twenty minutes a game, and he was collecting a lot of rebounds. In the first half against Lake

Superior, the lead kept changing hands. With three minutes left in the half, we trailed by a point, but we finished the half with an 8–0 run to take a 32–25 lead into the locker room. We added to the lead in the second half and eventually triumphed 81–69. On to the finals.

To be honest, I had mixed feelings about the win. If we had lost, our season would have ended. Our record wouldn't have been good enough to secure an invitation to the national tournament. And I wanted the season to end. Nothing about basketball was fun anymore. There was more disconnect between Coach Wesley and me than I had ever had with a coach before. Never in the past had I struggled so much to understand where my place was on a team. Back in Okemos, the gym had been my happy place. Now it was making me miserable. I didn't want to walk away from basketball, but I didn't see how I could continue at Grand Valley.

We weren't surprised to find ourselves facing Findlay in the finals. Their perfect streak had continued through the GLIAC tournament. After twenty minutes, an upset seemed in the making. We led 27–24, and a variety of guys had scored, including Nick, Przy, Alvin, and Toreau.

Findlay came alive in the second half, though, and demonstrated why they were the top-ranked Division II team in the country. Seven minutes into the second half, our three-point lead had become a nine-point deficit. They extended the lead to twelve. Then fifteen. Then eighteen. Pete Trammell and Justin Ringler made some shots for us to pull us within ten, but it never got any closer. Final score: 67–56.

Our season had been just good enough to slide into the national Division II tournament, so we still had some basketball left. Some guys saw the NCAA tournament as one last chance to win a few games and prove that Grand Valley was still an elite program. I dreaded more days of practices, more running. It was an extension of the most aggravating and unhappy season of my life.

Who did we draw in the first round?

Findlay.

A week after they defeated us to claim the GLIAC tournament championship, we traveled back to Ohio to play them for the fourth time that season.

We had another strong first half. Nick started at center, but Coach Wesley put me in early and played me for six minutes—the most first-half action I'd seen in a long time. I made my only shot attempt, so I contributed two points and a rebound. With twenty minutes to go, we were tied.

Unfortunately, history repeated itself: Findlay scored the first eight points of the second half and never looked back. The final score was 66–51. The season was over.

I'd also decided, with absolute conviction, that my career at Grand Valley was over. My life in Allendale was over. My years of rooming with Przy were over. My plan to form the Fab Five of Division II was over. I would walk away from my full-ride scholarship. Six weeks of school remained. After finals, I'd go somewhere else. I had no idea where.

When I was a preschooler running errands with Mom, I needed to know the name of every store we'd hit on an errand run. If she changed up the plan at all, I wigged out in the grocery store, the mall, wherever. One extra stop uncorked a meltdown.

And now? Did I know where I'd be attending school in the fall? No. Did I know if I could get a scholarship? No. Did I know what kind of future I had in basketball? No. Did I know where I'd be living, or who I'd be living with? No.

Coach Wesley met individually with each player after the season. Before my meeting I called my dad, and he reminded me not to get belligerent. "Don't raise your voice, and don't get offensive," he said. "Stay polite and see what happens."

I'd also been unloading my frustrations on Damon Arnold, my academic adviser. "I think I'm done here," I warned him.

"Why don't you wait and see, A.I.," Doc said. "I'd hate to lose you. Try to have a good talk with Coach. See what he has to say."

In the meeting, I asked Coach Wesley about my playing time. Why did it go up and down so much? I tried not to sound whiny or accusatory. I wanted to know.

"I can't believe you have the gall and the audacity to ask me that question," Coach Wesley said. "You don't take responsibility for yourself or for your actions. You never consider how you might be the problem. Your playing time is on you."

Way back during preseason conditioning, he said, my lackluster running was sucking the life out of the team, and he'd wanted to kick me off right then and there. My post game wasn't very good, he added. "You're nothing more than a rec league player, A.I.," he said.

In fairness to Coach Wesley, I will say this: a lot of college coaches play mind games. Depending on the player and on the coach, mind games can work. Coaches have to figure out how to coax more effort out of good players who often have an abundance of confidence. Different strategies work on different guys. For some players, calling them a "rec leaguer" might be just the insult they need to fire them up, piss them off, and inspire them to charge onto the court and prove the coach wrong. But in my literal brain, if Coach Wesley was calling me a rec league player, then there could be only one explanation: he really thought I was a rec league player. And if that's what he thought of me, there was definitely no point in me staying with the team.

Three days later I returned to Coach Wesley's office. "I'm here to ask for my release," I announced.

* * *

For a fleeting second, I thought about transferring to Davenport and rejoining Coach Paddock. He knew how to communicate with me; he knew everything needed to be straightforward and literal with me. I considered some other small schools—Division III programs like Adrian, where my mom had played. Spring Arbor heard I was leaving Grand Valley and reached out to me. Those possibilities were tempting. I would have had a scholarship at a smaller school, and probably lots of playing time.

But Division III was never my dream. In fact, no *division* was ever my dream. My dream had always been one school and one school only: Michigan State.

Two years earlier I could have walked on at Michigan State. I'd passed up that chance. Do I regret it? No. I needed to move away from home and learn some independence. East Lansing was too close to Okemos. The MSU locker room was too close to my dad's office. If I had gone straight to Michigan State, I doubt I would have learned to do laundry or figured out how to cook, let alone advocate for myself as a student with a learning disability. If I'd gone straight to Michigan State, I never would have met Przy, and without Przy I may have remained the shy kid who never left the dorm room and couldn't make friends outside the halls of Okemos High School.

I scheduled a meeting with Coach Izzo in late April, after I'd emptied my apartment and said goodbye to Grand Valley for good. I had no idea whether a walk-on spot still existed. Coach Izzo had made that offer almost three years earlier.

# 22

## GETTING BACK UP

TWENTY-FOUR HOURS AFTER RETURNING TO my parents' house, I was in Coach Izzo's office in the Breslin Center. After noon light came through the big window. Framed photos filled his walls and his shelves: of his family, of past teams, of people he had mentored.

When Coach Izzo and I sat down, I got right to the point. "A few years ago you advised me to go to Grand Valley and take the full ride," I said. "And that's what I did. Now it's time to listen to my heart. Coach, you know it's always been my dream to play for you and to play for Michigan State. I don't want to put my dream aside this time."

Coach Izzo frowned. "I'll be honest with you, A.I.: I've had some conversations with Coach Wesley about you. He called me and told me some things that were kind of a surprise to me. He said he wasn't too impressed with your work ethic. He used the word 'lazy.'"

"That's not me. You've known me for how long," I said. "Since I was a kid. I promise you right now, I'll give you a hundred percent and more every day. I will work my butt off. And if I'm slacking, you tell me, and I'll pick it up even more."

"I once offered you a jersey and a locker here, and that offer still stands," he said.

"I'm here to accept it."

"Now, before you do, you need to listen. First, you know it's a walk-on spot, right?"

"I know."

"Well, here's the deal. You know I'm going to push you. I'm going to push you to the limit. You'll work harder than you ever have before in your life."

I said, "Coach, I accept that challenge. Maybe that's what I need."

We didn't talk at all about playing time. We didn't have to. I knew I probably wouldn't see much action. That was fine. I wasn't transferring to Michigan State to play more minutes or score more points.

"I can't give you a scholarship," Coach Izzo told me. "I don't have one to give. Now, down the road, a year or two from now, you might earn one. But that's on you to earn it."

We talked about something else that meeting, too: my dad.

Tom Izzo is a direct communicator. He is the most straight-forward coach I've ever played for. He tells it like it is, and he never once tried a mind game on me. So he didn't ignore the fact that my dad was one of his athletic directors. "You know some people are going to give you a hard time," he warned me. "They're going to get on your case and think that you don't deserve to be here."

"I know."

"They're going to say your father is the only reason you're on the team. And you need to fight through all of that."

"I'm prepared for that. I'm not going to let it get to me. And if it does, I'll let you know, and you can yell at me for letting the talk bother me."

Coach Izzo looked like he was thinking about that.

"I belong here," I insisted. "I know I do. You know how much I love this program. I'd do anything for Michigan State."

Coach wasn't finished being blunt. "I'm not going to treat you any differently because of your autism."

"I don't want you to."

"I will treat you how I've treated every other player who's ever come through here, whether it's Antonio Smith, Morris Peterson, Drew Neitzel, or anybody else. No special attention, no breaks."

"I understand."

He offered his hand. "Welcome to the Spartan family."

As soon as I got home, I changed my Facebook profile picture: me in an MSU shirt. People could figure it out. I didn't do anything else to celebrate, because there wasn't anything to celebrate yet. I hadn't dressed for a practice yet, let alone a game. I hadn't proven to a single person that I could keep up on the court or in the classroom. I hadn't earned the jersey.

* * *

I'd met Mike Vorkapich a few times when I was a kid, and he had struck me as *intense*. He was the basketball team's strength and conditioning coach. During games he sat in the row behind the bench, and he traveled with the team. Vork led team workouts and supervised lifting sessions. Dad and I passed by the weight room once when Vork was demanding more effort from some of the basketball players. He was thick and muscular, and so was his voice. Over time I started to see other sides of him. My whole family was on the court after a game once, and Vork was friendly with all of us. A gentleman, really. When Vork heard I was transferring, he scheduled an optional workout so I could meet the team and participate as soon as possible.

A few days before the workout, I went to a party with Austin Thornton, my old teammate from the Michigan Mustangs. Austin, a guard, had redshirted his freshman year. We'd stayed in touch, both in high school and college. I had gone to a few of his high school playoff games, and we messaged regularly when I was at Grand Valley.

"You ready for this?" he said to me at the party.

"Yeah, I'm ready for it. I know it's going to be a step up, and I've got a lot of work ahead of me, but I've got guys like you in my corner to help me get through it."

"It is going to be a lot of work, but you'll be fine."

Two-thirds of the team showed up for Vork's optional session. Austin was there. So was Mike Kebler, my old Okemos teammate. Keebs had gone to MSU as a walk-on. People who followed the program weren't expecting him to ever see much playing time, but Coach Izzo and his staff were unlocking all kinds of potential in Keebs, and he had really grown as a player in the two years since we'd been high school teammates. Vork didn't push us too hard that day; the point was to welcome me, not make me regret transferring. As we were winding down, senior guard Isaiah Dahlman said to me, "We need a nickname for you." He made a few weird suggestions: the only one I can remember is "Ian-to." There were others, and they were all bad.

Draymond Green walked up behind Isaiah. "It's A.I.," he declared. "OK? It's A.I. Nothing different." Draymond and I had played together for a few weeks back in AAU. I wasn't sure he'd even recognize me, let alone remember my nickname.

Two weeks later our summer lifting and conditioning sessions began in earnest. We worked out in the Duffy Daugherty Football Building. It's a large facility on the west side of campus, a block south of Spartan Stadium and a few blocks southeast of the Breslin Center. Some of the facade is glass, giving those parts a sleek, futuristic look.

"I want you putting in thirty extra minutes of cardio every day," Vork told me. "We'll mix it up: speed bike, elliptical, a fast walk on the treadmill with a pretty good incline."

"Is there going to be a long run, like a two mile?" I described the trouble I'd had at Grand Valley. "If I don't make my time," I said, "I get freaked out over it."

"We don't really do long runs here. Mostly we run in spurts. We'll time you, but if you miss your time here and there, I'm OK with that, as long as you're not BS-ing me. If I know you're giving it your all, we're good. If you slack in the least, though, I'm going to lose my mind."

Vork said it like he meant it.

One rite of passage I endured that summer was a wall sit. Vork varied our exercises and lifts, to keep things interesting and to improve our entire bodies. We did leg presses, dips, box jumps, core exercises, and plenty more. He generally avoided squats and other moves that put a ton of stress on our knees, but everything else was fair game.

"It's time for A.I.'s wall sit," he announced at one of our first sessions.

I went to the wall and set my feet, ready to start.

"Oh, no, there's more to it than that," he said. Vork and a couple of other guys came over with hundred-pound sandbags. "These are going in your lap, for five minutes."

I lowered my butt to a sitting position, and Vork put three sandbags in my lap and started the timer. Soon my legs burned and my whole body trembled. I started sweating. I had to fight through the pain. I had to show people that I wasn't soft and I wasn't lazy. I trembled more. I don't know how the bags even stayed in my lap. Halfway through, I collapsed. I took a breath and shakily braced myself against the wall again. Vork set the bags back on my lap. My teammates all began their own wall sits as a show of solidarity, but without the sandbags.

"Do! Not! Fall!" Keebs yelled.

"You got this, A.I."

I fell again, and somehow got to my feet and resumed the wall sit. My legs gave a third time. I pushed myself up and put my back on the wall.

When Vork called time, I fell and didn't try to stand for a long time. Eventually I tried to walk, and I looked like a newborn gazelle in a nature video: uncoordinated, wobbly, and frail.

Vork put his hand on my shoulder. "You weren't the first person to fall. What I love is that you got up. You found a way to get it done."

\* \* \*

That May I made a return trip to Ms. Freeman's room at Okemos High School. Her classes were again reading *The Curious Incident of the Dog in the Night-Time*, and she wanted another set of students to hear about my experiences on the spectrum. I described how often things would go wrong in high school whenever I tried to be funny or clever in the halls. This time around, even more of her students were old friends and former teammates. Among them was Travis Bader, the guy who had called me "The People's Champ." Travis was getting ready to join Johnathon Jones at Oakland University. He and I talked afterward.

"A.I., why didn't you ever tell me this?"

"One, I didn't feel I needed to tell you guys. It didn't change who I was, because it was only a label. I was the same person either way. And two, I didn't know how you were going to react to it. I was worried. I thought you might treat me differently. I've been bullied and teased and disrespected a lot. I didn't want it to happen again."

"You should know better," he said. "We're your guys. We're your boys. We don't care if you have a disability. It doesn't matter."

*Shame on me*, I thought, *for ever doubting them.*

I realized that day just how good it felt to declare, "I am on the autism spectrum. This is who I am, and I am not afraid to put it out there."

\* \* \*

My major at Grand Valley had been communications. When I'd started college, I saw myself one day becoming a sports broadcaster. Whenever I watched sports, I studied the broadcasters' play-by-play. I paid attention to their timing, their catch phrases, their use of statistics. I took a speech class and improved my public speaking, and I took a communications class that focused on the technical side of broadcasting: sound levels, camera cues, and so on. I also made friends with a few guys who hosted radio shows on Grand Valley's student radio station. They took me behind the scenes, showed me how everything worked, and invited me to cohost a few shows with them. "I'd love to do it," I told them, "but don't have me on as a basketball player. Don't ask me questions about being on the team. I want to be like you guys. I want to be a fellow fan." They agreed, and I went on and had a great time discussing the NBA and college football.

When I transferred to Michigan State, my academic adviser asked me about my major.

"I'd like to keep my major communications, if possible."

The adviser, Elliott Daniels, shook his head. "I'll tell you right now, our comm classes here at Michigan State are difficult. And for somebody like you, and where your disabilities lie, I don't think you would have success in that program."

I appreciated his frankness, but I was dealing with enough changes. Would I have to change my major, too?

Elliott had played football at Eastern Michigan University, so he understood what it meant to be a student-athlete. He handled academic coordinating for the basketball team and some of the football players. Before long I thought of Elliott as "Dr. Arnold 2.0." Elliott was equally caring and equally motivating.

"What do you think of sociology?"

I confessed, "I don't even know what the heck it is."

Sociology, he explained, is the study of people: cultures, traditions, behaviors, and conflicts. The more he described sociology, the more I liked it. "I think that's my area," I said.

As Elliott started the paperwork to change my major and select my classes, he said, "Every single resource that's offered to you, you need to utilize it. If there is ever a sign that you're slacking, I'll push you."

*Use your resources.* I'd heard that before, and I knew from experience he was right.

*  *  *

For our first summer practices on the court, the other post players and I trained separately from the guards. We worked on post moves I knew already, like the drop step and the up-and-under, but the coaches also had us do things that weren't part of my game, like moving away from the basket out to the wing—nearly to the three-point line. That was far from my comfort zone. Catch the ball, they said, pivot toward the hoop, put the ball on the floor for one dribble, move aggressively toward the basket, and cash in on what should be an easy layup if you do it right. I was used to playing with my back to the basket, and I created separation by moving away from the hoop. This went against everything in my arsenal.

The other forwards and centers and I played one on one, up to five baskets. The coaches told us to use everything we'd been doing in drills. I tried to keep my games close. If I could lose 5–4 or 5–3, it might look like I deserved to be there. Some games I did keep it close, and I even won a few. I still relied on my hook, but I mixed in other shots, including turnaround jump shots off the glass.

I hated that people believed my dad got me a spot on the team. But I'll admit there was a situation where Dad came in handy: finding a roommate.

Dad was talking to one of the football coaches about me, and the coach knew a player in need of a roommate. His name was Arthur Ray Jr. The fall semester was approaching, and neither one of us was in a position to be picky, so the first time we met was at the Spartan Village leasing office to sign our lease. Afterward, we went to lunch together. I sensed immediately that it would work out fine. Arthur is one of the most sincere and passionate people I've ever met. Whatever he cared about, he cared about deeply. He was passionate about his faith and read the Bible daily. He was passionate about football. He was passionate about his classes and took studying seriously. In our time living together, I never once heard him say a critical word about someone. He never went negative. I take that back. He could talk a little trash when we were on "the sticks," playing *NCAA Football* on our Xbox. But he laughed so hard when he insulted me that even I could tell there wasn't a drop of meanness in his words.

Not long after we moved in, Arthur started calling our apartment "The Lions' Den." Calling ourselves lions was no act of machismo on Arthur's part. I've never met anyone more deserving to be called a lion. Late in Arthur's senior year of high school, he was diagnosed with bone cancer in his leg. For two years he underwent surgeries and treatments. People weren't sure whether he'd live, let alone play football again. Arthur was an offensive lineman—how was his leg supposed to handle that kind of punishment?

Arthur wasn't ready to play that fall, but he was working to get his strength and endurance back. He pushed his leg and the rest of his body as far as he was allowed to, and maybe even beyond. He rarely complained. Arthur knew he would put the Spartan jersey on and make it back to the field. He never doubted it.

Arthur considered me a lion, too, because I was busting my butt in a new program, trying to find a role for myself after walking away from a scholarship, from a team where I played at least a little, and from a group of friends who cared about me and were in my corner.

"We need to do something with this place," Arthur said one day. "We need some posters. What do you think of a giant picture of a lion in here?"

"It is the lions' den."

"Right!"

We drove together to Meijer and flipped through the posters, but we couldn't find any lions. Michael Jackson had died that summer, so Art and I chose MJ tribute posters instead. Mine went up in my bedroom, along with Allen Iverson and the Muhammad Ali poster from Mrs. Shafer. We kept our eyes open for a lion poster but never found one. We agreed on a few Michigan State sports posters for our living room.

One night that fall Art and I were watching TV in our living room when I said, "You know what, man? You're not the only underdog in this room."

And that's when I told him that I was autistic. I didn't say it like it was a pissing contest—seeing who had the bigger story of overcoming hardship. My diagnosis has never been potentially fatal. Autism never caused me to spend a season watching my team from a pediatric oncology unit in a Chicago hospital. I told Arthur because I didn't want any secrets between us. I knew he had my back.

\* \* \*

That fall, Coach Izzo didn't waste a second. There was never a moment of standing around in practice. Every practice was fast-paced. It was hustling, and drilling, and more hustling and drilling. And a lot of swearing, too. Coach Izzo didn't tolerate mistakes, especially dumb ones. He wanted perfection on every play, even if it was a rebounding drill in October. We had a shooting exercise we called the Marquette. We shot for four minutes, barraging the basket from the outside edges of the free-throw line and the corners. Together we had to sink a hundred. Individually, no one could miss more than two in a row. As soon as my third straight thunked off the rim, Coach blasted me. He swore and said, "You're a better shooter than that. You're not focusing, A.I. Get your focus back on and make the next shot."

Coach Izzo was keeping his promise: he cussed me out the way he would anybody else.

\* \* \*

When I was a kid, I knew Spartan Stadium and the Breslin Center, but other parts of campus didn't mean much to me. My classes took me to new buildings, and I walked new routes. One fall afternoon I passed Beaumont Tower on my way to a lecture. I stopped and looked up. The brick tower was almost a hundred years old, and it looked like it could have been attached to an ancient cathedral. For many it is almost a holy place. *I am officially here*, I said to myself. *This is all real.*

I said the same thing to myself a few weeks later when the MSU men's and women's teams threw their annual Midnight Madness pep rally. Midnight Madness is energizing and also a lot of fun. The men's team had reached the national championship game the previous year, so we raised the Final Four banner. Women's coach Suzy Merchant dressed as a cowgirl because the women's Final Four was being held in San Antonio that year.

Coach Izzo drove out in a mini racecar wearing a driver's helmet and fire suit. The men's Final Four would take place in Indianapolis, and Coach Izzo assured the 15,000 fans that we intended to be there.

The band rocked the fight song, and Sparty stomped around the court flexing his muscles. The cheering and the hype were for my team. I wasn't rooting for the Spartans anymore. I was one. Alongside my teammates, I signed autographs for fans. I was on the team poster with our schedule, and I appeared in the media guide.

When we took the floor for individual introductions, players picked their personal theme songs. Mine was "My Time" by Fabolous. The lyrics fit the moment:

> I'm a put it on the line cause it's my time
> I gotta stay on my grind cause it's my time, my time, my time.

Well, they fit the moment briefly. It wasn't my time in every way. The night finished with two scrimmages, first the women's team and then ours. NCAA regulations said I couldn't play in the scrimmage. Because of transfer rules, I had to wait a year.

But I didn't care about the scrimmage. I'd seen myself on the team poster. That was my face. *It's official*, I told myself. *You are a part of this.*

# 23

## SITTING OUT

"I AM NOT IN A good mood," Vork yelled, his low voice carrying to the far end of the weight room. "You guys better get off to a good start this morning. I haven't had my coffee, so if I don't see you busting your asses, I'm gonna lose it."

He stepped into his office and came back a minute later with his Styrofoam cup. He paced between us, calling off calf raises and box jumps. "Great energy, guys!" Vork barked. "You're doing awesome."

He made his way down the row toward me and quietly said, "You're doing fine, A.I. I was being sarcastic there."

"OK."

He patted my shoulder. "Some of the guys weren't giving much, but you're doing good."

I'm glad he didn't cut back on his sarcasm, just because I was around, but I was grateful when he clarified his cracks for me.

Michigan State hosted my former team, Grand Valley, for a preseason game. This was my second MSU-GVSU exhibition game in three seasons, and I'd played for both teams. I chatted with Przy and some of my other friends before the game. I wouldn't be playing in the game—the NCAA's transfer rules prohibited me from wearing a jersey all year—but I wore a warm-up suit and cheered from my spot at the end of the Spartan bench.

After Michigan State won, Przy and I talked longer at center court. We were still there when people in the upper deck started calling my name. I looked up. It was all of my friends and acquaintances from the bonfires at Grand Valley: football players, volleyball players, soccer players. "Hey, A.I.!" they called down and waved. I'd had some anxiety before the game, but all that warmth from my former teammates and from my friends in the upper deck washed away my stress and reassured me that everything was cool.

"Before I go," Przy said, "now that you're on a big-time team, you think you can hook me up with some gear?"

I laughed. "Sorry. You're on your own. Go to the store."

\* \* \*

Two classes that fall were especially challenging: sociology and theater. Nothing the sociology professor said was intelligible to me. I panicked. Had I changed my major to something I would never understand? I vented to Art: "We're supposed to write these summaries and reports about all of these concepts. I can't keep them all straight. Social constructs. Social action. Everything is 'social something.'"

"You can handle this, A.I. Take it one day at a time, one assignment at a time. Break it up small. Don't feed the stress, putting it all together and thinking about it all at the same time. Just continue to be the great person you are. You've got this."

Art was right—just like Mrs. Shafer was right when she gave me the same advice in high school: one assignment at a time.

As for the theater class, I wasn't eager to take it, but it satisfied an English requirement. We read and watched plays throughout the semester and were required to attend on-campus productions. That fall the MSU drama department staged *The Rocky Horror Picture Show.* I don't know if it was my autism or just my tastes, but nothing about that show made sense. The word play confused me. The plot took turns I didn't follow. Every minute in my seat, I just wanted to leave. My favorite comedies were movies like *Superbad*, *Bruce Almighty*, and *Semi-Pro*. What was happening on stage, and why was it supposed to be funny?

\* \* \*

I could practice with the team and I could sit on the bench at home games and wear warm-up clothes, but I couldn't travel, and I couldn't wear a jersey, not even when I was sitting right there on the bench at the Breslin Center. The transfer rules, I thought, were ridiculous. What did it matter if I wore an actual jersey, as long as I stayed on the bench? If there was an empty seat for me on the bus or the plane, why couldn't I use it?

We opened the season with four home games and won all four. Our fifth game was in New Jersey, against Florida in the Legends Classic. I wasn't allowed to go. I felt abandoned. I belonged in Boardwalk Hall in Atlantic City with my teammates, but instead I watched the game at a sports bar and grill with my family. We lost, 77–74.

The team stayed in New Jersey and beat Massachusetts in the tournament's consolation match. The game wasn't televised, so I listened to it on the radio. The Spartans then traveled to North Carolina to face the Tarheels on their home court. It was a rematch of the previous spring's national championship game. I watched us lose with a friend in his dorm room. When the team finally returned, Austin texted me: "Practice at 3 tomorrow." Everyone else had been told in person.

I gave it everything I had in practice. I hustled and crashed the boards, because that's all I was going to get that year: practices.

As inspirational as it was to live with Art, I still let myself get down. Road games were the worst. It was such a contradiction.

I was a Spartan—I was on the team. But they were in Madison, Wisconsin, and I was with Art in our apartment. The team was in Iowa City, and I was in front of a TV in a friend's dorm room. Whenever I started feeling too sorry for myself, though, I had Art's story to give me perspective. I knew for sure that after one year of sitting I'd get my uniform. Art had no idea when, or if, he would be cleared.

* * *

Years ago, Mom had found a hair salon that she liked in Canton. Canton is a western suburb of Detroit, so Mom had to drive almost an hour to get there, but for her it was worth it. Mom urged me to give the salon a try. "They don't just do hair," she said. "They do back waxes and back massages, too."

I don't want to dwell on this point, but I'll say this: I'm Italian, and my back could only benefit from a back wax.

So in November, when the basketball team flew to Atlantic City, I drove to the salon and had them work on my back. A month later the team traveled to Austin, Texas, to play the Longhorns. I decided to enjoy another back massage and then get home to watch the game on TV. Texas was the second-ranked team in the country at that time, so I didn't want to miss a minute of the game.

The woman who was working on my back knew my mom, and apparently they talked enough for Mom to share with her that I was single. "I've got a possible date for you," she told me.

I groaned. "I appreciate it, but I've had a couple of teammates try to set me up in the past. Blind dates haven't really worked out for me."

"No, no, no," she said. "This is different."

She started telling me about one of her coworkers, a young woman named Kelly. "She is really outgoing. She loves to laugh. She is the nicest girl you'll ever meet. And she loves sports. She's a huge fan. All the Detroit teams: Tigers, Lions, Red Wings, Pistons."

I liked what I was hearing.

The woman finished up with my back. I said, "I don't want to do this blind date stuff. How about I meet her now?"

"She's here, but let me check if she's with a client."

She was. All I could do was wave to her as I headed toward the lobby.

She was really good-looking.

She waved back.

At the counter I asked for Kelly's business card, and I wrote my name and my number on it and left it for her. Two days later I still hadn't heard from her, so I found her on Facebook. I gave her my number and told her I thought she was really attractive, and that I'd heard a lot of nice things about her.

Less than five minutes later, she wrote back with her number.

We spent two hours on the phone that evening. As soon as we hung up, we each thought of more things to say, and we texted for another three hours.

The day after Christmas, she agreed to drive to East Lansing to visit me and watch a movie together. That afternoon a blizzard hit Michigan. I assumed the date was off, but Kelly ventured into the snow and made it to Spartan Village. Her drive back home to Detroit that night took well over two hours. This was new—for someone to be that eager to know me.

We saw each other twice more that week: on New Year's Eve to watch the ball drop and on New Year's Day for dinner at Applebee's. After that we were Facebook official.

She made regular trips to Spartan Village that winter, and we watched a lot of movies. One night we watched something with Adam Sandler—I think it was *Grown Ups*. We'd been together about a month. When the movie ended, I said, "There is something I want you to know about me." I had nothing preplanned;

it just came out. "I am on the autism spectrum. My parents found out when I was four. I didn't know until later, but there it is: I am autistic."

A few other times on dates, I'd told girls about my autism. It had never gone well. But with Kelly it was different. First, she said she was surprised. Nothing about me so far had struck her as out of the ordinary. Then she started asking questions, showing genuine curiosity. She wanted to understand me better. This was a good sign.

Kelly started coming to MSU's home basketball games. She knew she wouldn't see me play—she wouldn't even see me wear a jersey. (Some people may have assumed I was a trainer or a grad assistant, since every game I was at the end of the bench in my warm-ups.) Still, the Spartans were my team, and she wanted to support my team. This didn't come naturally for her. She'd grown up in a family of Wolverine fans, and she rooted for Michigan, too. But she came. She cheered for us. And it wasn't long before she was rocking the green and white with everyone else in the Bres.

\* \* \*

Basketball courts and locker rooms can be some of the most sarcastic places in the world. Jokes, insults, boasts, silly raps, nicknames. Over the years, I improved a little in my ability to distinguish between what was sincere and what wasn't, but I remained miles behind everybody else. By far the most sarcastic guy I've ever played with is Draymond Green.

He had his rivals in the sarcasm department—Derrick Nix, to name one. But Day Day (Draymond's nickname since he was little) was the biggest jokester I knew. His sarcasm was great for team chemistry. It loosened guys up and made things fun. The way Day Day joked, he could inspire guys to hustle and get them to laugh at the same time. The problem was, what worked for everybody else on the team didn't work for me. When was he joking? When was he seriously trying to light a fire under me? Because of my autism, I couldn't tell the difference.

Draymond would be leading a workout session in the weight room. We'd do several sets of curls, or lunges, or whatever. Draymond would take us through our final reps and then look around the room and see how tired we were.

He'd announce, "You know what? Let's do a few more."

I'd pick my weights back up and get ready to start. Nobody else joined me.

Austin Thornton would quietly say to me, "He was kidding, A.I."

Austin often served as my translator at Michigan State. I lined up next to him whenever I could. Draymond might say at the end of practice, "We got an extra session of free-throw shooting tonight. Everybody better be here."

As we each headed our own way, I'd grab Austin and ask, "Hey, do we really have to come back tonight?"

"Yeah, we gotta be here."

I never outright said to Austin, "I'm asking you for help because I'm autistic," but he could tell where my struggles lay.

One night we were eating as a team at Champps. We'd just had a grueling practice, and the trainers ordered a "training table" dinner for us. Plenty of proteins and produce to choose from and absolutely no desserts. We ate like this most nights of the week but rotated restaurants.

Day Day was only a sophomore, and he almost never started (he was the best sixth-man in the Big Ten that season), but he held court at team dinners like he'd been the team's captain for years. When he heard me order the barbecue chicken salad, he shook his head. "They have other food, you know."

"I like it."

"You can like your barbecue chicken salad, but that doesn't mean you have to order it every single time we come here. You've got to live a little, A.I." He caught the eye of a few other guys near us. "Isn't that just weird? Has to have the exact same thing every time we come here. Next week I'll order for you."

I boiled. I had the urge to jump over the table and grab him. Why the hell was he giving me a hard time? Why was he bullying a guy on his own team?

Everybody else on the team heard the lightness in his voice. They recognized the affection. But not me.

Austin sensed my anger. He started texting furiously under the table. (Austin told me this afterward.) "Back off A.I.," he wrote to Draymond. "He can't tell you're kidding. He's getting ready to choke you."

\* \* \*

Our 14–4 conference record gave us a share of the Big Ten title—Ohio State and Purdue had identical records. We'd beaten the University of Michigan both in their gym and in our own. We'd lost a few games that maybe we shouldn't have, but the Big Ten had a lot of parity that season, and you had to respect everybody.

The team traveled to Indianapolis for the Big Ten tournament, hoping for a title we didn't have to share with anyone else: Big Ten tournament champs.

Our regular season finish earned us a first-round bye. In the second round we faced Minnesota. We'd defeated them twice already, but both games had been close: 60–53 in East Lansing in mid-January and 65–64 when we played them in the Barn ten days later.

I didn't get to ride on the team bus to Indianapolis for the Big Ten tourney, so I drove with my parents. Our seats in Conseco

Fieldhouse were ten rows off the court, across from the team. I could see my teammates' faces and the spot at the end of the bench where I was supposed to be.

All game long we missed shots that normally went in for us. Minnesota hit their jumpers, and our perimeter defense wasn't as sharp as it could have been. We trailed for much of the game, and were fortunate to be tied at the end of regulation. In over-time, Minnesota went on a 10–0 run and eventually beat us 72–67. After one game, the tournament was over for us.

*  *  *

"Nothing that has happened this season matters anymore." That was Coach Izzo's message to us after the loss to Minnesota. "Forget both the good and the bad. Focus on the next game and the next game only."

We still had an NCAA tournament left to play, and we weren't going to let one loss to Minnesota drag us down.

We opened March Madness in Spokane, Washington. Przy's season was over—St. Joseph's College had knocked out Grand Valley five days earlier—so I drove to Przy's apartment in Allendale, and we watched the Michigan State game together. Our regular season finish was good enough to earn us only a five-seed that year, so we opened the tournament against twelfth-seeded New Mexico State and won a tight game, 70–67. On to Sunday. We faced a tough Maryland team to see who would advance to the Sweet Sixteen. I went back to my parents' house for that game. The Spartans maintained a small lead for much of the first half, pulled ahead by fifteen in the second half, and still had a twelve-point advantage with under five minutes left and a nine-point lead with two to go. Maryland pressed hard, created turnovers, and somehow cut the lead to a point. A turnover later, Maryland took the lead and seized all of the momentum. With twenty seconds left, Draymond hit a long jump shot, and we reclaimed the lead, only for Maryland to score with seven seconds on the clock. Draymond rushed down the court, pulled up near the three-point arc, and shoveled a pass to Korie Lucious. Korie dribbled once and shot from behind the arc as time expired. Good! We won! My teammates swarmed around Korie, celebrating: Austin, Draymond, Keebs, Derrick Nix, and all the rest. I was relieved, elated, drained . . . and I'd watched the game in Okemos, two thousand miles away from the court.

Our third-round game was in St. Louis, and I flew down on my own. Dad had traveled with the team, so we shared a hotel room. Michigan State reserved a banquet room for our team meals and meetings, and we walked through plays on the carpeted floor. I joined the team for the meetings, but I couldn't step onto the court for our practices or shootarounds. Our first game of the weekend we faced Northern Iowa, who had upset top-seeded Kansas to advance. We knocked off Northern Iowa, 59–52, to advance to the Elite Eight. The team returned to our banquet room to briefly savor the victory before preparing for the next game. There was pizza and other food. Technically, I wasn't permitted to eat it, but Day Day grabbed a slice for me. "Here you go, A.I. I'm trying to lose weight, and you deserve something."

I was flying back to East Lansing the next morning, so before bed I texted Draymond: "Do me a favor, cut down a piece of the net for me tomorrow."

We faced Tennessee for a spot in the Final Four. I could have stayed for the game, but I had decided when I bought the plane tickets to fly home before the Sunday game. I knew that if we won, the team would fly back to Lansing after the game and go straight to the Breslin Center to celebrate. Thousands of students and other fans would be there. If I stayed in St. Louis for the game, my flight would arrive after the team's, and I would miss everything.

We defeated Tennessee, and a few hours later I drove to the Breslin Center to meet my teammates. I waited by the tunnel for the team bus, and gave high-fives to everyone as they stepped off. I hugged Draymond. He reached into his pocket and handed me a piece of the net from St. Louis. We lined up to take the court. Above us the crowd roared and the music thumped.

Three weekends in a row, regulations had cut me off from my team, but now I was one of them again.

\* \* \*

Indianapolis was hosting the Final Four that year, so Mom, Dad, and I had an easy four-hour drive to join the team. We stayed in the team hotel, but I shared a hotel room with my parents and slept on a rollaway cot, just like I had so often in middle school when we traveled for my sister's volleyball tournaments. I joined the team for a meeting and some film. If we won the national championship, I could go on the court, celebrate with the other guys, and get on the ladder and cut a piece of net for myself.

Our opponent in the semifinal was Butler. Like us, Butler was a five-seed. They'd beaten the top two teams in their region, Syracuse and Kansas State, to reach the Final Four. We would be playing without Kalin Lucas, the one-time star of the Orchard Lake St. Mary's team during my junior year of high school. Kalin had gone down with an injury during our second-round win over Maryland, and he was out for the year.

The contest started well for us. Back-to-back threes from Korie Lucious gave us a 6–0 lead. We maintained a small lead throughout the first half until the final minute, when Butler tied it up 28–28. We scored the first points of the second half to re-take the lead, but it didn't last. Butler pulled ahead a few minutes into the half and kept the lead. We trailed by three, then four, then seven, then four. Butler couldn't build a big lead, and we couldn't even it up. With two minutes to go we were down 48–46. Butler had the ball. They missed their shot, but grabbed the offensive rebound and scored the second-chance points to go up 50–46. Durrell Summers drove the lane for us on the ensuing possession and drew a foul. He went to the line and made the first free throw. His second shot hit the back of the rim, but Delvon Roe seized the rebound for us. We trailed 50–47 with a minute and ten seconds left. A three-pointer would tie the game. Draymond got a pass in the post but was fouled before he could shoot. He went to the line for a one-and-one. Fifty-seconds on the clock.

Draymond made the first. Then he sank the second. We were down by a point.

We'd spent the entire tournament in close games. Nobody was nervous. Dad and I were sure we'd pull it out.

We played tough defense on the next possession, and Butler missed their shot. Draymond got the rebound. We had a chance to win.

We called timeout with twenty-three seconds left to set up our play.

My parents and I didn't say a word to each other. We sat in our own private trances, completely focused on the moment. We weren't casual fans, eating popcorn and enjoying the action. We were, each in our own way, extensions of the Spartan team.

We'd won our share of close games that year, and I had every reason to believe we'd pull off another victory. Still, we were losing to a great team, and time was running out. A loss would end our season.

We inbounded the ball and kept it outside for a few seconds. Then we fed it to Draymond, who had his back to the basket. He tried to work his way into the paint. He made his move and put it up, but Butler jammed the lane and contested the shot, and Draymond didn't get much of a look. The shot wasn't close, and Butler grabbed the ball. I prayed the refs would call a foul and send Day Day to the line, but there was no whistle.

We fouled Butler instantly, and they came down and made their free throws. Now it was 52–49. Six seconds left.

We tried to set up a three-point shot, but Butler fouled us intentionally so we'd only get two free-throws. Korie Lucious made the first one. Now we were behind 52–50. He intentionally missed the second, hoping we could grab the rebound and put it back, but Butler seized the ball, and the game was over.

Mom and Dad knew to leave me alone. I needed to process the loss in silence, the way I always did. I walked back to the hotel alone.

\* \* \*

We didn't stick around for the national championship game. My parents and I packed up the next morning and drove home. So did the rest of the team. We'd been so fired up when we'd checked into the hotel, so sure MSU would be hoisting the trophy. Now we were tossing our bags into the car and returning to East Lansing, while Butler and Duke still had a game to play.

Being an underdog myself, of course I root for other underdogs. Duke was a number-one seed that year and is always among the best teams in college basketball, so I pulled for Butler. Plus, there is a little consolation in knowing you got knocked out by the best. Some Spartans reluctantly joined me in rooting for Butler. Other guys were too dejected to care and didn't even watch the final.

Butler's magic didn't last, and Duke won the national championship game 61–59.

So often that season I'd felt separated: sitting ten rows or two thousand miles away from the team, wearing the wrong shirt. I knew how NCAA transfer rules worked when I made my choice, but I still hated being left out. All year, though, people had found small ways to assure me I belonged. They remembered my nickname. Asked for my autograph. Patted my shoulder. Offered me a slice of pizza. Cut a piece of net.

# 24

## THE JERSEY

OFF-SEASON TRAINING STARTED ALMOST AS soon as we returned from Indianapolis. We had something like a week and a half of rest between the final meeting of the 2009–2010 season and the first weight room session for the 2010–2011 team. We conditioned through the end of April, until final exams arrived.

For twelve months I'd been training and practicing more intensely than I ever had in my life, yet I hadn't pulled an official game jersey over my head since leaving Grand Valley. I was burning out. Did I really have enough left in my tank for two more years of this? I was a walk-on player. No money was on the line. Maybe it was time to take a break from basketball.

I told a few friends that I was losing the fire. I also confessed to my academic coordinator, Elliott Daniels, that I was tempted to call it quits.

"I know it can be tough," he said. Elliott told me he'd had his moments of exhaustion on Eastern Michigan's football team. "But think of all the good things you'd miss out on, A.I. You guys have some great road games this year. You're going to Duke. You get to travel this year, and who knows? Maybe another Big Ten championship or two and another couple of tournament runs."

I also talked to Kaleb Thornhill about my dilemma. Kaleb had graduated from MSU a few years earlier and had served as a captain on the football team his senior year. He'd already completed a master's degree in education, and he was in the process of taking a job with the Miami Dolphins as their director of player development. In short, he was a hell of a mentor and a great guy to ask when you had one of life's big questions.

After graduation, Kaleb worked with my dad in the athletic department while he earned his master's degree. I still played for Grand Valley at the time, and Dad described to Kaleb the tough times I was having. Kaleb started sending me encouraging texts. Once I transferred to Michigan State, Kaleb and I met in his office from time to time.

"If you walk away from basketball," he told me, "here's what you're going to miss. You'll miss your teammates, for one. There is a bond there that maybe you don't fully appreciate, but trust me, when you stop playing, you miss those guys. Second, you'll miss out on all the experiences. Some of the most exciting things that happen on this campus happen on that basketball court, and you only get to be a part of that if you stay. The other thing to consider is how you'll feel years from now. I'm so glad I played football for this program. Not just for me, but for my future kids. I get to tell my future kids and grandkids what it was like to play for Coach D., what it was like to compete on the field at Spartan Stadium and to win in front of a sellout crowd. It doesn't matter if you play thirty minutes a game the next two seasons or zero minutes. Whether you score twenty points a game or no points, you get to tell your kids about your time on one of the best teams in the country. Don't deny them that, and don't deny yourself that."

Kaleb's words motivated me. I was staying, no matter what.

Soon after I decided to stick with basketball, I found out someone else might be leaving.

\* \* \*

"What's he gonna do?"

I was standing in line at China Express in Haslett, a restaurant fifteen minutes northeast of Spartan Village and not far from my parents' house. A stranger had entered behind me. He noticed my height and saw my Michigan State T-shirt and must have assumed I was on the team.

"What?"

"Is Izzo going to the NBA?"

"Honestly, I don't know," I said. And I didn't.

Even if I had a guess about my coach's future, I wouldn't have shared it with a stranger at China Express.

Coach Izzo traveled to Cleveland in the first week of June to discuss the head coaching job. The Cleveland Cavaliers had recently been bounced in the second round of the playoffs, and LeBron James's contract was up. LeBron was threatening to leave, so Coach Izzo didn't know if the team he'd inherit would come with or without its superstar.

Coach Izzo returned to East Lansing and called a team meeting for early the next morning. We had to pass through a small camp of news trucks to enter the Breslin Center. The media had been staking out the basketball offices since word had leaked that our legendary coach might be departing.

The meeting was a somber one. Coach Izzo didn't keep anything from us. He acknowledged he'd been to Cleveland and he told us how much money was on the line (a five-year contract worth about six million dollars a year, which would have doubled his salary).

"I want to know what you guys think," he said.

Nobody said a word.

We were all in a state of shock. I suspect everybody else was thinking the same thing I was. *He's gonna go. Thirty million dollars, and no recruiting, and none of the complex regulations that come with running a college program. Why wouldn't he go?*

We tried to go about our day after that: a scheduled weight session, lunch, and classes for some of us.

Someone called another meeting that day. Players and assistant coaches only. Mike Garland, who'd played with Coach Izzo in the 1970s at Northern Michigan University and had worked as an assistant for Izz since 1996, got fired up.

"You guys need to do something," he ordered. "If you sit there and say nothing, he's going to leave."

We all looked at each other. What were we supposed to do?

Draymond stood up. "This is ridiculous," he said. "Let's go over there and get our coach back."

We drove as a caravan back to the Breslin. As we pushed past the media throng, the reporters stuck cameras in our faces and started firing questions at us. *Go away*, I thought. *Go back to your trucks.* We marched through the arena's hallways and into our basketball offices.

We didn't sit in our usual swivel chairs. Instead we bunched together at the front of the room, sitting on tables or standing. We needed to be close to each other, and close to Izz.

Coach Izzo joined us and let us talk.

We don't want you to go.

You *are* Michigan State.

You're part of our family, and you're stuck with us.

Draymond did a lot of the talking. "Michigan State wouldn't be the same team or the same school without you. This group of guys you're looking at, we still have a lot left to accomplish, and it wouldn't be right for us to achieve it without you."

Coach scanned the room. We all met his gaze and nodded.

When the meeting broke up, I stayed behind. I wanted to talk with my coach personally. "I didn't come to Michigan State just to play basketball for Michigan State," I said. "I came to play *for you*. I didn't leave Grand Valley State just to be a Spartan. I transferred because I wanted you to be my coach. You're the only Michigan State coach I've ever known. Draymond was right. You *are* us. I came to play for you."

Quietly, he said, "I know you did. And I'll remember that."

A few days later Coach Izzo announced that he was staying. He told the media that LeBron's uncertain future as a Cav was a big factor but not the only one. Three weeks after that, on national television, LeBron declared he was moving to Miami.

We had our coach back. We also knew who our undisputed leader was: Draymond Green.

*　*　*

When fall semester started, I kept my apartment in Spartan Village. Some of the football coaches wanted Arthur Ray to share an apartment with a new player. I'd miss Art, but I couldn't blame the coaches. Art would serve as a fantastic mentor. He'd been like a preacher to me at times during our year together, and his story and his positive attitude kept things in perspective for me.

Another lineman on the football team, Antonio Jeremiah, had lived next door to Art and me, and we'd become friends, so he took Arthur's room. The year was starting off to be a good one. Coach Izzo was back. I'd soon wear a real game jersey for the first time. There was hype around our team—some polls had us ranked as the second-best team in the country. Plus, Kelly and I were getting along great; it was by far the most serious relationship I'd ever had. I was completely used to all of the campus and knew to the minute how long it took to get to my buildings: the Comm Arts building, Berkey Hall for my sociology classes, and Bessey Hall for the Resource Center for Persons with Disabilities.

Then, on October 19, 2010, someone entered my Uncle Nick's apartment and shot him multiple times. When the police found him, he was already dead.

Uncle Nick was named after his father, my Grandpa Nick. Uncle Nick was two years younger than my dad. Though he was married for a time, Uncle Nick never had kids of his own, so I was the closest he ever came to having a son. He was my godfather, and he was always generous with me. Uncle Nick had followed my dad to Michigan State and had graduated from MSU's prestigious James Madison College. From there he had gone to law school.

I had just finished a paper at the Clara Bell Smith Center when Dad called me. "You need to go home tonight, Ant," he said.

"Why?"

"I don't want to get too much into it. Your mother will tell you what's going on. I'm at your grandma's now."

I sensed that someone had died, but I didn't know who.

I drove to my parents' house, but it was empty. Mom texted that she'd be home in ten minutes. I paced the kitchen. I tried to prepare myself: *Our family may have lost someone.* I hated to speculate who it was. Finally Mom came in. "Sit down, Ant."

"No. Just tell me what's happening."

"Uncle Nick . . . Your Uncle Nick was shot and killed."

"What?"

"He was at home. And someone killed him."

"Who? Why?"

"They don't know yet."

I had to leave. I had to get in my car and drive.

How could Uncle Nick possibly be gone? I started my car, sobbing. I pulled out of the subdivision I'd grown up in, barely able to see through my tears. *"Who would do this to us?"* I screamed. *"Who would do this to our family?"*

Uncle Nick was one of the biggest Michigan State fans I've ever known. In just a few weeks, he was supposed to watch me, his godson, take the floor for the first time. This year I'd wear the real jersey. Number 44. Green and white. Instead of seeing me on the floor at the Breslin Center, we'd be burying him. It was impossible, and unfair, and cruel.

I headed for the Breslin Center. It was already evening, and I had no idea if anyone was still there. I started checking offices. Coach Izzo's was empty, but I found Kevin Pauga, our director of basketball operations. I was crying, and it took me a minute to find any words.

Kevin immediately called Coach Izzo and handed me the phone.

"I'm here for you, A.I.," Izz assured me. "This is a terrible tragedy, but we're all with you. I'm here for you. We can talk anytime you want."

Coach Izzo stayed on the phone with me for another ten minutes, and we agreed to talk again in his office the next day.

I missed some classes for the funeral. Then, for the first time, I started missing more classes, and for no reason. I was checked out. School didn't matter much. I slept late, often until nearly noon. I showed up for one o'clock study sessions and tutoring, and attended enough morning classes not to get kicked off the team, and went to practices and games, but whenever I could, I just stayed in bed.

I'd always needed stability and routine in my life. In elementary school Mom warned me if we were going to have a special assembly or a substitute teacher. Until the end of middle school, I refused to spend the night at friends' houses. Now I had to deal with the biggest threat to stability and routine that life can throw at any of us: death.

My whole world suddenly felt vulnerable. Were my parents safe? Was Kelly?

It especially haunted me that he was killed in his own home. He had an apartment in Novi, a nice suburb northwest of Detroit. As a lawyer, Uncle Nick had his enemies, and I know that he never opened the door for somebody he didn't know. So, whoever took his life was no stranger. It was someone Uncle Nick trusted enough to invite inside.

*  *  *

We had two exhibition games on the schedule that year: Saginaw Valley and Nebraska-Omaha. Both were at the Breslin Center. Though I was still deep in mourning, I was charged with pride and adrenaline as I bolted through the tunnel and onto the court as a full-fledged member of the Spartans for the first time. The previous season I'd elected to walk through the tunnel, allowing for a little distance between my teammates and myself. But not this year.

We built a big lead against Saginaw Valley, and in the second half Coach Izzo gave me the nod. I was going in. Our first possession down, Draymond spotted me in the paint. He lobbed it to me, and I put it up and in. The Breslin Center went crazy.

As I trotted back on defense, I pounded my chest and stuck out my tongue the way Michael Jordan used to. After the game, Kelly congratulated me on the win and the basket but told me never to stick out my tongue like that again.

We beat Nebraska-Omaha easily, too, to finish up the preseason.

We opened the regular season with two more home victories against Eastern Michigan and South Carolina. Next on the schedule was a three-game tournament in Maui. All last season I'd hated missing the road trips. I'd felt so disconnected from the team whenever I watched them on TV. And my first road game would be in Hawaii!

*  *  *

"I don't think I should go to Maui," I told Coach Izzo.
He looked surprised.

"My grades are dropping," I explained. "I've been skipping classes. I'm not doing my job in the classroom."

I knew that Coach Izzo had punished players in the past by refusing to let them travel to Maui and other fun tournaments. The way my academics were sinking, I didn't deserve to go.

"If you think this is a fitting punishment, A.I., then I'm on board. But I'm leaving it up to you."

If I had gone to Hawaii, I would have missed several days' worth of classes. They would have been excused absences, but that didn't matter.

I think there was a second reason I chose to spend the week on campus instead of Hawaii. Uncle Nick had been gone only a month, and Thanksgiving was approaching. (We played our third and final game of the Maui tournament the day before Thanksgiving.) Hawaii was too far, too soon. My family didn't need me on a plane, flying halfway around the world. They needed me close. We needed to be together. We had to reassure each other that nobody else was going anywhere. We were all safe and healthy and would stay that way.

\* \* \*

We won our first game of the Maui tournament, but the next night we were upset by Connecticut. So much for being the second ranked team in the country. A few games later we traveled to Duke to play in one of college basketball's legendary arenas. We lost 84–79. Two games later Syracuse beat us in Madison Square Garden. We came back to Michigan and almost lost to Oakland University. We followed that game with a 90–51 blowout victory over a weak Prairie View A & M team. I played two minutes against Prairie View and scored the first regular-season basket of my Spartan career. The next game we lost by twelve to Texas at the Breslin Center.

We were 8–4 headed into Big Ten conference play. We remained ranked, because we'd lost to other ranked teams (with the exception of the Connecticut game), but it was way too early in the season to have four losses already.

If I had to sum up our season in one sentence, it would be this: It sucked.

We never won more than two games in a row during the entire Big Ten schedule. In one six-game stretch, we lost five times. We lost to Michigan. Twice. We went to Iowa and lost by twenty. Four days later we were in Madison, Wisconsin, and the Badgers crushed us, 82–56. Toward the end of February, Purdue embarrassed us on our home court, 67–47.

I played my role as well as I could. I had to be the enthusiastic guy near the end of the bench. I had to cheer louder than anyone and dance whenever we scored a big basket. I couldn't care what I looked like. It was up to me to generate positive energy. But not everybody wanted my cheers and dancing. Russ Byrd, a freshman, started to mock my celebrations. He laughed at the way I danced and muttered that I looked ridiculous. I wanted to tell Russ to chill out, that jumping and waving my arms was my job, but I worried it would come out wrong.

As the season continued, Russ got to me more and more. He had arrived as a quiet guy, a kid who was three years younger than I was, and I'd been ready to take him under my wing and help him adjust to life in our program. But he grew more boisterous in the locker room, and more sarcastic. It was like he was joking in another language. If somebody is joking to your face in Italian, and the only Italian words you know are *arrivederci* and *ciao*, you don't know if the jokes are gentle are cruel. When they laugh, you don't know if you're supposed to laugh, too, or if you should take real offense and knock the smile off of their face. I assumed the worst, every time. I couldn't let it go. A few times I stormed out of the locker room ready to punch something.

* * *

I still grieved for Uncle Nick, but I went as hard as I could in practice. We ran a rebounding drill called the War Drill, and I crashed into teammates and battled for each ball. I spun, jammed my shoulder into theirs, and fought for each rebound like a national championship was on the line. Some of my team- mates told me to ease up, that I was making a fool of myself, but I ignored them. They were going to start in games that mattered, and I had to get them ready. Plus, I wanted them to remember me as one of the toughest SOBs they ever faced on the court.

At Grand Valley practices I had fought for playing time, un- successfully. Now I was fighting for our program.

Sometimes my intensity annoyed Draymond, too. Whenever I defended him, I played with desperation. I refused to give an inch, planting my feet and blocking the baseline. Time after time, he knocked me over, and a coach blew the whistle on him for charging.

"Why do you have to take charges in practice?" he yelled at me. "This isn't a real game."

"But that's what you do. You drive the baseline and some- times you run people over. It's my job to take it away from you."

"A.I., that's weak."

"No, it's not. I'm gonna take charges on you whether you like it or not."

"Weak, man."

"It's called getting you prepared."

* * *

As a member of the scout team, I had to mimic the big guy on whatever team we faced next. I adjusted my play so that I moved the way the opponent did, defended the way he did, and shot the way he did. That year Syracuse's starting power for- ward was Rick Jackson, so during practices leading up to the

Syracuse game, that's who I pretended to be. Jackson used his hook shot a lot, so when my scout team faced the starters, I went to my hook right away.

Coach Izzo blasted his whistle.

"No, that's not right," he yelled. "That's not what the scouting report says. What do we know about Jackson?"

I didn't answer.

"He's left-handed. He's gonna shoot that hook with his left hand. So that's what you're going to do."

The rest of the scrimmage, I shot hooks as a lefty. They weren't pretty, but at least it was the same arm that Rick Jackson used.

\* \* \*

We ended the regular season with a 17–13 record. Our Big Ten record was only 9 and 9. We hadn't even finished above .500. If we had a bad showing in the conference tournament, we were in danger of not going to the NCAA tournament.

The win-loss record wasn't our only problem that year. Two guys had been kicked off the team. Chris Allen was gone before the season started, and Coach Izzo dismissed Korie Lucious in January.

Korie's departure was a tough one for me. He was one of the funniest guys on the team. He was always cracking us up—even me. I may not have understood all of the jokes, but I caught enough of them to appreciate how hilarious Korie was. "A.I., my guy!" he always said to me, warbling his voice. Korie was my road roommate, so I'd grown used to sharing a hotel room with him. I didn't blame Coach Izzo for dismissing Korie; we all knew Korie was doing things that were hurting the team and himself. Still, you never want to see a likeable, talented teammate clean out his locker in midseason.

Even among the guys who stayed, the chemistry was bad. Players didn't really care about each other or about the program. Selfishness prevailed.

* * *

We were in danger of missing the NCAA tournament—
something that hadn't happened to Michigan State since 1997.

In the first round of the Big Ten tournament, we beat Iowa to
advance. The next day we defeated a good Purdue team, 74–56.
The lopsided score may have been just enough for us to secure a
line in the NCAA brackets.

Penn State knocked us out in the Big Ten tournament semifinal, 61–48.

When the NCAA announced its tournament teams, I held
my breath.

We were in. As a ten-seed. We drew seventh-seeded UCLA
for our first opponent.

The Bruins built a lead early, and we trailed by eighteen at
the half. At the end of the bench, I tried to sound encouraging.
Given the season we'd had, though, I don't think my heart was
in it. Not completely.

UCLA increased their lead to twenty-three in the second
half. *Yet another blowout*, I thought.

And then we started making some shots. And UCLA couldn't
find the basket. We played aggressive defense, willing to get
called for fouls. UCLA started missing a ton of free throws.
Somehow we shrank the lead to ten. Then the gap was in the
single digits.

With time running out, we trailed by one.

The next foul, UCLA made the first free throw but missed the
second. Unfortunately, we couldn't get the ball up court for a
last-second shot, and our season ended with a 78–76 loss.

What I remember more than the game was the conversation
I had with Draymond Green and Austin Thornton afterward.
The team had a short, dejected bus ride from the St. Pete Times
Forum in Tampa back to the hotel. Austin and Day Day got off
the bus together and headed toward the hotel entrance. They

were next year's seniors. So was I. There was no way I wanted my final year at Michigan State to be a repeat of the season that was just ending. I hurried up to them and put my arms around their shoulders.

"We're not going out like this next year," I said. "I refuse to let this happen. Day Day, I know you refuse it. And Austin, I know you refuse for it to happen. We are going to put Michigan State back where it rightfully belongs, among college basketball's elite. We're going to win the conference, go to the Final Four, and who knows? Maybe get another national championship."

Draymond and Austin agreed. They made the same vows.

"I may be just a walk-on," I said, "but I'm going to be a leader with you guys. I'm going to be vocal. I'm going to play my role as a senior, whether I'm on the floor or not. I'm gonna do whatever it takes in practice, whatever it takes on my end of the bench, to make sure we go out the right way."

# 25

## "I'M SCREWED UP"

SPRING EXAMS WERE A DAY away, and Coach Izzo called a team meeting in the film room, mainly to encourage us to finish strong academically and prepare diligently for our finals. I claimed the same leather chair in the second row that I'd had throughout the season. Coach held reports on every one of us: our finals schedule that week, our current grades, and our attendance record for the entire semester. He started naming individual players, telling them to make sure they were ready for specific tests. Coach Izzo wasn't doing it to embarrass anyone; he wanted to push us.

Then he came around to me.

"You need to be ready for these exams, A.I. You've slipped this semester—I see a lot of absences here. Maybe you've been wrapped up with your girlfriend. Maybe you're going home too much and hanging out there when you should be studying. I don't know what's happened, but you need to be ready. Get focused and finish strong, OK?"

His words didn't carry an ounce of meanness, but I only heard cruelty. I snapped.

I stood up and pointed my finger right at Coach Izzo. "Don't you bring my girlfriend into this!" I yelled. "Don't bring my family into this!" I started throwing every swear word in the book at him. I blurted that he had no right to shame me in front of the team. He was out of line, mocking my academic struggles.

When I finished, the room fell silent. No player had ever snapped at Izzo like that before—especially not a walk-on. Draymond Green quietly spun his chair around to face me. "What are you doing?" he whispered. "Do you even want to be here?" His stunned look asked another question: *Do you want to walk out of this room alive?*

I ignored Draymond's questions. I was way too upset to acknowledge him. Besides, I didn't understand the explosion any better than he did. Was I trying to get kicked off the team, so soon after I'd promised to be a leader on it?

Izzo gave me the evilest look anybody's ever given me in my life. "Don't you ever talk like that to me again," he snapped. "Office. Now."

Dane Fife, an assistant coach who'd been with the team for only a week, followed me out—maybe to make sure I didn't hurl anything through a window. Fife was still getting to know the players, and this was his introduction to me.

"Whatever it is, you seem like you're going through a lot," he said as we walked. "But whatever the issue, you can't pull what you just did with Coach. That can't happen in the film room. If you need to vent, you find me, and we'll go for a walk. Not in the film room."

Coach Izzo wrapped up the meeting, came to his office, slammed the door, and sat across his desk from me. Before he could say a word, I started bawling.

"Coach, my god, I'm so sorry," I blubbered. "I didn't mean for that to happen. I just feel like everything is spiraling out of control, ever since my uncle was taken from me. Mentally I'm just checked out. Nothing seems important. Classes don't matter. I can't get into anything. I don't even know who to go to about this. I can't tell my family that I'm feeling like this. I don't want to share it with any of my friends or my teammates. I'm desperate, Coach. I need help. I'm screwed up."

I buried my face in my hands, afraid to look at my coach. The tears kept coming.

Coach Izzo pulled his desk chair around so that he was sitting next to me. He put his arm around me.

"I know what they said about you when you were younger, A.I.," he said. "I know you weren't supposed to ever make it here. But that's the past. Let's talk about now. You've been on a path this year that isn't working, and if you stay on that path, you won't be here at Michigan State in the fall. You're going to be gone. And you'll come back to campus in the fall for a football game, but you won't be here as a student, and everyone who's ever doubted you and made fun of you, they'll finally be right about you. They always said you'd fall short, and they'll finally get to see you fail."

He kept his arm around me.

"So you need to walk out of my office tonight with a mindset you haven't had in a long time. You need to be hungry for success. And that includes academic success. You need to prepare hard for your finals, and a few weeks from now, when you come back for summer workouts, you need to tell yourself you're going to have the best year of your life.

"And before you go, I'll tell you this. May fifth next year is the day you graduate, right here in the Breslin Center. And you *will* walk across the stage that day, and you *will* get your diploma, and when you've made your way to the other end of the stage, somebody's going to be waiting there to shake your hand and hug you. And that's going to be me. I'll be the very first person to congratulate you on being a college graduate."

We stood together, and Coach guided me out of his office. We shook hands once more, and I exited the Breslin Center, alone. Thirty minutes later I flopped onto my couch, still not sure how to handle my exams. I considered calling Kelly, but I didn't want to admit what I'd done in the film room. Finally I told myself, *Coach is right. If Coach Izzo believes you can do this, you can do it.*

That spring my exams all fell on different days, with room between each for cramming. It made my studying priorities obvious and allowed me to focus on one course at a time. I arranged for extra sessions with the team's tutors, and that week I rarely left the Clara Bell Smith Center, the academic support facility for student-athletes. When the week was over, I had passed everything—though in a few courses, I'd cut it close. Never again would I jeopardize my eligibility, I vowed.

My tirade in the film room was one of the most visibly autistic moments I'd had in a long time. I had misinterpreted language. I'd been socially inappropriate. I'd launched into an emotional outburst. Coach Izzo had responded in just the right way, though, and I left his office more eager to succeed than I had ever felt in my life.

\* \* \*

Draymond frequently led our lifting and conditioning exercises. One day the team was in the Duffy doing lunges. Day Day called off the sets. As we finished, Coach Vork reminded all new team members—freshmen and transfers alike—that today was their VO2 Max test. The test checked new players' heart and lung health. I'd done it two years earlier, when I'd first transferred, and it had been brutal. When the test administrator first hooked me up with sensors, I'd jogged slowly on the treadmill, but then he sped it up, and sped it up some more, to the point where I was gasping and didn't know whether to collapse or throw up. The test is a kind of rite of passage.

"They want you, too, A.I.," Draymond said. "Your VO2 workout is today."

"No, it isn't."

"They said your name."

"No way."

It didn't make any sense. My score hadn't been great, but once was once. They tested the new players, and I wasn't a new player.

"I don't want you to forget, A.I. They said your test is at 11:30."

I froze. Did I really have to get on that treadmill today?

Guys started laughing. I swiveled toward Draymond and got in his face. "Shut the hell up!"

I cussed at him, and he bumped me back.

My teammates dropped their weights and hurried toward us. Nobody laughed now.

"You need to learn how to take a joke," Draymond spat. "You can't take a joke, you shouldn't be here."

I wanted to shove him. And punch him. *Don't talk to me about taking jokes. Do you know how many jokes I've taken in my life?*

Coach Vork stepped between us. "Listen," Vork said to Draymond, "the thing about A.I. is, he's autistic. He's not always going to catch when you're kidding."

Vork looked at me. Regret flashed in his eyes. *Shit,* he must have thought, *maybe I wasn't supposed to say anything.*

"I should have asked you first," he said. "It's out of the bag now, though, so is it OK if I explain?"

*Out of the bag. . . .* There was a time when even that would have confused me.

"Go ahead," I said, still fuming. "Do what you gotta do."

I strode out, not sticking around to hear Vork's explanation. I was still in fight mode, not heartfelt moment mode. It was weird having my autism revealed this way. It was nothing like at Grand Valley, where I'd told the team myself. This time I wasn't even in the room to hear Vork describe how the spectrum worked.

The next day Draymond pulled me aside. "How come you never told me?" he said. "All that could have been avoided."

"I didn't know how you or anybody else would take it."

"Come on, A.I. You should've known we'd be cool. But kudos to you. You've had to overcome some odds, man."

That summer, Draymond started taking more time with me in practice. When we ran new plays, Draymond paced me through my movements and responsibilities, down to the smallest detail. "Set the pick right here," he demonstrated, guiding me to the top of the key, "and don't set it early. Move for your spot here exactly with the pass, not before."

During conditioning, I was always one of the slowest and ugliest runners—the same as at Grand Valley. This time, though, I had one of the best players in college basketball cheering me on. "You got this, A.I.," Draymond encouraged. "Keep it going!"

Although I'd initially been the butt of Draymond's VO2 Max joke, the story took a turn after I left the room.

The next lifting session after my near-fight, I showed up early, and Vork had a chance to talk with me alone. "Want to hear what the guys said after you left?" he asked.

"What did they say?"

"Derrick and Draymond were talking," Vork said, meaning Derrick Nix, a center who had played high school basketball at Detroit Pershing. "And Derrick said, 'I don't understand what the big deal about A.I. is. You know, I'm artistic, too.'"

Vork had double-checked: "What did you say?"

"Artistic. That's what you said, right?"

\* \* \*

The basketball team sits together for football games at Spartan Stadium. We share a block of seats about forty rows from the field with other Spartan athletes, recruits, and alumni who once played for Michigan State. For many of my teammates, their first time in the stadium was on a recruiting trip, but I'd grown up spending fall Saturdays here with my family. My parents' seats were still in section 23, directly across the field from my teammates and me. This felt significant, trading one seat for another. As a boy I was just a fan, and I was just Greg Ianni's kid. Sometimes I abandoned my seat and tagged along behind my dad, especially when he worked from the club section in the stadium's tower of offices and suites. Now, gathered with the other athletes, I sensed that I was a part of something larger than myself. I represented MSU. The public address announcer often acknowledged our team's presence, and people around us cheered. I wore the green and white not as a fan but as an ambassador.

The first Saturday of September, our football team played its home opener against Youngstown State. The Spartans began the season ranked seventeenth in the country, and the game was expected to be a warm-up for us. While everyone focused their attention on the team's stars—guys like quarterback Kirk Cousins and wide receiver B.J. Cunningham—my eyes focused on one number, 73, the number of my old roommate, Arthur Ray, who for the first time was cleared to play. Our first offensive possession, I saw him take the field.

Arthur was starting.

"That's my boy!" I yelled to anyone around me who would listen. "Seventy-three, that's Arthur Ray! He's starting." I turned to Travis Trice, who was next to me. "He was my roommate! The Lions' Den!" I told Travis about Arthur's bone cancer, and the surgeries on his leg, and how he wasn't expected to ever play again.

Art's dedication had paid off. He was healthy and on the field. As soon as the game finished, which Michigan State won easily, 28–6, I sent a lengthy text to Arthur. I told him how excited I was to see him on the field, and how proud I was of him. He'd worked so hard to get there. Others would have given up. Others wouldn't have had his mental toughness, and would have let doubt and pain get the best of them. When people think of dramatic moments in sports, they think of championship games and last-second heroics. I think of those things, too, but I also think of number 73, Arthur Ray, jogging onto the field against Youngstown State to line up at left guard.

Truly, all signs pointed toward a great senior year for me. Coach Izzo had promised he would see me receive my diploma, Draymond had assured me he had my back, and now the other lion from the Lions' Den was inspiring me to never give up.

\* \* \*

The energy in the film room had changed. It was barely September, and our first game was still two months away, but a brotherhood was forming. Guys joked more warmly than they had the previous season. We chatted with more affection: about that summer's NBA finals, about the MSU football team, about our classes that semester. We knew how hard we'd worked that summer on the court and in the weight room, and we were eager to show the world what this year's team could do. The Associated Press preseason poll hadn't ranked us in the country's top twenty-five, and the Big Ten's prognosticators had placed us somewhere in the middle of the pack. Free from the burden of high expectations, we were loose—and ready to show the forecasters how wrong they were. As we took our leather chairs, groups of us made plans to buy textbooks together that evening and to grab dinner afterward. These groups were noticeably larger than the previous season's.

I felt like a different person, too. I'd taken four classes that summer, and I'd earned nothing but 3.5s and 4.0s. My life seemed to have purpose now, and any obstacles seemed puny. Thanks to Draymond and others, I grasped our playbook better than I ever had before. Already I knew what my role on the team would be: the most vocal guy on the bench, the guy who never stopped hustling in practice, the guy who treated each scrimmage like it was a Final Four game. It wasn't the role I'd wanted for myself when my college career began, but I had come to embrace it fully.

Coach Izzo's meeting was a short one. He went over the preseason workout schedule and made sure everybody's classes were in order. Coach must have enjoyed the chemistry that afternoon, too. He recognized that he had a tight-knit group on his hands.

After Coach concluded the meeting, he said, "A.I., I need to see you."

I followed him to his office, and he shut the door.

"I want you to know," he said, "that I am 99.9 percent sure that you are on scholarship this year."

"Say that again?"

"You're on scholarship. You worked your tail off this summer. All the hard work you've put in, on and off the court, the improvement you've shown since your little explosion in May— the scholarship is part of the reward. Now, there will be bigger rewards. This team is going to do great things this year, and you're going to help get us there. You'll graduate in May. Those are rewards, too, but right now your reward is a scholarship."

"Thank you," I managed. "I . . ." What could I say? "Coach, thank you."

"You busted your butt to get this, A.I., but don't forget: the work is just starting."

"I know, Coach. I won't let you down. I promise you. Whatever you want from me, you got it. I'm going to keep playing my role."

Coach Izzo smiled. I sensed not just his happiness but his pride in me. "I know you will, A.I."

Afterward I turned out of his office and walked down the hallway, still numb, still not believing I was a scholarship player. My green-carpet route through the Breslin took me by photos of past teams: championship teams, teams with future NBA stars. My status had changed—I *belonged* more. My place in this chain of players that extended back in time was more secure.

The afternoon was still bright and warm, and the sun gleamed on the bronze statue of Magic Johnson: palming the ball, scanning the court, youthful and leading the Spartans to a national championship.

I turned around and faced the Breslin Center.

The Bres.

We had come into this world together, the Bres and I. The Spartans had played their first home game here late in 1989, ten months after I was born. Like me, the Bres was an unknown, its future a 15,000-seat mystery. Michigan State had briefly flashed on the national basketball scene in 1979 thanks to Magic Johnson, but the national title was receding by the time the Breslin Center opened. The Spartans had a few good years in the 1980s, but we weren't elite. We weren't the kind of team that had a permanent invitation to the NCAA tournament. It wasn't impossible to beat us on our home court. But as we settled in at the Bres, our ascension began. We won the Big Ten title in our first season in the new arena. In 1995, MSU promoted Tom Izzo from assistant coach to head coach, and three years later we tied for the Big Ten championship. We won the conference outright in 1999, en route to the Final Four. In 2000 we claimed the national championship, and in 2001 we returned to the Final Four. Since the Bres has become our home, we have reached the Final Four eight times and counting. We now are mentioned in the same breath as programs like Duke, North Carolina, and Kentucky.

Nobody could have imagined my story in 1989, either. My parents never would have believed that their newborn son was on the autism spectrum. And no one could have guessed the journey I would take to reach this moment: a child who wasn't supposed to play sports or go to college, a tall but uncoordinated boy who didn't catch anyone's eye in middle school, an improving high school player who saw offers from midlevel schools fall through, a recruit who committed to Grand Valley State but never found a place, and a transfer to MSU who joined the program as a walk-on and stayed home when the team traveled. Finally, I was a full-fledged member of the Spartan basketball team.

I started my car, but before I could pull out, I began to cry. I was a scholarship player. For two years I had tried to ignore the talk on message boards that I hadn't earned my place on the team. I'd read it all: that I was just another Okemos kid who sat on the end of the bench, that Izzo let me wear the jersey as a favor to my dad. One post even accused my dad of buying my spot on the roster. I tried to remind myself that most of these messages came from people who'd never played a game of basketball in their life. But now? I was a scholarship player. The NCAA permitted teams only thirteen scholarships a year, so Coach Izzo had to spend them wisely, and he'd offered one to me. I'd earned it. It didn't matter what high school I'd played for or who my dad was. Scholarships were too precious to burn on acts of generosity. I belonged to the team as much as anybody did now.

I thought about Uncle Nick. Even though he was gone, he was with me in that moment. He was savoring the news as much as I was. As I continued to cry, sitting there in my maroon Oldsmobile in the Breslin Center parking lot, I felt everyone I'd ever met join me in the car. The doubters and haters were seeing how wrong they were. The people who had mocked me when I swore I'd play for Michigan State would have to admit they'd been mistaken. My parents and teachers and Kelly and Geoff and

Przy and Grandpa Nick and everyone else who had ever supported me got to celebrate with me. They'd had my back every step of the way, and it had paid off.

*I did it*, I told them all. *The year's just starting, and I know I have a lot more to do, but I did it.*

The Rudy of Michigan State basketball.

Rudy opens rejection after rejection from Notre Dame's office of admissions. He applies one last time, and the answer arrives by mail. He carries the still-sealed envelope to a stone bench near the banks of the St. Joseph River, across from the university's Main Building and its iconic dome. Alone, he opens the letter. The music builds, and Rudy weeps. "Oh, thank god," he says.

This was my *Rudy* moment. This was my envelope. I was in my car, but in a way I was in South Bend, Indiana, looking across the river at the Golden Dome.

# 26

## THE *CARL VINSON* AND THE GARDEN

MY SENIOR YEAR BEGAN ON an aircraft carrier.

Where I met the president of the United States.

On Veterans Day 2011, we faced North Carolina on a court assembled on the deck of the USS *Carl Vinson*. The game was billed as the Carrier Classic. We traveled to San Diego, where the ship was in port, a few days before the game. Service members led our team on a tour of the ship. We met the captain and went up on the bridge and took in the view: the city's skyline, Coronado Island, San Diego Bay, the immense Pacific Ocean, and the gleaming hardwood floor and the basketball hoops directly below us. Sailors showed us how they lived and the work they did. I met some armed-forces members from Michigan, and they assured me that they'd be rooting for the Spartans. The sailors showed us the galley, and I admired its order. The sailors explained their precise schedules to us and the odd hours when they had to squeeze in sleep. They described their routines to the minute. The exceptional structure of their lives reminded me of my own childhood and how much order and predictability I had needed.

We were told we'd get to meet President Obama before the game, but we didn't know exactly where or when. We were on the court warming up when US Secret Service agents instructed both teams to follow them to a tent behind the bleachers. The agents lined us up in the tent and told us not to move. The president and the first lady would walk down each line and shake our hands, an agent said. "Stay where you are. They will come to you. When you meet the president," he said, "you will say, 'Hello, Mr. President, my name is so-and-so.' Refer to him as 'Mr. President.'"

When President and First Lady Obama entered the tent, we were all starstruck. Some of the players were stars themselves, within the world of college basketball, but being in President Obama's proximity left us in awe. A few of my teammates bounced on their feet like they were in line for Santa Claus. We weren't supposed to move, but as the president made his way down the North Carolina line, my teammates and I leaned to get better views, and we bunched up our line. Secret Service agents had to put us back in place.

As the Obamas started greeting Coach Izzo and the first of my teammates, I thought about my connection to him: I was wearing number 44, and I was about to shake hands with the forty-fourth president of the United States.

The funny thing is, I could have met a different US president on a different occasion, but didn't. In 1995, President Bill Clinton spoke at Michigan State's commencement in Spartan Stadium. My parents and sister attended, met the president, and took a picture with him. I'm not in the picture because they left me at home with my grandma. I was in kindergarten at the time, and my parents feared I would wig out. A meltdown in Target or my school was one thing, but they didn't want to take that chance when meeting the president.

President Obama reached me. I was looking at the president of the United States, face to face, each of us meeting the other's eye. I put my hand out. "Hello, Mr. President. My name is Anthony Ianni."

"Hey, Anthony, it's nice to meet you," he said. "Good luck this year. I hear you're graduating."

"Yes, sir."

"Best of luck to you."

After such honors—meeting the president, touring an aircraft carrier, and meeting so many men and women in uniform—we had to remind ourselves that we still had a game to play. This was no exhibition. This was game one of the regular season, and we wanted to start with a victory.

We kept a small lead for a good stretch in the first half, but then North Carolina pulled ahead 21–19. A free throw, a Spartan turnover, and a fast-break bucket later, we trailed by five. The Tar Heels extended the lead in the closing minutes of the half, and at the break we trailed 36–25.

They added to their lead in the second half, but we went on a 10–0 run to reduce the deficit to ten. The Tar Heels scored when they needed to, though, and beat us 67–55.

When the game was over, Draymond called together all of the players from both teams. We huddled at center court like we were a single unit. I stood next to North Carolina's Harrison Barnes. Draymond said, "Let's take these jerseys off and give them to the wounded. We can get other jerseys for ourselves later." He pinched his uniform. "These game one jerseys should go to the men and women of the armed forces."

Everyone, Spartans and Tar Heels alike, immediately agreed.

I found a seating area where some of the wounded were. I approached a man in a wheelchair, pulled off my jersey, and signed it.

"I want you to have this," I said. "Thank you for what you have given to our country."

\* \* \*

A few days later, we flew from Lansing to New York to face Duke in Madison Square Garden. It was one of the craziest and toughest starts to a college basketball season ever. North Carolina was ranked the best team in the country, and Duke was ranked sixth. Instead of starting at the Breslin or in someone else's gym, we faced opponents on an aircraft carrier and at the Garden.

We went to New York to take care of business and win a basketball game, but we still hoped to enjoy the surroundings a little. Our hotel wasn't far from Times Square, so some of the guys walked there to see the commotion and buy souvenirs. Austin, Day Day, freshman Travis Trice, and I wandered around the block until we found a pizza place. We wanted to try authentic New York pizza.

The moment I walked into the Garden, I felt its history. The hallways featured photos of people who had competed or performed there: not just New York Knicks like Patrick Ewing and Walt Frazier and New York Rangers like Wayne Gretzky, but also Muhammad Ali, WrestleMania, Garth Brooks, and so many more. In our locker room, I wondered what other teams had dressed there. What stars had sat where I was sitting, pulling on my shorts and tying my shoes? When I stepped onto the court for our first shootaround, I started to list the NBA greats who had played on this same floor: Michael Jordan, Kobe Bryant, Magic Johnson, Allen Iverson, Shaq . . . I could have gone on and on.

Another historic moment was possible that game, and we wanted to stop it. A Duke victory would make its coach, Mike Krzyzewski, the winningest coach in college basketball history. It was on our minds. *He can set the record against somebody else.*

The game stayed close throughout the first half, and Draymond scored the first points of the second half to give us a 35–34 edge, but the Blue Devils surged ahead and built a twenty-point lead. We made it close with a late run but lost 74–69.

We were 0–2, but we didn't feel like an 0–2 team. There was so much camaraderie that year. We cared about each other deeply, and we all knew what our team was capable of. Starting the season with two losses didn't shake us. We still had twenty-nine regular season games left to play, a Big Ten tournament, and an NCAA tournament. Of course we wanted to make a statement by winning at least one of those first two games, but a pair of losses would not define us.

"Let's learn from these games," Coach Izzo told us in the Madison Square Garden locker room. "Let's improve every day. Use every practice and every workout to improve, and we're going to get on a roll."

The work started as soon as the plane left New York. Coach Izzo and Day Day watched game film together in the back of the plane. Other coaches watched film with other guys. Nobody sulked, and nobody pointed fingers.

The loss to Duke happened on November 15.

We didn't lose again for two months.

*   *   *

When I was a sophomore at Okemos High School playing on the varsity team, the juniors and seniors took me under their wings and assured me I belonged. The same thing happened when I was a freshman at Grand Valley: seniors like Bean, Tommy Fellows, Joel Whymer, and L.J. Kilgore looked out for us. Now I was a senior. It was my turn to be the big brother for young guys like Travis Trice, Branden Dawson, Dan Chapman, Alex Gauna, Colby Wollenman, and Keenan Wetzel.

One thing I could do for those guys was be their chauffer. Among players with a car, I had the ugliest one. My maroon

Olds 88 was a hulking eyesore. It was missing a hubcap, and it rattled. Austin told me you could stand in the Breslin Center parking lot and listen for the racket. "Here comes A.I.," guys said when I was still blocks away.

My car was legendarily ugly, but also legendarily comfortable. During one ride, Dan Chapman said to me, "I'll give your car this, A.I.: the seat feels like you're chilling on a couch. It's like you've got a La-Z-Boy in here."

Often on Sunday nights after a workout, I drove the younger guys to a dorm cafeteria, and we all ate together. I explained what they should expect as we got deeper in the season: what Big Ten road games were like, how intense our rivalry was with the University of Michigan, and what to anticipate come March Madness.

I was captain of the scout team my senior year. Our job was to look as much like the next opponent as possible. If our next opponent was Florida State, we played defense the way Florida State did, and we ran their offense. As captain, I had to make sure we were all in position, running the plays correctly. I also had to bring as much energy as possible to the scrimmages. Sometimes it's hard to manufacture game-time intensity in an empty gym, but that's where I came in. Once I started clapping, yelling, fighting for rebounds, and stepping into the lane and taking charges, every guy out there—starter and scout team player alike—knew this was for real. It had to be.

We played our next three games at home and won all of them. I appeared briefly in all three, late in each game. Against Milwaukee, one of their players came into the lane for a layup. I anticipated the move and had a sick block. Our bench went nuts for me.

There was a scenario in which I would play a little more: I was a scholarship player now, and one of our forwards, Delvon Roe, had retired because of knee problems. If we had a game with a perfect storm of injuries and foul trouble, Coach Izzo might need me to give a few meaningful minutes. I talked about my dilemma with Coach Izzo. "Of course I want to be ready if you need me," I said. "But I've got a job as scout team captain, too. I think that should still be my focus."

"I agree," he said. "Keep the scout team your priority. Doing everything you can on scout team actually will prepare you, but keep your attention on the dirty work. What you're doing is crucial."

Our next game was against Eastern Michigan. Technically it was a road game, but plenty of Michigan State fans showed up at the Convocation Center in Ypsilanti. We built a big lead, and my scout team partner Alex Gauna and I took the court together late in the game. We'd played together so much already against the starters that we had a strong chemistry. One possession, Travis Trice hit me with a pass in the short corner near the baseline. I immediately feathered a no-look pass to Alex, who was cutting right where I knew he would. Alex dunked it, and I had one of the best assists of my career.

We played another three games at the Breslin and won all three, improving our record to 7–2.

Final exams approached, and so did the deadlines for major assignments. I had to write a lot of papers that semester; all of my sociology classes demanded essays.

I was using every resource at Michigan State available to me. Basketball gave me access to the Smith Center's Student Athlete Support Services, and I had the Resource Center for Persons with Disabilities—the RCPD—to help me overcome learning difficulties connected to my autism. I worked frequently with a woman named Gretchen Paige. Gretchen already had a master's degree in counseling, and she was working toward another master's degree in education. She reminded me of the two resource room teachers who had helped me throughout middle school and high school, Mrs. Hall and Mrs. Shafer. *One assign-ment at a time.* How many times had Mrs. Hall and Mrs. Shafer told me that? With Gretchen, it wasn't just one assignment at a time. It was one paragraph at a time. One *sentence* at a time.

"Don't just start writing your paper," she said one tutoring session. My assignment was to explain the historic tensions be-tween Irish people and Italians and offer ways in which the dis-like could have been addressed. I took the class with my friend Jared McGaha, an offensive lineman on the football team who was Irish and proud of it. Jared and I joked that we might have to stop being friends because of the assignment.

"Here." Gretchen handed me a lined sheet of paper. "Make a list of everything you want to say in the paper. Don't worry about the order or about spelling. Just list your ideas."

Once I finished, she read it over. "Now let's figure out where all of these ideas should go. An outline will make this a lot easier." She pointed at one item. "That should go in paragraph one, for example." We went through my list and decided where to put each idea. Once we created the outline, the actual paper flowed onto the page. When I finished, I could tell it was one of the best essays I'd ever written.

If you look back at how much I lagged behind my classmates in elementary school, writing a college-level paper was as great an accomplishment as making the basketball team.

Other guys had papers and exams, too. One day, because of players' class conflicts, the only time we could practice was 5:30 in the morning. And that meant dressed, on the court, and ready to go at 5:30. I set my alarm for 4:30 and was in the locker room by 5:00. A few of my teammates were already there, and a couple more came in with me. A minute after I took my seat, I heard the locker room door bang. "Let's go!" someone bellowed. It was Alex Gauna. Everyone laughed. The rest of campus was asleep, and we were about to play basketball. A more divided team would have complained and slacked through practice, but not us.

Kelly knew my exams were coming up. Our two-year anniversary was only a few weeks away, and things were fantastic between us. Usually. For a long time my Facebook profile picture had been of the two of us together. Often Kelly used the same photo for her profile picture, or a different one of us together. But sometimes she changed it up. Once, she switched it to a picture of her with her niece. As soon as I saw it I freaked out. I called her in a panic and asked her what it meant.

"I just wanted to show off my niece," she said. "Don't worry about it. It's not a big deal. We're as good as ever."

I give Kelly so much credit. She didn't insist that I make her my top priority. In fact, she did the opposite. "If you're in class," she told me, "you better not be texting me. Whatever you need to say can wait." Basketball was the same. When you're in the gym, she said, focus on practice. We have the rest of our lives to be together.

\* \* \*

We'd begun the season unranked, with some justification. Day Day was our best returning player. After that, our lineup looked uncertain, at least to people outside of East Lansing. Delvon Roe's knee issues had ended his career. Travis Trice was a true freshman. No one knew what we would get from transfer Brandon Wood. Nobody even picked us to finish near the top of our conference. At a preseason media day, I told a reporter from the *Lansing State Journal* that our physical toughness would bring us the Big Ten championship, and the reporter threw me a doubtful look.

When we boarded our plane for Spokane, Washington, to face Gonzaga, not many people thought we had a chance. Gonzaga was ranked twenty-third, and they'd lost only six times at home since 2004. Our second night in Spokane, we gathered in a reserved room at a steakhouse and had one of my favorite meals as a member of the Michigan State basketball team. It was nonstop joking and razzing, and I was catching all of the humor, or enough of it. The bonding reminded me of the best team dinners back in Okemos, when my mom and JJ's mom cooked together.

Draymond put us on his back that game. He shot from everywhere, and he scored from everywhere. We led 35–34 at the half and built a bigger lead in the second half. Draymond swung outside on some plays, and he hit four three-pointers and missed only once. We won 74–67, and Day Day finished with thirty-four points.

*I think it's time for us to be ranked*, I said to myself on the flight home.

The polls agreed. They ranked us twenty-first.

# 27

## THE BIG TEN

WE FINISHED OUR NONCONFERENCE SCHEDULE with three more victories at home, improving to 11–2. The Big Ten season began December 28. We hosted Indiana.

The day before the Indiana game, the scout team was scrimmaging the starters. I went up for an offensive rebound in a crowd of players. Coming down, I landed on someone's foot and violently rolled my right ankle. I hopped to the sideline and waited for a trainer. Immediately the ankle swelled to the size of a softball. The pain scared me; I was sure I'd broken something. People helped me to the training room. *God, no*, I thought. *Not this, not now. I'm not ready to be done. I don't want to end my career like this.*

The X-ray came back negative: it was just a sprain. A few weeks of rest and rehab. But, I couldn't lead the scout team as we prepared for road games at Nebraska and Wisconsin. And I couldn't give Coach Izzo any minutes if everything went wrong for the guys ahead of me.

During practices I alternated between the treadmill and the sideline. Sometimes I cheered on the scout team and tried to keep up the intensity, and other times I stayed in the weight room and managed to do a light jog and test the ankle.

We won all three of those games: Indiana, Nebraska, and Wisconsin. I still wasn't ready to rejoin the scout team as we prepared for Iowa, but it didn't matter. We defeated them soundly, 95–61. It was our fifteenth straight victory.

Second semester began. I needed to go to the bookstore to load up on course materials, and I invited Colby Wollenman to come with me. Colby was a freshman and a walk-on. Colby had played basketball in Big Horn, Wyoming, but had come to Michigan State on an academic scholarship. His plan was to be a doctor, not a basketball star. Everyone in the gym could tell from his first day of tryouts that he had the size, toughness, and intelligence to make the team. As we drove, I told him about growing up so close to Michigan State, and he told me about Wyoming. "There is a lot of space," he said. "Wide-open space." His graduating class had about thirty kids in it. Big Horn High School sounded nothing like Okemos.

He asked me, "What have you gotten out of being on scout team? Are you glad you've done it?"

"Absolutely. I love my role. Scout team is the best way I can help this program. If we don't play hard and play physical, our starters won't be ready."

\* \* \*

My ankle still wasn't fully recovered as we prepared for a road game against Northwestern. Even if I had been completely healthy, the coaches wouldn't have used me much. Northwestern didn't really have a big post player. Instead, they used a lot of quick guards who were good outside shooters. One name I recognized in the scouting report was Davide Curletti. Curletti had played for Orchard Lake St. Mary's with Kalin Lucas. I remembered our state semifinal battle. The report said that Curletti, listed as a six-foot nine-inch center, came off the bench and made the occasional three-pointer.

In practice I called out encouragement from the sidelines, but in retrospect I should have pushed the scout team harder and brought more intensity to our last few practices.

We started off hot, making a lot of early shots, but cooled off later in the first half. We also weren't adjusting to all of

Northwestern's picks and movement. They had space, and they made the most of it. At halftime, Northwestern had a 39–37 lead.

Curletti got a rare start that game, and he seized the opportunity. His shots were going in, and away from the ball he hustled. He hauled down rebounds on both ends of the court. Northwestern pulled away in the second half and beat us 81–74. Curletti's 17 points and 36 minutes had been the difference.

We bussed back from Evanston, and I was about to unlock my apartment door when my phone rang. It was after 11:00, and the number was unknown. Something told me it was Coach Izzo from his home phone, so I answered.

"A.I., what did I do wrong?" he said. "What happened today?"

"We didn't prepare as well as we should have," I admitted. "That's on the scout team. We should have had our guys ready, and we didn't. You can blame me. I know my ankle is still slowing me down, but I should have been better on the sidelines during scrimmage. I should have been more vocal."

"You think it's fair to blame the scout team?"

"You have every right to be hard on us. It's our responsibility to get guys ready. And Michigan is next. I guarantee you that tomorrow, scout team is going to be at another level."

I did not like the University of Michigan. It was personal for me. When I was little my cousins had taunted me, declaring that Michigan was the better school with the better teams. Most of my dad's siblings rooted for the Wolverines. I sensed that Michigan people arrogantly looked down on MSU. My parents went to a Michigan–Michigan State football game in Ann Arbor in 1996, and a Michigan fan spat on my mom, just because she had an MSU jacket on. Every game since then, no matter what sport, has felt for me like an opportunity for revenge. Baseball, hockey, soccer, football, basketball—it didn't matter.

The rest of the scout team and I watched a lot of film, and we replicated Michigan's offense. That meant a lot of ball screens. Sometimes I set a pick at the top of the key for a guy going left to right and then pivoted and faced the opposite way for another pick as the ball came back from right to left. It was tricky, and it was fast.

The previous season, Michigan beat us both times we played. The year before, we'd won both, but that was the season I'd had to sit out. I wanted a victory as a full-fledged member of the team. Two losses in a row was enough.

Michigan scored first and kept the lead throughout the first half. It was a streaky game. They went on a run to build a lead. Then we responded with a run to trim the deficit. We didn't have our first lead until the middle of the second half. We held a 57–53 advantage late in the game, only to squander it. Michigan regained the lead, 60–59, on a layup with 37 seconds to go. We couldn't make our last shots, and that's how the game ended.

My third loss in a row to Michigan.

\* \* \*

With my ankle recovered, I resumed my duties as the most fired-up guy on the bench. I danced and pumped my fists, celebrating every good play. Keenan Wetzel and I lifted a handshake from the Fresh Prince and performed it every time we hit a three-pointer. I didn't care if I was over the top. If guys laughed a little at my antics, then I was doing my job. If they chuckled, or even if they rolled their eyes, they were outside their own heads. When Travis Trice went through a string of missed shots and a few turnovers, I put my arm around him and pestered him with my optimism. "You're gonna make them. They're gonna fall. I believe in you, and you're gonna be just fine. Just keep shooting." I didn't believe in leaving people alone. I had faith in our guys, and I told them so over and over. Russ Byrd, I could tell, was still irritated by me at times, but I let it go. The team needed my exuberance, and a few comments from one guy didn't matter. Besides, Russ was frustrated. Foot injuries had hampered his development at MSU. I tried to remember that.

We won our next two Big Ten match-ups against Purdue and Minnesota. Then we traveled to Illinois. Both Brandon Wood and Draymond were dealing with food poisoning on the way down. They were throwing up on the plane and on the bus, and both spent their down time in bed. The game was weird and ugly, and neither team made many shots. Draymond was feeling better, but he hurt his knee with four minutes to go and had to sit. We held a late lead but let it slip away and lost 42–41. On the trip back, I worried more about Day Day's knee than I did the loss. We had a rematch against Michigan next. Draymond had to be healthy.

The next day we had a film session. Just the players gathered and watched the Illinois debacle. "We're watching this once, and we're putting it behind us," Draymond declared to the room. His knee was already feeling better.

Every mistake on the screen was a mistake we vowed not to repeat against Michigan. I sensed that some of the younger guys, especially the younger guys from out of state, didn't fully appreciate the rivalry. "This is our last chance," I said to the room. "Michigan beat us three times in a row. For us seniors, we can't go out like that. If we lose again, we're going to have to live with that for the rest of our lives. Our program is better than theirs. We have to win."

I worried that some of the guys still didn't appreciate the rivalry's bitterness. I asked Jordan, our video coordinator, to find the clips of Michigan's Mike Hart and Michigan State's Mark Dantonio. Michigan's football team pulled off a comeback win in 2007, and Hart, the Wolverines' running back, had said this in his press conference afterward: "Sometimes you get your little brother excited when you're playing basketball and let him get the lead. Then you just come back and take it back."

He had the nerve to call us "little brother."

In response, the Spartans' Coach Dantonio said during a press conference, "They need to check themselves sometimes.

Let's just remember, pride comes before the fall." Coach Dantonio's voice was calm, but there was fury behind it.

I'd seen both clips a dozen times or more, but watching them with my teammates a few days before we faced Michigan on the court, it was like I was seeing the videos for the first time. My anger was raw.

It was a beautiful game. We scored the first points and never trailed. Draymond, who had guaranteed a victory, was incredible, especially on the boards. We led by eight at the half, and at one point in the second half, we pulled ahead by seventeen. We were winning 64–54 as the last sixty seconds began to tick off the clock. The Izzone was going crazy—it was as loud as I'd ever heard it. With about twenty seconds remaining, Coach Izzo put me in the game. I stepped onto the court and savored the moment. As we slowly brought the ball up, I walked along the sideline and started tugging at my jersey. My message to the Breslin Center was clear: *THIS is the top basketball team in the state. THIS team will not be disrespected. THIS team is going to win the Big Ten.* That entire section of the arena went wild.

Draymond finished with sixteen rebounds; the entire Michigan team combined had fifteen.

We'd beaten Michigan, but we still had a Big Ten title left to chase.

* * *

Prepping for Ohio State was a blast. My job was to pretend to be Jared Sullinger, one of the best big men in the country. Sullinger shot lots of turnaround jumpers, could put the ball on the floor for strong drives, and tried the occasional three-pointer. He also caught the ball in the post and fired creative inside-out passes to wide-open guys. I got to do all those things in scrimmage. When I hit a three-pointer, my teammates gave me a lot of cheers.

"You should think about using me as a three-point weapon more often," I told Coach Izzo.

He shook his head. "Stick to the post."

I give a lot of credit to Jordan Ott. Even though he was our video coordinator, he had the patience and the instincts of a special education teacher.

I didn't grasp an opponent's plays as quickly as Colby, Dan, and the other scout team players did. I also took longer to mimic a specific guy's moves and tendencies. Jordan was generous with his time. He and I watched a lot of film together, just the two of us. Before the Ohio State game, he showed me a lot of clips of Jared Sullinger. He slowed down the film for me. "Watch his feet," Jordan said. "Watch where his right foot goes."

I stood and tried to copy the move.

"Not quite," Jordan said.

Bubbles of frustration began to rise in me.

"You'll get it. Watch again. Pay attention to the spin . . . there."

I stood up. "Like this?"

"Exactly. That's it."

In special education classes, they call this an accommodation. The idea is that a student with a disability can have success, given more help and adjusted instructions. Jordan just thought of it as a little extra coaching, but it worked.

We traveled to Columbus, knowing a win would put us in a tie for first place. We played our best defense of the season and held Sullinger to seventeen points and forced him into a lot of turnovers. We led 35–25 at the half, let the Buckeyes get within four points once in the second half, and pulled away and won 58–48.

From there, we kept on rolling, beating Wisconsin at the Breslin Center and Purdue on the road. Then we flew to Minnesota for my final game in the Barn. We took a one-point lead into the locker room at the half, but we didn't look good. Minnesota surged ahead after the break and took a 48–39 lead. They stayed ahead until late in the game, but we mounted a comeback and squeaked by with a 66–61 victory. My dad was on the trip, and he hugged me on the court after we won. "It feels like your journey started here," he said, and I knew what he meant. Thirteen years earlier I'd been a ten-year-old ball boy, and I'd watched the Spartans come from behind to win. Now I wore the jersey, and history had just repeated itself. Dad said, "We closed the circle."

With two games to go, we had first place to ourselves. We were 13–3 in the Big Ten, and Ohio State and Michigan were both 11–5. We controlled our destiny.

We traveled to Indiana and lost to the ranked Hoosiers. Michigan and Ohio State both won.

That set up a showdown: Ohio State was coming to the Bres for the final game of the season. If we won, the Big Ten title was ours and ours alone. If we lost, we had to share it with Ohio State and Michigan. We hadn't lost in the Bres all season: a perfect 17 and 0.

For the seniors, the last home game of the season also meant the last home game ever.

In the days leading up to Senior Day, local news outlets wrote individual stories on each of us: Draymond, Brandon Wood, Austin Thornton, and me. "MLive" is a website run by a Michigan newspaper chain, and a story about me went up the day before the Ohio State game. I knew it was coming; the reporter had interviewed me for it. And even though I'd answered his questions, I wasn't fully prepared for the article's focus.

It was almost entirely about my autism.

He'd interviewed not only me but also my parents, and they'd provided him with many of the cardinal moments of my life as an autistic athlete: my initial diagnosis, the initial IEP meeting during my kindergarten year, the elementary school bullying, and the peace I discovered on the basketball court.

The article was scheduled to go online the night before we played Ohio State, while we were having one last practice. After practice ended and I'd showered, I went to my car and checked my phone for the article. It was up.

I was stunned to see paragraph after paragraph emphasize my life on the spectrum.

I wasn't stunned for long. The article flowed so well and told my story so clearly that I mainly felt happy to see how good it was.

One line, though, did make me wince:

"He has also emerged as a gregarious presence in the locker room and on the bench for the fifth-ranked team in the nation—a jolly giant in green relishing his role in helping the Spartans win."

*Did he really just call me a green giant?*

The sentence awoke some bad memories, but I knew the mistake was an innocent one, and since the whole point of the article was that I'd proven the bullies wrong, I didn't mind.

Two quotes in the article caught my eye. The first was from Coach Izzo.

"What he's done for us, not many people can do," the article quotes him as saying. And this is the part that made me swell with pride: "He bangs Nix and Payne and Gauna and Day-Day every day, and that's no fun job. He does the dirty work, and that's what I respect about him the most."

The article closed with a quote that was even more emotional for me. It was from Dad: "I've had two heroes in my life—my dad and Anthony. If I could be more like anyone in the world, it'd be Anthony."

# 28

## TOURNAMENTS AND AWARDS

THIS IS HOW SENIOR DAY was supposed to go: First, we would beat Ohio State. Then we would celebrate winning the Big Ten regular season title. Then, still elated from the win and from raising the Big Ten banner, we would begin the ceremony for the seniors.

The game began exactly the way I wanted it to. Ohio State started cold, and our shots were falling. We roared ahead early and at one point led 24–9. At halftime we held a 38–29 advantage. We were twenty minutes away from the Big Ten championship.

The Bres was rocking, especially the Izzone. The Izzone had witnessed seventeen straight home victories that season, and we were about to make it eighteen. I was my usual vocal self, clapping and cheering wildly.

We came out of the locker room and let the Buckeyes score the first six points of the second half. The rest of the game was back and forth: their lead, our lead, tie.

Twenty seconds remained with the game again tied. Ohio State had the ball and would get the last shot. We defended like crazy and forced their shooting guard, senior William Buford, to put up an off-balance jumper. He had one foot on the three-point line, his arms weren't right, and Keith Appling was in his face, but somehow Buford's shot went in. Ohio State 72, Michigan State 70.

We would have to share the Big Ten title with Ohio State. We also would have to share it with Michigan, who claimed their third of the honor by beating Penn State that day.

It was bittersweet. We were still champions, and it was still Senior Day, but we didn't want to share anything with anybody, least of all Michigan.

The seniors retreated to the tunnel for the ceremonies. I lined up with my parents and my sister, waiting for my introduction. I cried for so many reasons: because we'd blown a lead and lost on our own floor, because we had let Ohio State and Michigan claim a share of the title, and because I was saying goodbye to the Breslin Center. We still had some games to play, but not here. Not on my home court. Dad took me by the shoulders and said, "You're still a Big Ten champion. Don't you ever forget that. And you have plenty more work to do."

I was the first senior to be introduced. My parents and Allison escorted me onto the court as my name and the number 44 flashed on the ribbon board. My highlight reel played on the main scoreboard; it included my bench mob celebrations and my blocked shot against Milwaukee. I dropped to a push-up position and kissed the Spartan head at center court. I stood and said to myself, *Your dream is officially achieved.*

\* \* \*

I returned to the Breslin Center the next night for our team banquet. The arena's crew had pulled up the basketball court, rolled out carpet, and set up tables. The team sat at a long table on a stage; I was next to Day Day and Adreian Payne. At the tables below, hundreds of people joined us: parents, school administration, faculty, donors, and dedicated fans who paid to share the dinner with us and watch our awards ceremony. I scanned the program for an award I might win. I knew I didn't have a chance at most of them: MVP, defensive player of the year, scholar-athlete award, or the "Jumping Johnny Green Chairman of the Boards" award for the team's top rebounder. The previous year I'd won the Tim Bograkos Walk-On award, but this year I was on scholarship.

The event's keynote speaker was Brian Calley, who was Michigan's lieutenant governor and also an MSU alumnus. I'd never heard of Brian Calley before that night, and he had heard of me only because of the MLive article. When Mr. Calley read the feature, he didn't just see the Ianni family. He saw his own. Brian Calley and his wife have three children. Their middle child, a daughter named Reagan, is on the spectrum. For years, Mr. Calley had been a public advocate for autism awareness. He was involved in the Autism Alliance of Michigan, and that spring he was pushing for legislation that would improve health insurance coverage for children with autism.

He sought out my parents among the tables, introduced himself, and explained why my story meant so much to him. Through my parents, Mr. Calley invited me to the Autism Alliance of Michigan's annual gala to speak about my experiences as an autistic athlete. Mom and Dad assured him that I would call.

The first award of the night went to my fellow Okemos native, Dan Chapman, who received the walk-on player award. Next, Vork took the microphone to announce the Unsung Player winner. It was the only recognition I thought I had a shot at.

Vork began to describe Derrick Nix: how he'd worked to lose weight and improve his game. I was disappointed that I hadn't won, but I knew Derrick was just as deserving.

Then Vork said that Derrick was sharing the honors with a second recipient:

"Anthony Ianni."

Since Derrick and I shared the award, Vork told the story of when he lit it slip in the weight room that I was autistic. The MLive article had been up for a few days, so my autism was public knowledge by then. When Vork recounted that Derrick had heard it as "artistic," he got one of the biggest laughs of the evening.

After I returned to my seat, I said to Draymond, "That's two awards for Okemos and zero for Saginaw."

"You just wait."

Draymond was right. The ceremony continued, and he picked up one award after another: the rebounding award, the inspirational player award, the players' MVP, the media's MVP, and the "Antonio Smith Glue and Guts Award," named after Big Tone, my first Spartan hero.

After he was recognized for the third time, Draymond said to me, "You want to tally up that score again, A.I.?"

Despite the ceremony and the awards, we still had some games left. A lot of games, if both tournaments went the way I wanted them to.

\* \* \*

A few days later, we were on our way to Indianapolis for the Big Ten Tournament. Indy is a short drive for many schools in our conference, so fans show up and make noise. We'd earned a first-round bye, which meant four teams were knocked out on Thursday while we rested and went through plays in our hotel's banquet room on our taped court.

Friday saw no upsets. The Big Ten's four best teams—us, Ohio State, Michigan, and Wisconsin—all won. On Saturday we defeated Wisconsin and Ohio State beat Michigan, setting up a rematch with the Buckeyes—a chance for revenge. Ohio State had won the Big Ten Tournament the last two years, and we hadn't won since 2000, the year we claimed the national championship.

During warm-ups that Sunday, I thought about that tournament in 2000. I'd been an eleven-year-old fan sitting with my family, a youth-league basketball player who was tall but unremarkable. Now I was on the court, in the layup line, wearing a jersey. The journey from the seats to the floor had been a long one.

The entire game against Ohio State was like an extension of our previous match's second half. The lead kept changing hands. Play was physical, especially in the paint. Our two guys assigned to Sullinger, Adreian Payne and Derrick Nix, fought him for every inch. We led 34–32 at the half, but Sullinger and the Buckeyes started the second half strong and built a 52–45 lead. We scored the next ten points to go back on top. Day Day's shots weren't falling, but Brandon Wood was having his best game of the season.

Minutes ticked off. We led by three. By five. By three.

Austin made a free throw with thirteen seconds on the clock to give us a 68–64 lead. Elation surged through me when his shot went in. A two-possession lead! No last-second shot from Buford or any other Buckeye could get us now.

Thirteen long seconds later, the horn blared. It would have rattled me when I was in kindergarten. Now it was the best sound ever. We spilled onto the floor. I hugged every teammate I could find. I grabbed a camera from MSU's media team and pointed it at my face and bragged, "We don't have to share anything with anybody now!"

A ladder was opened underneath the basket. The last time Michigan State cut strings, I was hundreds of miles away and Draymond had to snip my piece for me. Now I climbed the ladder myself and cut my own piece of the net. I was a Big Ten champ! Kelly and her brother had traveled to Indianapolis for the weekend and were staying in our team's hotel. She got to see me gather around the trophy with my teammates and pose for pictures.

I knew Dad would be in the swarm of people on the court, and I moved through the crowd looking for him. I found him near the sideline by our bench and gave him the biggest hug ever. "We did it!" I said. "We did it!"

*  *  *

When I was in tenth grade and just starting to play varsity basketball, college seemed a long way off. Visiting Grand Valley for the first time, I thought my college career would last forever. After I transferred to Michigan State, so much basketball still remained for me. But now it was just about over. March Madness is cruel to seniors. A loss ends your career. Out of the sixty-eight teams that played in the NCAA tournament that spring, sixty-seven ended the season by losing, and sixty-six seasons ended abruptly, before reaching the finals.

The NCAA bracket-makers awarded us the number-one seed in the West. We would play our first two games in Columbus, Ohio, giving us a home-crowd edge. Our first matchup was against Long Island University–Brooklyn. We were heavily favored, but upsets happen every March, and anytime you underestimate an opponent, you're setting yourself up to lose.

We were still in the hotel when we saw that the second-best team in our region, Missouri, had been upset by fifteen-seed Norfolk State. We hadn't even arrived at the arena yet, and I was already thinking that our path to the Final Four had just gotten a little easier.

Long Island kept it close through the first half. The last thing we wanted was for them to start believing an upset was possible, but at intermission we led by just five: 42–37.

We surged ahead in the second half, building a 66–50 lead. Then it was 74–54.

On the bench, I kept an eye on the scoreboard as it posted results from other games around the country. Then I saw Duke's score: they'd lost to fifteen-seed Lehigh, 75–70. I elbowed Dan

Chapman, who sat next to me, and pointed: "Duke is out! That's huge."

Chap and I both went in with a few minutes left and the game already decided. All season I'd vowed to assist him on the first basket of his college career. It hadn't happened yet, but the NCAA tournament was a great time to change that. Two Okemos kids could end up on the stats sheet together.

"Cut backdoor, and I'll get it to you."

I caught the ball near the edge of the free-throw line. Chap faked a move toward me, then burst toward the hoop. I led him with a bounce pass . . . and he missed the layup.

"I could have had an assist," I teased him after. "Chieftain to Chieftain."

"I know. I shouldn't have missed it."

It's easy to joke about those things when you win by twenty-two.

Two days later we played our region's nine-seed, St. Louis. This one was much closer—we won 65–61—so Dan Chapman and I stayed on the bench. Kelly drove to Columbus for the game, so after our victory, I waved to her and blew her a kiss.

With the victory we advanced to the Sweet Sixteen.

*   *   *

We flew to Phoenix for our contest with Louisville. A victory would put us in the Elite Eight, a win away from another trip to the Final Four.

Louisville was a perennially strong team, and they'd had a good season. Not a great season, but a good one. All week in practice, Coach Izzo stressed the importance of rebounding. Louisville would miss some shots. We had to grab the misses and not give them a second chance.

Sure enough, Louisville started slowly, missing shot after shot early. The problem was, we couldn't score, either. Louisville had a big man from Senegal named Gorgui Dieng who shut down everything inside and blocked one shot after another. Their stifling defense drained us.

We held them to twenty-three points in the first half.

But we'd managed only eighteen.

In the second half we fell behind 35–25. We made it 35–29 with a basket and two free throws. On our next trip down, Day Day slammed home an offensive rebound to make it 35–31. We had all the momentum. We defended fiercely on the next possession, and the shot clock ticked down. With just a few seconds left to shoot, Louisville got the ball inside and made a layup. We tried to respond with an inside play of our own, but Gorgui Dieng blocked Adreian Payne's shot, and just like that, our momentum fizzled.

A few minutes later the Cardinals extended their lead to 46–33.

When I was little, I had that saying: "Nobody wins and nobody loses." That got me through a few tough losses as a fan. But the chant wouldn't work this time. Somebody had to lose. The clock ran down. A comeback was unlikely. Then impossible.

With twenty-eight seconds left and the game out of reach, Coach Izzo sent me in for Day Day. It wasn't how I wanted either of our careers to end, but in a way, it fit. For three years I'd busted my butt in practice in order to make Day Day a better player. I'd taken his charges, and I'd battled with him for rebounds. We'd fought for position in the paint in scrimmage after scrimmage. This was the final thing I could do for him: sub in for him so our fans could applaud as he stepped off the court. All of the Spartan fans in the Phoenix arena stood and gave Draymond an ovation. I hugged him, grateful to have had him as a teammate and a leader.

In the locker room afterward, some guys were pissed and others were just sad. There were tears. This had been a special team, and not just because of the victories and the titles. We had been brothers, all of us. I went around the room to every single guy and hugged them and thanked them for everything. The other seniors and I had a group hug. Yes, we said to each other, we came up short, but we accomplished a lot, and we put Michigan State back among the elite teams of college basketball, and that was something.

\* \* \*

A few days after the loss to Louisville, my head was clear enough to think about the Autism Alliance event.

"OK," I said to Mom. "You can tell the lieutenant governor I'd like to speak at the gala."

\* \* \*

For the first time in fifteen years, I had no basketball season to look forward to. I took a break from workouts and hit some of the East Lansing bars with Jared McGaha and other friends. I wanted to have one month of life as just a typical college kid in East Lansing.

Graduation approached. Soon I would have a sociology degree. But what was I going to do with it?

My broadcasting dreams had faded. I'd done nothing with them since transferring from Grand Valley. I hadn't spent any more time on radio shows, and I'd already forgotten the little I'd learned about radio and TV technology.

Sometimes guys in my position went to Europe and played basketball. That's what JJ had done the previous year. After graduating from Oakland and going undrafted, he signed with a team in Slovakia. I kept in touch with him while he was abroad and met him once when he was home on break and working out in the Okemos High School gym. If your heart wants to keep playing basketball, then Europe is OK, JJ told me, but the money isn't good, and the off-court hours are lonely. I gave little thought to basketball across the Atlantic. I'd miss my family way too much. And what about Kelly? I couldn't ask her to leave everything behind and join me in Slovakia, or Macedonia. Besides, think of all the communication problems I'd had over the last five years, and we were all speaking English. What would happen in Greece? How would I fare in Poland?

The most tempting career path was to follow my dad into sports management. The previous year I'd started to learn about the field. I'd shadowed some of MSU's people at soccer games and volleyball games. I took a sports management class and wrote reports on what I was learning at the games. When the MLive reporter asked me about my career plans, I told him I wanted to follow in my dad's footsteps.

That spring I helped with game-day management for our softball games. I unlocked the visitors' locker room, checked on the reporters in the press box, and made sure the concessions stand was running smoothly. When Indiana's softball team came to East Lansing, their parents disagreed with a few of the ump's calls. Indiana's supporters grew increasingly belligerent and vulgar. They swore at the umps . . . and our players, and our coaches, and our fans. "Go stand in their section," my supervisor said. "If they say anything that bad again, they've got to go."

As soon as I reached their section, I became their newest target: "Looks like the rent-a-cops are here!"

I wanted to go into game-day management and have the special moments with my kids that my dad had had with me, but at the moment, I was nothing more than a bouncer.

\* \* \*

The Unsung Player Award wasn't the only recognition I received that spring. The Resource Center for Persons with Disabilities held a reception that April in a club room at Spartan

Stadium, and the RCPD honored me with a perseverance award. My longtime academic coordinator, Gretchen Paige, had nominated me.

My grades were in order, and I was set to graduate, but Gretchen's work with me wasn't done.

"Can you help me write a speech?" I asked her.

I told her about the upcoming Autism Alliance gala in Detroit. Together, we worked on my remarks. My speech would be autobiographical—about my journey from that kindergarten IEP to the Michigan State locker room. Gretchen encouraged me to expand on a few moments.

"Don't talk too fast," Gretchen advised. "Take your time."

As I rehearsed my speech with Gretchen, and then again and again back in my apartment, I thought about Kirk Cousins. Kirk was Michigan State's star quarterback. At a Big Ten luncheon the previous summer, he had spoken on behalf of all of the football players in the entire conference. Cousins had expressed so much humility and gratitude in his speech. "It has been a privilege to play football in the Big Ten," he told the assembled media. "It has been a privilege to play college football, and to do so in the greatest conference in the country. While many children dream of playing college football, relatively few have the opportunity, and to be living that dream is a privilege. It has been a privilege to play home games in Spartan Stadium, in front of the fans that make up the Spartan Nation, who live and die, figuratively speaking, based on our team's performance each Saturday in the fall." Kirk included some good jokes but also stressed that athletes who have had his privileges should develop a sense of responsibility, not a sense of entitlement.

When he finished, the room stood and clapped for a long time: reporters, coaches from other teams, Big Ten Network people, everyone. I watched it on TV, and it was the best speech I'd ever seen by a young athlete. Soon every athlete on campus knew about it. Coach Izzo had us watch Kirk's speech that fall when he hosted the basketball team at his house.

I called my sister a few days before the gala and told her how much I'd been practicing. "I'm going to get my Kirk Cousins standing ovation," I told Allison.

"You don't know the crowd," she said. "Even if you are great, they might not stand. If they don't, it's not a big deal."

"Kirk showed how much pride he had in being a Spartan and a football player in the Big Ten. I want to say the same thing with autism, that I am extremely proud to be a member of the autism community. I'll get them to stand."

While I worked on my speech, the Michigan legislature finalized its autism bill and sent it to the governor's desk for final approval. Governor Rick Snyder was overseas visiting Michigan troops in Afghanistan at the time, so Brian Calley would sign the bill into law. Brian Calley's office called Mom and invited our family to the signing at the governor's mansion. Mom and I attended and stood nearby as Mr. Calley put his signature on the document. Also in attendance were Mr. Calley's wife and his daughter Reagan. I wore a suit—one that my Uncle Nick had bought for me. It was my way of having him join me in that moment.

As the gala approached, I didn't feel nervous. Three years of playing for one of the most high-profile college basketball teams in the country had adjusted me to the spotlight. I knew the crowd would be on my side—even the people who had gone to the University of Michigan.

Tuxedos and dresses were everywhere that night. The gala was held at the DTE Energy headquarters lobby. The room was bright and open with huge floor-to-ceiling windows that overlooked downtown Detroit, just to the east. Lots of corporate donors attended, and it occurred to me that someone might appreciate my speech and offer me a job.

Brian Calley hosted the evening's ceremonies, but broadcaster Frank Beckmann introduced me. As I took the stage, I reminded myself of Gretchen's advice: *Not too fast.*

I told the crowd my story, starting with my diagnosis and the low expectations set for me in kindergarten. I'd given this narrative before, in Ms. Freeman's class and for the MLive article, but never for such a large crowd, and never with so many people in the audience who had similar stories: Their own child's diagnosis. Their own child's first IEP. Doctors' predictions about their own son or daughter.

Being on the autism spectrum isn't a curse, I assured them. I am proud of it. Being autistic makes me who I am. And if someone says autism will prevent me from reaching a goal, I'm going to prove them wrong.

The applause filled the room—and everyone rose to their feet.

Frank Beckmann kept me on stage for some questions. We talked about life as a student-athlete at Michigan State, my family's tireless support, and my relationship with Kelly. "You and I both jumped out of our skis a little bit when it comes to the women in our lives," he joked.

Frank had been the voice of Michigan Wolverine football for more than thirty years, but he graciously admitted that the U of M–MSU football rivalry had tilted in the Spartans' favor in recent years. (Frank didn't use the term "little brother," but Michigan State had won all four games since the "little brother" interview.) Frank was warm and genuinely curious.

When Frank presented me with a plaque for being the autism advocate of the year, something clicked in my head. I wasn't just a person with autism. I was a champion for the cause. I could help others. I could inspire.

I was driving Kelly back to her family's home in northwest Detroit when I said, "I think I know what I'm supposed to do now."

Kelly waited.

"The autism community has Temple Grandin," I said. "Name somebody else besides her who is serving as a role model for people with autism."

"I can't."

"Me, neither. I think that's my calling. I need to step up and be the next hero. I can be another person that kids on the spectrum can look up to."

"Go out and do it, then," she said. "You've got the right mindset and the right story. I think you should try it and see what happens."

# 29

## COMMENCING

WHEN I PLAYED FOR MICHIGAN State, our floorboards were the same boards that the Spartans had won the 2000 national championship on. The university had bought the court from the RCA Dome in Indianapolis and had installed it at the Breslin Center. A plaque noting the floor's history was embedded on the baseline near the tunnel. Every time I emerged from the tunnel during my three years as a Spartan, whether it was for a game or a practice, I veered over to the plaque and tapped it with my foot.

On the morning of May 5, 2012, Kelly and I drove to the Breslin Center for the College of Social Science commencement ceremonies. My usual parking lot was already full, so we settled for a more distant space. I put on my cap and gown, and Kelly and I walked to the entrance together. She left me at the elevator. When I stepped into the elevator alone, it felt like I was going to just another practice. Pushing the button to go down was muscle memory for me. For most of the graduates, this might be the only time they ever used the Breslin elevator, but I'd taken it literally hundreds of times.

I found my buddy Jared in the tunnel beneath the stands. He was graduating with a degree in sociology, too, so when the commencement organizers separated us by our majors, Jared and I stayed together.

When the band began "Pomp and Circumstance," the moment felt more real to me. *You really are graduating. You, Anthony Ianni, an autistic student who wasn't expected to take a single college course, are about to receive a diploma from Michigan State University.*

As I stepped out of the tunnel, my instinct was to swerve toward the plaque and tap it one last time. But the court was stored away and there was no plaque. I stayed in line and marched toward my seat with the other sociology majors. I walked under all of the basketball program's banners, including the ones I had been a part of: the two Big Ten regular season championships, the 2012 Big Ten tournament championship, the 2010 Final Four appearance. My legacy was in those banners and would stay there in the Breslin's rafters long after I graduated. I was part of the building's history now. Once we reached our seats, Jared and I watched the other graduates enter. We looked for friends from the soccer and wrestling teams who had other majors in the College of Social Science. I scanned the arena for my parents and found them after a minute. It was weird seeing them several sections away from our family's usual seats—the seats where I used to wig out from the lights and the screaming crowd. While the last of the graduates marched in, my phone buzzed. I considered ignoring it, but I pulled it out from under my gown and glanced quickly. It was a text from Coach Izzo: "Hey there buddy, looking good." I couldn't spot him on or near the stage, but he had seen me.

There were welcomes and introductions and speeches. Finally, it was time for us to receive our diplomas. Other degrees went first: anthropology, criminal justice, history. I grew nervous. What if I tripped on stage?

Then it was the sociology majors' turn. Jared and I stood and lined up with the other graduates next to the stage.

"Anthony James Ianni."

As I crossed the stage, I saw Coach Izzo waiting at the far end. He was standing right where he said he would stand. Coach hugged me and shook my hand. "I'm so proud of you," he said. "You did it."

When the commencement ended, I found my parents outside the Breslin Center in the congestion. This was their moment, too. I graduated from college because of them. They never accepted the idea that I wasn't capable of this. They sacrificed for me. They pushed me. Every resource available, they made sure I got it.

"You're officially a Spartan forever now," my dad said. People said I'd never be a Spartan. I'd never go here at all, they said, let alone play basketball and earn a degree.

Dad had it right, not my critics.

*  *  *

My first job as a college graduate was a familiar one: paint crew.

Spartan Stadium needed a fresh coat of paint, so I spent a lot of my time there. The columns in the concourse I painted white, and I paired up with another painter and did the stairs. One of us took the green paint, the other took gray, and we alternated the two. I had two friends on the paint crew, Durant and Justin. Durant ran for the track and field team, and Justin was trying to get a grad assistant position with the football program.

I didn't worry about my career prospects. For the moment I was using my degree in sociology to paint Spartan Stadium in the summer heat, but I was confident it was temporary. Between autism advocacy and game-day management, something would work out.

Durant, Justin, and I were on break one painting shift in Spartan Stadium when I asked them for advice: "How do you guys think I should propose to Kelly?"

"What about during a Tigers game?" Durant said. I'd talked about Kelly enough for them to know what a sports fan she is.

"Nah. She doesn't really care for the spotlight. She wouldn't want me to pop the question in front of forty-one thousand other people."

Justin said, "You know, you could ask her at Comerica Park when the Tigers are on the road and the stadium is empty. Propose to her on the pitcher's mound."

"That's a pretty good idea!"

The Tigers' head groundskeeper, Heather Nabozny, was an MSU grad, and Dad knew people who knew Heather.

Heather and I met over email, and we looked at the Tigers' schedule. At the end of June the Tigers would be in Tampa Bay for the weekend, finishing a ten-game road trip. Perfect.

I booked a room at the Renaissance Center's hotel in downtown Detroit. I told Kelly I just wanted us to have a weekend away, but she may have suspected something.

That Sunday Heather met us near the park's front office entrance. We hopped into her cart and she drove us down toward the field entrance. As we neared the entrance, one of her crew members stopped us to ask Heather a question. While they chatted, the crew member looked at Kelly and me and said, "What's going on here?"

"He's here to propose to his girlfriend." Heather didn't flinch or cringe or apologize. She had no idea she'd just spilled the beans!

Kelly gave me a big smile and put her arm around me.

Heather dropped us off at the edge of the tunnel. "Stay off the grass, since it's being watered, and don't go on the infield dirt. We're pretty careful about that. But go ahead and check out the dugout. You can walk along the foul line out to the bullpen. Take your time."

Kelly and I took seats in the Tigers' dugout and looked out on the field. Then I got down on one knee.

* * *

After Kelly said yes, we walked along the edge of the field toward the bullpen beyond the outfield. The seats were empty; the stadium was ours. We'd seen a lot of games here together as a couple, but now we were engaged. We were promising to spend the rest of our lives together.

Eventually we reunited with Heather, who apologized over and over. "I can't believe I said that. I didn't even realize what I said!"

Throughout my years as a Spartan, Kelly had made drive after drive in the Michigan winter to watch our games. She was living in Detroit at the time, which is almost a hundred miles from East Lansing. She voyaged through blizzards to back me. The drives weren't Kelly's only show of support. Raised as a University of Michigan fan, Kelly never would have cheered for MSU before meeting me. But she'd started rocking the green and white for me and my team. It was one more indication of how special she was. (She still pulls for the MSU basketball team, but football is a different story.)

In the years we dated, Kelly educated herself about autism. She talked with my mom and asked her a lot of questions, and she spent plenty of time on the computer doing research. She learned how vast the autism spectrum is and how different we members of the autism community can be from one another.

It took Kelly time to understand me. It's not every day you enter a relationship and, a month or two in, find out that you're dating someone on the spectrum. She showed patience. She was willing to get to know me and learn about me. Not every person would go through that.

The best decision I ever made was asking her to marry me.

* * *

My career path was still up in the air, but there was no doubt about Draymond's. He was going to the NBA. The only question was which team.

A few days before Kelly and I became engaged, I drove to Saginaw for Draymond's draft party at the Dow Event Center. Most of our team and coaching staff were there, as were a lot of guys from the MSU football team, Day Day's family, and his old Saginaw friends and teammates.

TVs showed what was happening at the actual draft in Newark, New Jersey. Picks were announced every five minutes. I was with Coach Fife and also with Kevin Pauga, who had been at his desk in the Breslin Center the night I learned about Uncle Nick's death. K.P. had a brother who worked for the San Antonio Spurs. Every time he looked at his phone, he had inside information.

"The Wizards are taking Bradley Beal."

"The Pistons are picking Andre Drummond."

I ordered K.P. to put away his phone. "You're spoiling it for me," I said, gesturing toward a TV.

"It's not a movie, A.I." But he put his phone away.

I sort of wanted Draymond to go to the Detroit Pistons, because I could see him bringing back the toughness of the Bad Boys teams of the late 1980s and early 1990s, but mainly I hoped he'd be drafted by a well-run team where he could have an impact right away. I also wanted to see him picked in the first round, because I thought he deserved it. Most of the people at the party thought Day Day would go late in the first round, but nobody could figure out which team would take him.

Team after team passed on him. Each time a pick was announced, a small wave of disappointment went through our crowd.

Oklahoma City passed on him.

The Chicago Bulls chose somebody else.

In the last pick of the first round, the Golden State Warriors selected Festus Ezeli, a Nigerian player who had played at Vanderbilt.

Draymond would not be a first-round pick.

By the time the draft entered the second round, K.P. had his phone back out. Another pick, and another, and another.

"Marquette's Jae Crowder is going next," K.P. said.

While the TV was catching up to Kevin and Twitter, a new buzz shot through the room.

*Golden State's going to take him.*

*Day Day's going to the Warriors.*

Draymond had avoided the large room all night, watching the draft from a smaller, quieter room and waiting for his phone call. When he emerged with a smile on his face, we knew what it meant. The room erupted.

A few minutes later Draymond's draft was announced on TV, and we cheered all over again.

When I hugged him, I said, "I'm so proud of you, man. Now go out and prove some people wrong. Show them you should have been a first-rounder."

If you look at the list of draft picks who went ahead of Draymond—guys who are in Europe now, or in the NBA's developmental league, or who are in the NBA but have never appeared in an All-Star game—it's safe to say he's done that.

\* \* \*

Finally, in August, I got a call of my own. The Autism Alliance of Michigan wanted me. I would be a public speaker for them: touring the state, appearing at functions, telling my story. Once I had some practice, they wanted to expand my tour to schools. This was the beginning of what became known as the Relentless Tour, a tour I continue to this day.

Kelly and I married in the summer of 2013, and Przy, my old Grand Valley teammate, served as my best man. Geoff Hall, my best friend from Okemos High School and the first person I ever told about my autism diagnosis, was one of my grooms-men. When Geoff's dad hugged me, he said, "Congratulations, Big Fella!" That old nickname, Big Fella, rolled off his tongue as if only a week had passed since I'd last shot pool and played video games in his basement. Kelly and I held our reception in the Huntington Club, the banquet room in Spartan Stadium overlooking the football field. A year earlier in this same room, I'd received my perseverance award from the Resource Center for Persons with Disabilities. Now Kelly and I were beginning our married life together here, celebrating the moment with all the friends and family who had gotten us to this point in our lives.

Kelly gave birth to our first son, Knox, early in 2015. Our second son, Nash, was born three years later. People have asked me whether I'm worried about passing on my autism to my kids. I have to explain that no definitive proof exists showing autism is passed directly from parent to child. Then I say, "If my kids are autistic, then great! I'm surrounded by experts. My parents have had an autistic son for thirty-one years. Kelly has known me for more than a decade. Who is more equipped than my family to take on the challenges of raising an autistic child?"

When I was a little older than my son Nash, my parents couldn't figure out what was happening with me. They had my ears tested. They entertained the possibility of Ritalin. Mom was some months away from taking me to Children's Hospital and learning what PDD-NOS stood for. From everything Kelly and I have seen, neither son acts anything like I did. My mom agrees and says there is no comparison.

Knox is a tall boy, though, and he does seem to be drawn to the basketball court.

＊  ＊  ＊

I have moved the Relentless Tour from the Autism Alliance of Michigan to the Michigan Department of Civil Rights, but I continue to speak at schools and appear at autism awareness events, trying to bring an end to bullying and encouraging everybody to dream big. I also have the privilege of speaking to sports teams and at universities. This job means I must relive my past often, including the most painful experiences of my life. I often return to those feelings of confusion and isolation. It still can hurt, but it's worth it. Once I become vulnerable with my audience—once I tell them about my past and admit where I'm still wounded—a huge sense of relief passes through the crowd. They've felt those same feelings. They've hurt that way, too. And they're learning that they're not alone.

The future looks bright for people on the autism spectrum. Society no longer assumes we all are wired just like Raymond Babbitt from *Rain Man*. Parents and coaches now realize we can contribute to our schools and our communities, and even to our sports teams.

Autistic athletes are reaching elite levels. Every season another athlete on the spectrum breaks down a barrier in hockey, baseball, NASCAR, running, or basketball.

In November 2016 *Sports Illustrated* ran a story about the recent progress autistic athletes have made. The piece led with the anecdote about Draymond and me: how I yelled at him for getting sarcastic with me, and how he barked at me for failing to take a joke.

Everyone I know bought that issue of *Sports Illustrated*. Some people picked up multiple copies. (The World Series–winning Chicago Cubs were on the cover.) I received all kinds of calls, texts, and emails congratulating me on my appearance in the magazine.

When I was a kid I dreamed of being on ESPN's *SportsCenter* and in the pages of *Sports Illustrated*. Whenever I conducted my postgame press conferences in the shower, I imagined that *SportsCenter* would air my comments and that someone from *Sports Illustrated* was in the scrum of reporters asking me questions.

These are common dreams among young athletes. Kids want to see themselves in *Sports Illustrated*, and they want to be on a *SportsCenter* highlight clip. For a long time, children on the autism spectrum weren't allowed to have those dreams.

Whenever I speak in schools, I assure the students that *every* kid is allowed to chase *every* dream. It's not always easy, I warn them. No dream will come to you. You have to be relentless, I urge, when you're attacking those obstacles.

Being on the spectrum could not hold me back. It could not keep me from playing college basketball or earning a degree. It didn't prevent me from appearing in *Sports Illustrated*. In fact, how did I end up in the magazine?

It was because of my autism.

ANTHONY IANNI played basketball at Michigan State University from 2009 to 2012 and was the first Division I college basketball player known to be on the autism spectrum. He now tours the country as a motivational speaker. He lives with his wife and two sons in Livonia, Michigan.

ROB KEAST grew up in Lapeer, Michigan, and studied journalism at Michigan State University. He has written for newspapers in Michigan and Illinois and has taught English in Tokyo, Japan. Since 2004, Rob has taught high school English in Wyandotte, Michigan. He has a teenage daughter.